More Praise for *It's How We Play the Game*

"In *It's How We Play the Game*, Stack demonstrates that he's playing a different game than other retailers, moving past all the clichés about 'giving back' and turning his support of local communities into a kind of killer app. . . . Few recent business books are as well-told or as rich in takeaways."
—Jim Rohr, former Chairman
of PNC Financial Services Group

"In *It's How We Play the Game*, Ed Stack makes the compelling case that leading with the values of sports—like hard work, teamwork, and selflessness—matters in business, and most of all, society."
—Adam Silver, NBA Commissioner

"Ed Stack is not just a great entrepreneur running a big, successful business but a courageous American who is willing to stand up for what's right. And he's a talented author."
—Gert Boyle, Chairman of Columbia
Sportswear Company and author of
*One Tough Mother*

"Ed Stack has created one of the greatest retail emporiums. . . . As this book shows, he is an entrepreneur, corporate steward, and leader of an engaged workforce, but first and foremost, he is always thinking about his customers."
—John Idol, Chairman and CEO
of Michael Kors

"Paints a fascinating picture of a man who is a fulfilled leader . . . Stack's name should be on the impressive roll call of men and women whose will to compete, and success in doing so, offers inspiration and wisdom."
—Jay Monahan, Commissioner of
the PGA Tour

"An awe-inspiring story of overcoming obstacles . . . If there were more people like Stack running companies, the world would be a better place."

—Jimmy Dunne, Senior Managing Principal
of Sandler O'Neill & Partners

# IT'S HOW WE PLAY THE GAME

### BUILD A BUSINESS.
### TAKE A STAND.
### MAKE A DIFFERENCE.

## ED STACK

#### CHAIRMAN AND CEO
#### OF DICK'S SPORTING GOODS

SCRIBNER

New York   London   Toronto   Sydney   New Delhi

Scribner
An Imprint of Simon & Schuster, Inc.
1230 Avenue of the Americas
New York, NY 10020

First Scribner hardcover edition October 2019

SCRIBNER and design are registered trademarks of The Gale Group, Inc.,
used under license by Simon & Schuster, Inc., the publisher of this work.

For information about special discounts for bulk purchases,
please contact Simon & Schuster Special Sales at 1-866-506-1949
or business@simonandschuster.com.

The Simon & Schuster Speakers Bureau can bring authors to your live event.
For more information or to book an event, contact the Simon & Schuster Speakers
Bureau at 1-866-248-3049 or visit our website at www.simonspeakers.com.

Interior design by Erich Hobbing

Photographs courtesy of the Stack Family and Dick's Sporting Goods

Manufactured in the United States of America

1   3   5   7   9   10   8   6   4   2

Library of Congress Cataloging-in-Publication Data
Names: Stack, Ed (Edward W.), author.
Title: It's how we play the game : build a business, take a stand,
make a difference / Ed Stack.
Description: New York : Scribner, [2019]
Identifiers: LCCN 2019013286l ISBN 9781982116910 (hardcover) l ISBN
9781982116927 (pbk.) l ISBN 9781508296676 (compact disk)
Subjects: LCSH: Stack, Ed (Edward W.) l Dick's Sporting Goods. l Sporting
goods industry—United States. l Businesspeople—United States—Biography.
l Social responsibility of business.
Classification: LCC HD9992.U54 D537 2019 l DDC 381/.456887092 [B]—dc23 LC
record available at https://lccn.loc.gov/2019013286

ISBN 978-1-9821-1691-0
ISBN 978-1-9821-1693-4 (ebook)

*Note to Readers:* This book is a memoir. It reflects the author's present recollections
of his experience over a period of years. Dialogue has been reconstructed
from the author's memory to capture the essence of conversations that transpired.

In memory of my father,
Richard John "Dick" Stack

# CONTENTS

# CONTENTS

# INTRODUCTION

It was midafternoon on Valentine's Day when I heard an early news report about the school shooting. The particulars drifted in as I hurried my way through a pile of work that needed attention before I left for a long Florida weekend with my wife: students and teachers killed, number unknown. Panic in the halls. A gunman armed with an assault rifle. My first reaction was: *Not again.*

I'd found myself thinking that too many times lately. Hadn't we all? Four months before, a lunatic had barricaded himself in a high-rise Las Vegas hotel, busted out his room's window, and opened fire on a crowd of thousands gathered below for a country music festival. He'd snuck fourteen AR-15s, a type of assault-style rifle, into the hotel. Twelve were fitted with hundred-round magazines. It took him just ten minutes to kill fifty-eight people. Another eight hundred fifty-one—an almost inconceivable number—were wounded by his bullets or in the panic he created.

A month later, a twenty-six-year-old misfit walked into the Sunday service at a Baptist church in Sutherland Springs, Texas, and let loose with an assault rifle, killing twenty-six people and injuring another twenty.

In the few years before those shootings, there'd been so many others: A June 2016 terrorist attack on a gay nightclub in Orlando that killed forty-nine and wounded fifty-three; the shooter there had used an assault-style rifle, too. A December 2015 attack by husband-and-wife terrorists on a San Bernardino County public health training event and Christmas party, which left four-teen dead and twenty-two injured. A July 2012 massacre in an Aurora, Colorado, movie theater. That same year, the brutal massacre at Sandy Hook Elementary School that claimed twenty-six children and faculty.

Mass shootings had become an all-too-familiar part of life in America. Their frequency seemed to be increasing. The number of dead seemed to ratchet upward with each new incident. And there seemed no end to it. No safe place left. And maybe worse, no one trying to deal with it—our political leaders seemed to lack the will for meaningful action. Their response to these tragedies had become depressingly predictable. One side would decry the availability of guns and call for a clampdown. The other would trumpet its broad interpretation of the Second Amendment—in which any regulation, any safeguard, was seen as a constitutional breach—and would drag out that old cliché that guns don't kill people, people do.

As I listened to the news on February 14, 2018, more details emerged from Parkland, Florida. The gunman was a former student at the school. Thanks to the weapon he'd chosen, a derivative of a rifle originally developed for military use, he'd performed his slaughter with grim efficiency, killing seventeen people in little more than six minutes. I left the office in a deep state of melancholy, not only at the day's news but, perhaps even more, at the realization that it would happen again—that this tragedy was a link in a chain that seemed without end. *Somebody has to do something*, I thought. *This has to stop.*

My wife shared my despair. On our way to Florida, Donna was as preoccupied with the shooting as I was, and we talked about little else. She was near tears. Somebody has to do something, we told each other. Somebody. Has. To do. Something.

Halfway through the flight, forty-two thousand feet over the Carolinas, I realized that somebody had to be me.

Because few people were better positioned for the mission. As the chairman and chief executive officer of Dick's Sporting

Goods, America's largest sporting goods retailer, I led a team whose annual sales of firearms were among the nation's largest. We sold thousands of rifles, shotguns, and handguns from our nearly eight hundred big-box stores in forty-seven states. And in our thirty-five outdoors-oriented Field & Stream stores, we sold the very style of rifle used in Parkland, Florida, that Valentine's Day, and in so many other mass shootings.

That made us part of the problem. But maybe, I thought, it could make us part of a solution, too.

What followed that epiphany would thrust me and the company into an emotional and, at times, even threatening national debate. My team and I did something that few retailers had dared to: we followed our consciences, even if that steered our company into short-term hardship. We took a stand that earned both applause and condemnation, and in the months since, my life—and the lives of many Dick's employees—hasn't been the same.

The mass shooting at Marjory Stoneman Douglas High School wasn't the first occasion on which we encountered such a moment. Looking back, one can see that this tendency of Dick's to go beyond the traditional role of retailer and get involved with the communities of which it's a part—sometimes in a way that alters people's lives for decades—is pretty ingrained. It all harks back to the store's embryonic days as a small family business in upstate New York. The company's founder, and the man for whom it is named—my father, Richard John Stack—recognized that he couldn't prosper unless and until the city around him, and thus his customers, did too.

Dick Stack wasn't always a lovable man. There was nothing cuddly about him. He could be spiteful, prickly, and willfully hard to deal with. But in that belief about a company's relationship with its surrounding community, he was right.

This is the story of that company my dad started, which my team and I grew from two stores to hundreds—a story that shows Dick's evolution from the humblest of beginnings to a classic American success story. The sporting goods industry is littered with roadkill, and its victims include giants. That we at Dick's have survived, let alone thrived enough to become the only national player left in the game, is a pretty remarkable tale on its own.

But alongside that story of Darwinian struggle, I'll also describe the rise of a corporate culture that has sought to do the right thing, time and again. You'll see that we're no angels: in business, we're in the game to win. We love street fights, and we're good at fighting them. Even as we've sought to defeat our rivals, however, we've striven to build a legacy of good corporate citizenship—to measure our success not only by how much we've made, but by what we've created.

Importantly, the account that follows isn't all about me. As the founder's son and, also, the company's leader for thirty-five years, I've been a key player in Dick's story, but only *one* player. Thousands of men and women have had a hand in the company's success. Even so, I've worked in the company since I turned thirteen, when it consisted of a single small store selling hunting and fishing gear, and most of my life has been indivisible from the business. Its DNA is bound up in mine, and mine in its.

Has this journey that my team and I have taken together been a great adventure with hard-to-experience lows and exhilarating highs? Most definitely. I hope you'll enjoy reading about it as much as I've enjoyed living it.

## CHAPTER 1

# "GO START THIS"

Richard John Stack: where to begin, explaining my father? He was a born salesman with the gift of blarney, a guy who could chat up pretty much anyone. He was a good, if conservative, businessman. He was an athlete in his youth and remained passionate about sports throughout his life. When I played baseball and football as a kid, he never missed a game. He defined customer service broadly: he believed that a business owed a debt to its community, and he made good on that debt in a number of ways. He did right by his hometown.

But he was a complicated man. He stood five-eight and never topped 150 pounds, but he was a brawler, unafraid to use his fists to make a point. He wasn't a particularly happy guy—he was driven more by a fear of failure than a desire to succeed, and he could be a humorless tyrant at work and home. He drank too much, smoked too much, didn't eat well or exercise, and his habits turned him old before his time. He could be great company. Just as often, he wasn't.

So, to be straight with you, right from the start: there's plenty of Horatio Alger to the story you're about to read, several episodes of rags-to-riches heroism, but the first protagonist of this tale was no saint. He was a child of the Depression with his share of demons, and his days were not always easy or pleasant, for him or anyone close by.

All that said, Dick Stack left imprints on me, his oldest son, and on the company he founded. Many were indelible and continue to color the way we do business today, more than seventy years after he opened his first store. Much of the culture we've built at the company that bears his name can be traced back through the years to the examples set by my mercurial, hard-living, often exasperating father.

The good examples, that is.

We'll set out on this journey where he did, and where I did twenty-six years later: in Binghamton, New York, a town that occupies a narrow valley in the state's "Southern Tier," the long stretch of rolling countryside that runs along the Pennsylvania border, north and west of New York City. Binghamton is nestled on bottomland at the confluence of two rivers—the Susquehanna, which crosses the town from west to east and is already fat with the outflow of upstream tributaries, and the smaller Chenango, which joins the Susquehanna from the north.

Downtown is tucked into the northeast crook of this confluence and is linked to neighborhoods to the west and south by a half-dozen bridges. The principal east-west street through town, US 11, is called Main Street west of the Chenango, and Court Street in downtown and the middle-class neighborhood of small shops and modest homes to the east. And it is in those rivers and on Court Street, in Binghamton's East Side neighborhood, that the Dick's story begins.

Or, to take the story back even further, it begins at 11 McNamara Avenue, across the Susquehanna on Binghamton's South Side, where my father was born on July 17, 1928.

The Stacks were Irish Catholic, and the South Side was a blue-collar section of town populated with other Irish, along with Italians and Eastern Europeans. Binghamton was half again as big as it is today, swollen with immigrants. They'd started arriving by the thousands shortly after the Civil War, first to make cigars. By the 1880s, Binghamton was the second-biggest cigar town in America, strange as it is to think of New York as tobacco country.

6

When the cigar boom passed, they made shoes. The Endicott Johnson Corporation ran huge plants in town, and in Johnson City, just west of Binghamton, and Endicott, a few miles farther west. "E-J," as the company was known, was the biggest employer around for decades, employing twenty thousand people in the twenties and even more during World War II, when it made virtually all of the shoes used by the US military. In the mid-forties, it was turning out fifty-two million pairs of shoes a year.

Newly landed immigrants showed up in droves, most knowing only enough English to ask, on arriving in town: "Which way E-J?" It became an unofficial Binghamton motto. In 1984, years into the company's decline, Ronald Reagan visited on the stump, and he opened his speech with those words. He was way behind the times and was met with complete silence. Still, it underlined just how big a deal the company once was. Endicott and Johnson City, which with Binghamton form the Southern Tier's "Triple Cities," were named for the company's two owners.

More quietly at first, another company was growing in the Triple Cities that would soon change the face of the region. It dated to 1901, when two smallish companies that made time clocks and time-card readers were bundled into a new enterprise that incorporated in Binghamton. A decade later, through a series of mergers with outfits that made adding machines and commercial scales, the company became the Computing-Tabulating-Recording Company, or CTR, based in Endicott. In 1924, CTR changed its name to International Business Machines.

So the town into which my father was born was a mix of heavy industry and high tech, with a workforce that reflected its shifting fortunes. During his youth, E-J was the biggest employer. By the time I came along, IBM dwarfed all. I can remember my dad saying, long before I understood what it meant, "If IBM leaves Binghamton, turn out the lights."

He did not have an easy childhood. Dick was the last of six kids born to Edward W. and Mae Stack, his dad the owner of a beer distribution business—which, during Prohibition, was a polite way of saying my grandfather was a bootlegger. That must have been an uncertain and dangerous way to put food on the table, though his grandchildren have come to view it as a swash-buckling, even romantic, chapter of Stack history.

Tragedy struck the family before Dick was born. When his twin siblings, Billy and Betty, were nine months old, they caught whooping cough. My grandmother took them to the doctor. Betty was frailer; the doctor said he wanted to keep an eye on her, that she had the worse of it. Billy was a chubby, big-cheeked baby, a robust little boy, with a head of thick, curly black hair. The doctor judged him to be almost back to health.

Once home, my grandmother took Betty inside and got her settled. When she came back to the stroller for Billy, she found he'd choked to death on his own phlegm. I'm not sure that any-one in the family got over that, especially my grandmother. My sister Kim was talking with her fifty-some years later, when my grandmother was in her eighties, and asked her about that day. "Some people say, 'You have these other kids. Be thankful,'" Mae, whom we called Nana, said with tears in her eyes. "I think about that baby every day."

Billy's death was a prelude to even greater pain. On August 1, 1935, when Dick was seven, his father was killed in a horrific car accident east of town. Family lore has long held that the crash was no accident—that Ed Stack Sr. was bumped off by mobsters looking to muscle in on his beer business, which by then was legal. The available record doesn't dispute that legend outright, but it does raise questions about it: in a front-page story, the local paper reported that my grandfather had taken a downhill curve at high speed, drifted into the oncoming lane, and smashed his sedan into a truck loaded with live chickens. He was crushed behind the steering wheel and died on his way to the hospital.

His female passenger, who was not my grandmother, was ejected from the car and "picked up unconscious in the center of the highway," but recovered. I don't know what became of her. Not long after, Nana lost the beer business. The reasons are murky, but it seems that Granddad may have been involved in some gambling, as well as booze, and she gave up control of the distributorship.

From that point on, my dad's childhood was one of deprivation. Ed Sr. hadn't carried a life insurance policy. The beer income was gone. Nana had to take in boarders to make the mortgage. Dick's upbringing fell largely to his father's parents.

When I think back to the time I spent with Nana as a kid, I'm always impressed by her toughness. She was kind and had a charming, warm way about her, and she was a tiny woman, no more than ninety pounds. But she had steel inside, a no-nonsense core beneath her softness. I guess that's inevitable, given everything she went through. She'd had her first five children in quick succession—my uncle Ed first; then, two and a half years later, twins, my aunt Rosemary and uncle Joe; and fourteen months after that, the second set of twins, Billy and Betty.

So at one point the oldest of her five kids was barely four years old, in an age without baby formula or disposable diapers. That'd toughen up anyone. Then she lost Billy. She had my dad five years after that, and almost lost him to rheumatic fever, a close call that left him with a mitral valve defect in his heart. She hadn't even put him in school when her husband died; her oldest, my uncle Ed, wasn't yet sixteen.

Faith and family saw her through those trials. She went to Mass every day, no matter the weather, no matter how tired she felt. And she held her children close. When I was growing up we'd go to her house a lot—the same house at 11 McNamara Avenue, where she lived into her nineties—or she'd come over to ours for Sunday dinner. I remember many cold nights when we'd build a fire after the meal and she'd call us around the fireplace to watch it. We sat there for what seemed like hours, watching the flames. It drove me crazy at twelve years old. *Are you kidding me? Why are we wasting time staring at a bunch of burning logs?* Now that

I'm older, I can imagine that those nights reminded her of easier times, before all the heartache, when she and my grandfather would sit with their kids in the parlor of that little house.

Dick grew up adoring his oldest brother, my uncle Ed, who was nine years older. Ed was a dashing character—handsome, charismatic, athletic, fun loving. He was more of a father to my dad than their father had been. But the real influence on young Dick was his paternal grandfather, who introduced him to fishing for trout in the Susquehanna and Chenango, and for bass in some of the lakes outside of town. They did a lot of talking, and I understand they caught a lot of fish, but I think my dad enjoyed being outside on the water, the solitude and beauty of their setting, as much as anything. It was enormously calming.

Which did him good, because my dad was a high-strung kid with a lot on his mind. When he was in junior high, my uncle Ed joined the Army Air Corps and was away for years. My dad felt that loss. Even before then, he wasn't doing well in school— he had trouble studying, and my siblings and I have long suspected that he had a reading disorder; he remained a poor reader throughout his life. He was deeply interested in sports, passionate about them. He landed a spot on Binghamton Central High's junior varsity football squad in his sophomore year and played intramural basketball for a couple of years.

His greatest passion, then and throughout his life, was baseball. He was a catcher, and a good one, with a strong arm and a quick glove, and for several years played for the team at St. John the Evangelist, our parish church. The squad played other parishes, and the competition was surprisingly fierce. But while good, my dad wasn't great. If he harbored any dreams of taking his game higher, like most kids he didn't see them pan out.

So Dick Stack had a chip on his shoulder. He was barely getting by in his classes. He felt as if he was falling behind, that he was struggling at tasks his classmates found easy. He found just one respite: he immersed himself ever deeper into fishing.

And he worked. Dad had a paper route for a while, worked in

an ice-cream parlor, then got a job with a guy named Irv Berglass, who ran an army-navy surplus shop in Binghamton. As the war ended, the surplus market was flooded with useful stuff the government no longer needed, everything from coats and boots to cook sets, sleeping bags, tents. Sportsmen loved browsing the store.

In January 1948, my dad graduated from Binghamton Central. He'd forever after say that it was "by the skin of my teeth," which is no doubt true. He said he wouldn't have made it without a passing grade—a flat-out gift—from an English teacher who told him, "I don't know what will become of you, Dick, but somehow I know you'll be a success." At the store, the supply of surplus goods was beginning to slow, and Irv Berglass was mulling a transition into sporting goods. He knew my dad spent a lot of time fishing and was good at it. So he said, Listen, kid. I know you're a big-time fisherman, and I want to get into the tackle business. Only I don't know what we should stock, so I want you to go home and put together an inventory of what we'd need to get started.

My dad went home and put a list together. He stayed up into the early morning giving it thought, winnowing the list to the essentials, so that it all fit on two sheets of paper from a legal pad. The next morning, he took the list to Irv. The boss looked over the papers, took out a pen, and started crossing out items my dad knew any fisherman would need. Dumb kid, Irv said to him. You don't know what the hell you're doing.

Did I mention that my dad was a hothead? He snatched the papers away, stormed out of the store, and never went back. He walked across town, angry at the boss and himself—now he was out of high school, with no prospects for college, and suddenly jobless—and stopped in to see his father's parents.

Martin and Mary "Mamie" Stack did not have a lot of money. Born in County Kerry, Ireland, they'd come to Binghamton during the cigar boom, and now they lived very modest lives, scrimping for every extra dime; they went so far as to erect a tiny cottage in their backyard, which they rented out. One challenge was my great-grandfather, who was a wonderful man liked by virtu-

11

ally everyone who met him—and was known around town as "Backy," for the tobacco he chewed 24/7—but who was also an Irish cliché in terms of how much beer he consumed at the local pub. In other words, the dimes didn't pile up.

My father showed Mamie the list he'd compiled, told her what had happened. She could see that he was torn up. After a while she quietly asked: "How much would it cost you to do this—to open this business for yourself?"

"Three hundred dollars," he answered. He might not have been a great student, but he was always handy with numbers.

With that, she crossed the kitchen, went to a cookie jar in the back corner, reached in, and pulled out a wad of cash. God knows how many years of saving that represented. She counted out three hundred dollars, handed it to him, and said: "Go start this business yourself."

As origin stories go, I think that's pretty good. Some details have proved variable over the years: With each telling, my dad would have himself staying up later to put together the list; it was midnight when I was a kid, and by the time he told my kids the story, he was pulling an all-nighter. Occasionally, press accounts of my great-grandmother's generosity have amplified the sum she handed over to $600, or even $1,200.

But my dad always insisted that it was with $300 that he started his business, and Mamie backed him up. That cookie jar of hers has become a lasting bit of iconography at Dick's Sporting Goods. Today, when an associate reaches twenty-five years of service with the company, we present him or her with a cookie jar, tucked inside of which is $300.

My dad stretched that cash. He found a tiny storefront for rent at 453½ Court Street. The family used to kid him that it was so small it didn't deserve a full number for its address. There, just months after his high school graduation, he opened Dick's Bait and Tackle. He was nineteen.

That original store remains an important piece of the company. Walk into any Dick's today, and you'll find a framed picture of the place. My dad is standing to the right, just inside a front window lined with fishing rods. Uncle Ed, natty in a bow tie and dress shirt, is to the left, with an elbow propped on homemade shelves piled high with small boxes of gear. The wall behind the shelves is cinder block. They hold rods that cross between them, and at their feet is a stack of wicker fishing creels. A display of hooks and lures occupies a table in the left foreground. More than one customer on the sales floor—the little bit of open space in front of the camera—would have crowded it. You hear people talk all the time about humble beginnings. *This* was a humble beginning.

My dad stocked the shelves with as much fishing gear as he could afford, and hoped to do enough business to buy more. On the days he did, he'd close up shop; drive sixty miles to the Eynon Drug Store in Scranton, Pennsylvania; spend the day's receipts on fishing gear; then drive back and stock the shelves.

Bear in mind, he was paying more than wholesale for this stuff. His markups had to be razor-thin, or he'd have priced himself out of business. And on many days, he made too little to put gas in the car. Decades later, my sister Kim came across some old register receipts from those days, and she cried when she saw how little business he did. Five dollars, some days. Six or seven on others.

On some of those lean days, his situation must have seemed almost cripplingly bleak. But like I said, he had a chip on his shoulder. He had something to prove. He wasn't going to give in willingly. And ever so slowly, his little shop started drawing some regulars who recognized that this skinny kid knew fishing, knew gear, offered good advice. The word spread around town.

I wish I knew more about those days. He didn't speak of them often, and I didn't press. This much is clear: pretty soon, he no longer had to drive to Scranton for his inventory—he was doing enough business to place orders with wholesalers or buy directly from the brands he carried. He broadened his offerings: by 1952, he'd renamed the place Dick's Army-Navy & Sporting Goods, and was stocking work clothes, a little sportswear, camping gear, and picnic supplies, along with an expanded array of fishing tackle. He was generating enough traffic to buy newspaper advertisements. He sponsored a monthly fishing contest that awarded forty bucks for the biggest fish. "Buy your equipment from an experienced angler," he wrote in an ad in April of that year, "who will demonstrate the proper use of each item sold."

My dad wrote all of the ads himself, and at times he got creative. One of my favorites was an ad that appeared in the Binghamton *Press and Sun-Bulletin* in February 1953 and resembled a boxed news story. "Warning! Fishing Pox," its heading blared. "Very Contagious to Adult Males. Symptoms—continual Complaint as to the need for fresh air, sunshine and relaxation. Patient has blank expression, sometimes deaf to wife and kids. Has no taste for work of any kind. Frequent checking of Fishing equipment. Hangs out in DICK'S Army-Navy store longer than usual. Secret night phone calls to fishing pals. Mumbles to self. Can't sit still, wants to buy the best Fishing Tackle at the lowest possible prices." The "treatment" was to "go Fishing as often as possible with tackle from Dick's."

In time he was doing well enough that he expanded into the other half of his store's half-address. It remained an unpretentious operation in the same low-slung cinder-block building, but now he had three big display windows looking onto Court Street. And while he'd so far done the bulk of his business during warm weather, when fishing in the Southern Tier didn't require hacking a hole through a foot of ice, he made a change that transformed Dick's into a year-round destination: he started carrying rifles, shotguns, and ammunition.

My father was an occasional hunter—very occasional—but he knew enough about firearms to get by, and hunting seemed a natural extension of his existing business. This is a point that will be important later in this story: Dick's has been in the gun business for at least sixty-seven years.

• • •

Successful as the operation seemed to be, Dick's Army-Navy was vexed by a problem all too common to businesses in Binghamton. An explosion of car ownership was transforming America, especially its cities, and Binghamton was no exception; the shortage of parking just in front of Dick's Army-Navy was soon frustrating customers.

So in December 1953, Dad decided to move the operation to larger quarters with off-street parking, about seven hundred yards to the west. A story in the paper—which read suspiciously like his own advertising copy—announced that the new place, at 389 Court Street, was "5 times larger than the present one and there is parking facilities for at least 300 or more cars. Just think how easy it will be to shop at Dick's, drive up anytime, park and shop."

The new store, while another single-story, concrete-block structure, was vastly larger, and set back behind a large parking lot. Business, it seems, was good—enough so that eleven months later, when a new shopping center opened a ten-minute drive north of town, Dad signed a lease on a second location.

Success seemed a safe bet. The Hillcrest Shopping Center was unassuming, by today's standards—a small, stone-clad strip mall anchored by an A&P supermarket and a big furniture showroom—but busy State Route 7 passed out front. The new Dick's Sporting Goods occupied the storefront next door to the grocery. Prime real estate.

My dad's business philosophy was as simple as it gets: "If I take in more than I spend, I'm okay." By such reasoning, it seemed the Hillcrest store couldn't lose. It opened in late November 1954, selling toys in addition to sporting goods.

That was a busy time for my dad. Earlier that year he had married my mother, and he was soon to become a father.

My mom, Mary Ann Boyle, grew up on McNamara Avenue, just four houses away from my dad's childhood home; the two families knew each other, so how my parents met is no mystery. To this day, though, I can't figure out what brought them together. This was not a case of opposites attracting. They were alike in all the wrong ways—both high-strung and quick-tempered. Neither was demonstrably loving. Words of reassurance, or tenderness, or comfort, were not in their vocabularies.

Like my dad, my mom went to Binghamton Central High School, graduating five years behind him. She was a kid. Still, they married in January 1954 and bought a modest little one-and-a-half-story bungalow on Binghamton's South Side. She'd worked as an operator for the local telephone company before they got together and kept working for a few months after the wedding. But just a few, because eleven months into their marriage, on December 27, 1954, I was born—Edward William Stack, named for my father's father and my uncle Ed.

It was an inauspicious time for a baby to arrive, because things weren't going as planned in my dad's business. The Hillcrest Shopping Center had been developed by Mart Development Corporation, which the local paper described as "largely the creation of William M. Viglione, the tax accountant." Viglione, a former IRS numbers cruncher, had little commercial real estate experience; he'd built a motel out west of Binghamton two years before, but nothing quite like a strip mall.

It showed. For all the traffic the highway out front seemed to promise, no great population surrounded the shopping center, and there wasn't much prospect that one would develop. The situation wasn't helped by Hillcrest's weird mix of tenants: a furnace company, an insurance agent, and the Minneapolis-Honeywell Regulator Company, which made thermostats. Not exactly the sort of neighbors that attracted armies of shoppers. Being next door to the A&P—usually a good strategy—didn't count for much, because the A&P was having trouble attracting customers, too.

Just four months into the two-store experiment, my dad

decided to shut down his Court Street location. It was almost certainly doing better than Hillcrest; I can only guess that his lease at the strip center was tougher to break, so he chose to consolidate his merchandise there, rather than in town. My dad wrote a big advertisement that appeared in the paper in late March. "We have moved our Court Street store to the HILLCREST SHOPPING CENTER," it read. "In combining the 2 stores, we will automatically cut our overhead. This means that we can offer you LOWER PRICES! Drive out, 'Always a place to park.'"

One feature of the ad conveyed the nervousness he must have been feeling. Down at the bottom, it listed the Hillcrest store's hours. Since opening his first store, he'd always operated from nine a.m. to nine p.m., Tuesday through Friday, and nine a.m. to six p.m. on Saturday. Now the store was open on Sundays until three p.m., and he kept it open until midnight on Thursday and Friday "for Your Last-Minute Tackle Needs and YOUR LICENSE."

The desperation that emanated from that ad was even more pronounced in those that followed. By the time I approached my first birthday, Dick's was advertising a "$50,000 stock reduction," with deep discounts on just about everything under the roof. Rifles priced at pennies on the dollar. Double-barreled shotguns, 48 percent off. A huge range of stuff, from fishing vests to sweaters to model airplanes, to work shoes, house paint, and tennis balls, all for half off or more.

This wasn't the behavior of your typical retailer nearly three weeks before Christmas. Struggling to survive, Dad had made a loss leader of virtually everything in the store.

CHAPTER 2

# "IF I HAD WHAT I OWE,
# I'D TRULY BE A WEALTHY MAN"

When my dad spoke of the Hillcrest store later in his life, it was with anguish and frustration—not only over what happened there, but because he'd allowed himself to be talked into the venture. He never identified who it was who'd persuaded him that it was a good idea. He never blamed anyone but himself. "I should have been content with what I had," he'd say. "I should never have opened that second store."

Actually, if he'd opened west of town, instead of to the north, he'd likely have been just fine. The suburbs were fast spreading to the west: subdivisions, gas stations, and strip malls ran unbroken past Endicott.

Hindsight. He didn't realize he was planting his flag in the wrong place. But by the time I reached my first birthday, it must have seemed inevitable that it would end badly, judging by those Christmas ads. The wonder, for me, is that the store managed to limp through the spring of 1956. Finally, on June 6, he took out a new ad in the paper. It was topped with an immense heading: "We Quit."

"We must sell out to the bare walls!!!!" it continued. My dad never was bashful about exclamation points. "To satisfy our creditors we are forced to GO OUT OF BUSINESS! OUR LOSS, YOUR GAIN. SALE STARTS AT 9 A.M. TOMORROW!" Below was the

19

now-familiar assortment of drastically discounted merchandise, the prices even lower than they'd been before Christmas.

The next three weeks were a living nightmare for my dad. He was already burdened by a deep and abiding inferiority complex: His close friends from high school had gone on to college and were now finishing their studies to be doctors and lawyers. In contrast, he'd set himself up as a shopkeeper, which he viewed as second rate next to their achievements, and now he was about to fail at that. He'd tell me later that his nights were sleepless, agonizing, that he was tortured by the thought that he'd blown his one shot at success. He couldn't provide for his family. Worse, his family was growing—he and my mom learned in the midst of the store's collapse that she was expecting again. His life, it seemed, was in chaos.

My dad padlocked his place on July 15, 1956. I've been past the Hillcrest Shopping Center a thousand times in my life; years later, it remains an outpost. The furniture store is the only survivor, and it moved into a bigger building up the road. A storefront church occupies the old A&P. The space where my dad set up shop is now a gym.

Dick Stack was a proud man, and he refused to declare bankruptcy. He could not abide the thought of making others pay for what he saw as his mistake. Instead, he returned what merchandise he could, then sold virtually everything he had—the house he'd only recently bought, his car, anything he could liquidate—to pay off his creditors. He succeeded: none of his suppliers lost money when Dick's folded. For my dad, and our family, his insistence on protecting everyone else promised a bleak future. He and my mom had no choice but to return to living with their parents. Four months pregnant, my mom moved herself and me into her folks' place on McNamara Avenue. My dad couldn't bring himself to live with his in-laws—in his heartsick state, that represented a step down that might have finished him off. He moved in with his mom, my Nana, just up the street.

Broke and desperate, he found a job at Montgomery Ward in

downtown Binghamton. And there this story could have ended. At twenty-six, my dad could have chosen the safety of a sure paycheck over any further risk. A lot of men, with the responsibilities he faced, would have taken that route. But my dad, for all of his shortcomings, was a resilient guy, toughened by the deprivations of his childhood and the uncertainties of his early years in business. He had that chip on his shoulder, that need to prove himself among friends and classmates who he thought were doing better. He had guts. "When you get knocked on your ass," I heard him say a million times, "you get back up, dust yourself off, and get back in the fight."

Not exactly original, maybe, but true enough. When you dig down into the roots of success, it has little to do with brilliance. I've known plenty of geniuses who didn't amount to much, and quite a few numbskulls who've done well. We all have. Life teaches that success also has little to do with talent—we've all met really talented, creative people who can't translate that talent into a successful career.

No, success is all about what's inside you, and the most important element of success is simple perseverance—often tedious, sometimes soul crushing, but the great differentiator in whether smarts, talent, and education add up to something bigger. Great musicians practice to perfection. Engineers refine and test, refine and test again. Athletes never stop training. And my dad, knocked on his ass, got up, dusted himself off, and got back in the fight.

The turning point came while he was on the sales floor in the Montgomery Ward sports department. A stranger approached—my dad had never seen him before, and never saw him after, but the guy had evidently known Ed Sr., my bootlegging grandfather, and recognized his son. "If you had half the guts your father had," this mystery man said, "you'd be doing this for yourself."

Then he walked off, leaving my dad stunned. The stranger's words, he told me, sliced straight into his soul. Emboldened, or maybe embarrassed, or a little of both, he quit Montgomery Ward a couple of days later and hit the streets to find a way to get back into business. He found a friendly ear at an East Side bank, whose lenders knew that he'd been successful on Court Street and were willing to underwrite his second chance, provided he returned to that part of town. His former suppliers, impressed by how he'd made them whole after the Hillcrest failure, stepped up to say they'd do business with him. In late August he was again advertising in the *Press and Sun-Bulletin*. This time, the ad featured a picture of my dad standing in front of a long rack of rifles and shotguns, under the heading "Dick is Back!" The address for the new Dick's Clothing and Sporting Goods was the same as the old: 389 Court Street. He reopened on September 1. His resurrection had taken just six weeks.

But the Hillcrest debacle never really left him. My dad carried scar tissue from that experience for the rest of his life, and it affected every aspect of his conduct in business. He was terrified of failure. He was deathly afraid of going broke.

He was not averse to spending money; to the contrary, he lived pretty large for a guy who ran a small local business. When I was old enough to have a clue about what was going on around me, I noticed that my dad bought a new car every two years, always a Cadillac Sedan de Ville. He kept a rustic weekend cottage on Page Lake, a few miles across the Pennsylvania line. He had boats and snowmobiles. And starting when I was very young, he and my mom spent a couple of months each winter in Florida. They left me, and the kids who came later, in the care of neighbors, who'd move into our house for the duration.

I don't know that my dad allowed himself to enjoy much of it. He was preoccupied. I'd come to see and feel that up close in the years ahead, and it could be enormously frustrating.

Then again, I didn't experience his close brush with ruin. I was busy learning to walk.


In the hands of my haunted, driven father, Dick's Clothing and Sporting Goods reestablished itself as Binghamton's go-to source for fishing and hunting gear, camping supplies, and outdoor clothes. I don't mean that it made anyone rich. That, it did not do. Dick's was always in debt to the bank and to the vendors that supplied the store with merchandise, and it always seemed to have too much inventory or too little. Throughout my childhood, the business was a bad month away from collapsing under the weight of that debt, so even as the store's reputation and clientele grew, there was a palpable air of nervous struggle about the place. My dad would sometimes ruminate on the dicey state of affairs and say to me—and I heard this many times—"Ed, if I had what I owe, I'd truly be a wealthy man." Even so, he almost immediately bought a new house—a split-level place with a walk-out basement, bigger than the last but far from large, at 16 Ardsley Road, on Binghamton's East Side.

My sister Kim came along in the midst of the store's rebirth, in January 1957. I'd just turned two. And pretty regularly for the six years after, my parents had kids roughly two years apart: my brother Rick, then my brother Marty, and finally, when I was eight, my sister Nancy. Our house had one bathroom and three bedrooms: one that my parents shared, another for my sisters, and the third into which I was shoehorned with my two brothers—a small room with a ceiling so low, and sloped so acutely, that even as kids, we could stand straight only in the middle.

We all worked, on and off, at Dick's during our formative years, but from early on it was clear that my dad expected me to join him in the business, and that assumption was woven into my entire upbringing. My childhood is inseparable from "the store," as it was always called at home. Some of my earliest memories are wrapped up in the place. I remember the garage stuffed with merchandise that wouldn't fit in the store's back room—Coleman coolers stacked high, Sorel winter boots, snowmobile oil, and case after case of propane tanks and white gas. The whole place was a tinderbox: one spark would have leveled the entire block. Nowadays, the state would take your kids away from you for less.

My dad broke me in early on retail. When I was five, and my

mom had her hands full with the younger kids, she'd sometimes have my dad take me into Dick's for the day. My dad had no time to babysit, so he planted me in the store's basement, where he kept the back stock of clothes and gear, along with ammo and gunpowder, and put me to work. My job: attaching prices to heavy cotton work pants, which involved pins and paper tags—not the easiest task for so little a kid. By the end of the day, my thumbs would be bleeding from dozens of pinpricks.

From about the same period, I remember going down to the store with him on Sundays, when the place was closed, and sitting beside him in his office while he did paperwork—stamping and signing checks, gathering deposits, filling out orders. During the winter, he'd have the TV tuned to football. I can picture watching the Giants on that small black-and-white screen.

When I wasn't at the store, I was hearing about it at the dinner table, where the conversations followed predictable themes: In the summer and fall, we talked about the Yankees and the store. In the fall and winter, we talked about the Giants and the store. If you couldn't jump in with a contribution to one of those subjects, you were pretty much shut out. Weather came up, but only because it had such an impact on the business: my dad always hoped for cold days in the fall, because it would bring in hunters looking to gear up on hats, coats, and long underwear.

The store came up during my parents' arguments, too. My siblings and I witnessed a lot of those. My mom wanted my dad home more, though looking back, it's clear that my folks were mismatched. My dad was self-absorbed and obsessed with his work. My mom, raised by doting, demonstrative parents and accustomed to constant attention, didn't get the devotion she expected. They bickered constantly. At night, as I drifted off to sleep, it was often to a soundtrack of loud, angry voices.

Alcohol looms large in my early memories, too: When I was five, Dad taught me how to fix his standard cocktail, a perfect CC Manhattan. He gave me a shot glass and told me to fill it up twice from the brown bottle—that'd be Canadian Club—and once from the green bottle of sweet vermouth. I'd add a splash of water and a cherry and take it to him. As I got older, I came to see that when he got into his third Manhattan of the night—with six shots of booze already in him, and three more headed that way—trouble was coming. He wasn't a happy drinker. He grew sullen, and sometimes flat-out mean. His patience, never ample, vanished entirely. He could blow without provocation. I made myself scarce.

When provoked, my dad sometimes forgot that he stood five-eight and weighed 150 pounds. Once, while attending a sporting goods convention, he was in the restaurant at a hotel in New York City. A group of guys sat at the next table over, and one, who was talking loud enough that my dad could hear, told his buddies, "That Dick Stack, at Dick's Sporting Goods, he doesn't pay his bills on time." He probably said more, but he'd already crossed a line. If there was one thing my dad was a stickler for, it was paying bills on time.

My dad's friend and coworker, Frank Gehrlein, was sitting with him, along with a few others from Dick's, and Frank could see that he was steaming. A while later, the loudmouth—evidently a manufacturer's rep—got up and crossed the restaurant to the bathroom. My father waited a minute or so, then got up and made for the bathroom himself. It took a few seconds for Frank to put together what was about to happen, and to hurry after both. He watched as the loudmouth stepped out of the bathroom and started back across the lobby. My dad stopped him halfway across, said a few words, then punched him right in the face. The guy flew backward over a couch, where my dad pounced on him. They were whaling away at each other when Frank pried them apart. "I knew what was going to happen," Frank told me long after. "I just couldn't get there fast enough."

That wasn't the only time my dad got into a fistfight. Truth be told, he was in quite a few.

• • •

I don't mean to paint Dick Stack as a bad man. I think he was self-medicating when he drank, trying to escape the suffocating anxiety that gripped him. And I don't mean to make it sound as if I had a Dickensian childhood, because like a lot of kids in the early to mid sixties, I didn't spend a whole lot of time in the house, anyway. Every morning from age five on, I was outside minutes after I woke. At first, my friends and I were small enough to squeeze our play into the backyard at 16 Ardsley. Though it seemed plenty big at the time, it was a tiny space, dominated by a weeping willow tree that dropped leaves and spiders constantly. A rusty swing set took up some space, too, but we scratched out a miniature baseball diamond in the remaining grass and managed to play some truncated form of the game.

The backyard was bordered by hedges, in most places so thick that you couldn't get through them, but thinner in spots. If you hit a ball to the left, it would end up in the Bagostas' yard, and you'd have to push through one of those thin stretches of hedge to get it. A shot into center landed in the Risleys' yard, and you'd go through the same routine of wading through the bushes. Ah, but if you hit to the right, and the ball sailed into the Laytons' yard, you were screwed, because if Mr. Layton saw our ball land on his property, he'd snatch it up and wouldn't give it back. One day my dad came home at dinner and wanted to play catch. I told him we couldn't—Mr. Layton had kept our ball. My dad walked into the backyard and through the bushes into Mr. Layton's yard. A few minutes later he came back with the ball. His knuckles were covered with blood.

We'd play Wiffle ball out front in the street, too. The center field fence was our roof: hit the ball on the porch for a double, onto the shingles above for a home run. As I got a little older, I'd jump on my bike and pedal to Fairview Park, about a half mile away, and spend the morning playing ball. I came home long enough to wolf down a peanut butter sandwich, a couple of Oreos, and a glass of milk, then rode back to the park to play more. My parents never worried about me during my long hours away. The East Side of my childhood was a close-knit neighborhood in which all knew their neighbors. Most were one-income households—policemen, insurance salesmen, IBM workers—with a parent at home during the day. Little happened outside without an adult taking notice. We had a lot of eyes on us. Then as now, Fairview Park had a full-size Little League diamond, a wading pool, and a big blacktop playground. It was the center of my universe. Between eight thirty a.m. and six p.m., I might have been home for half an hour.

Baseball. I lived for baseball. It filled my days and at night, my dreams. In 1962, the year after Roger Maris broke Babe Ruth's home run record, my uncle Harold took me to New York City to see the Yankees. We took the train out of Binghamton, and I'll never forget walking the concourse and passing through a tunnel, and the concrete around us opening to reveal the field and that great bowl of stadium around us. I'd seen Yankee Stadium only on black-and-white TV. In person the grass was a surreal green, the brightest and most saturated color I'd ever seen, and the dirt of the baselines was a deep cinnamon brown and perfectly groomed. The foul lines gleamed white. It was breathtaking. I wanted nothing more than to play on that field.

Soon, all my heroes were there: Maris and Mickey Mantle. Yogi Berra. The Yankees' catcher Elston Howard, who was the only player in the league—in those days before catchers wore helmets—to flip the brim of his hat up when he turned it around to put on his mask. I thought that was so cool.

Back home, I had a little transistor radio that I'd sneak into my bed, and on nights when the Yankees were playing out west I'd listen to the play-by-play. I couldn't get enough. Even now I can recite the Yankees' batting order from those days. In fact, in the bookcase behind my desk, I have a figurine collection of the 1961 Yankees' lineup. I'm looking at my hero, Elston Howard, as I write this.

• • •

Back then, baseball games were televised only on weekends, and I never missed a Yankees game on TV. Which brings up the other great love of my childhood: my grandfather.

My mother's parents had divorced when she was little, and her father, an Irishman named Thomas Boyle, had moved off to Florida. Her mom, Anna, had remarried an Austrian immigrant named Karl Krupitza, who'd moved to Binghamton in 1906, when he was nine. For reasons obscure, everyone called him "Dutch."

My mom, six or seven when they married, adored him, and I could understand why. I called him Grampa or Gramp, and when things were tough at home I could always count on him. He listened when I was upset or excited. He didn't say much but offered quiet advice when I needed it. And he was a master at companionable silence: we could spend long stretches of time watching the Yankees without a word passing between us, yet have a wonderful time together.

Gramp was my anchor, my refuge. He understood me when it seemed no one else did. He was a wonderful example to me in so many aspects of life. He was relentlessly upbeat. Unfailingly good-natured. Comfortable in his own skin. A true gentleman, too. I never once heard him say a bad word about another person. Never heard him swear. Never heard him boast. And his marriage was a revelation, because in stark contrast to my parents, he and my grandmother enjoyed each other like newlyweds. Every night after supper they went out to the Elks or Moose lodge for three beers apiece. They spent weeks each winter in Florida and flew to Las Vegas once or twice a year until he was ninety. My grandmother played bingo and the slots. Gramp played blackjack and poker. You want proof that age is just a number? Karl Krupitza was it.

Something else about him awed me. He was a little guy, bespectacled and slight, not at all imposing to look at. But I'll tell you what: he was a force to be reckoned with in any sport he took up. The first of those sports was baseball. In 1923 he started working as a "vacation fireman," filling in for city firefighters who'd taken off work. Two years later, he was appointed full-time to the department. Binghamton firefighters had a baseball team that played in the adult city league, and Gramp earned a spot as third baseman. He was good enough to keep the assignment into the mid-thirties, and in 1936 was elected the team's manager. By then he was taking an interest in bowling, and for more than twenty years he ranked among the city's top competitors. During that reign, he picked up a golf club for the first time, at age thirty-five. Four years later, he broke one hundred for the first time. Five years after that, he won the Broome County amateur title.

One good thing about being a firefighter is that you get a lot of free time. Gramp worked two days on, three off, and with rare exceptions, he played a full round on those open days, and often bowled in a league a few hours later. By the time he made fire lieutenant, in 1949, he was among the region's top amateur golfers; by the time I came along, years after he'd retired, he was playing five or six rounds a week.

I didn't often join him on the golf course—I was too busy with baseball—but I'd stop by his house to watch golf on TV with him. At about the time we moved onto Ardsley, he and my grandmother had moved from McNamara to Sunset Avenue, little more than a block away. To get to their house, I walked out our front door and across the street, cut through two neighbors' yards, and emerged on Riverview Avenue, right where it intersected with Sunset. I'm sure the neighbors didn't care for my shortcut, because I practically wore a groove into their lawns.

My dad was of the generation of fathers for whom the worst thing that could happen was to see a son grow up a sissy, and his approach to ensuring that I didn't was to be a ruthless hard-ass. He expected a flawless performance in everything I did, and when I let him down he'd let me have it—most often, about halfway through that third Manhattan.

But he was pleased by my interest in baseball. It became our common bond. He'd been a catcher when he'd played for St. John, so he set out to make me a catcher. His explanation was, and remains, good counsel. An outfielder might never field the ball in the course of a game, but a catcher was involved in every pitch. It was an exciting position, dependent on speed, arm strength, and smarts. You called the pitches and directed the infield; you led the defense. You were a key to winning or losing games.

When Dad came home for dinner, he and I would play catch in the yard before we sat down to eat. These weren't casual games. I'd play catcher, and he'd pitch to me—burning fastballs, each one harder than the last. Then he'd start throwing the ball in the dirt, and I'd scramble to dig it out. If I missed and had to run into the bushes to retrieve the ball, I'd turn back to find he was gone. The message: If you can't catch it, we're done. Don't screw up.

I was pretty good at fielding wild pitches by the time I was seven. My dad put me to an even greater test when I'd visit the store. He'd show me off to the staff and customers by positioning me with one of the big plate-glass windows at my back, then firing a baseball my way. They weren't throws *to* me—he threw high, low, to my left and right. I never missed a catch. If I had, we'd have taken out the window.

Such was my apprenticeship. And my fielding skills were further sharpened by a ritual we followed for years. After dinner, my dad would devote a few minutes to quizzing me about baseball. "You're playing second base, there's two outs and a man on third, and you have a ground ball hit to you," he'd say. "What do you do?" Or: "There's one out, a guy on first, and you're playing shortstop. The ball is hit to you. What do you do?" I was expected to answer without pausing to think about it. "I'd throw the ball to second, and the second baseman would go to first base for the double play."

The more we played this game, the faster he expected me to be. I don't recall ever giving a wrong answer. This wasn't always true of my work in school, then or later, but when it came to baseball, I was an A student. My dad's questions spurred me to *study* the game. From an early age, I didn't merely watch the pros on TV, I dissected their fielding decisions. Analyzed every play. Strove to understand why they did what they did.

So while my dad's coaching and quizzing weren't fun, exactly, they left their mark. Our games of catch sharpened my reflexes and my eye. His quizzes taught me that fielding should be intuitive, instantaneous, performed without thought. I grew into a much better player. That's what makes Dick Stack such an elusive figure to pin down. He could be tough as nails at times—maybe most of the time—but I don't doubt that his intentions were usually good. I believe he honestly wanted to help me improve my game. It's just that his tough-love approach to parenting emphasized the "tough" part.

His efforts heightened my passion for baseball. As much as I loved the game early on, as I got better at it, I loved it even more.

Whatever shortcomings my dad displayed at home, his conduct in business was farsighted, smart, and—when you consider he'd lost everything just a few years before—surprisingly bold. In January 1960, about the time he introduced me to mixology, he took out a bank loan and quietly bought two Court Street lots from a Binghamton couple, and an adjoining corner tract from a used-car dealer. Four months later, he bought another two lots on the same block from a business associate of his brother Joe's, giving him two acres of land a half mile west of his current store, and closer to downtown.

That July, he obtained a permit to erect a freestanding building of cinder block and brick near the block's southwest corner, and over the summer spent $29,200—about a quarter million in today's dollars—creating a new Dick's at 345 Court Street. "The new store will be filled with new stock, new ideas, and fantastic bargains for all," my dad promised in an August ad. "WATCH and SEE." It opened that September, just before hunting season.

31

It was a humble place, by modern standards—five thousand square feet, with a flat roof and floor-to-ceiling glass running the width of its face. But it was his, and he customized it to his specific needs. The vinyl-tile sales floor was parceled into departments for hunting and archery, camping, fishing tackle, and a newcomer—golf. Smaller sections were devoted to bowling balls (custom-drilled on the premises) and tennis. Lots of tables and racks displayed clothes, including a large assortment of work wear—Carhartt, Woolrich flannels, men's underwear.

Extra inventory hung from pipes attached to the ceiling; when a customer asked if he had a shirt in another size, all he had to do was look overhead, then snatch it down at the end of a pole. Behind the rear wall, a stockroom ran the width of the place. In the back right corner a small, low-ceilinged office occupied an enclosed balcony, with a window overlooking all.

This is the store in which I grew up. This is where I got my start in the business.

Once the new operation was up and running, my dad's most pressing need was to reduce his overhead, particularly the mortgage on the building and lots. He accomplished this pretty creatively. First, he put up a wall inside the store to create a small, independent space that he leased to the Sports Mate Diner. Dick's and the Sports Mate had a nice symbiotic relationship: we brought each other customers.

Then he caught wind that Acme Markets, a Philadelphia-based chain of grocery stores, was looking to open a supermarket on Binghamton's East Side. Court Street was the neighborhood's main drag and a natural home for such a business, so he suggested the unused eastern half of his block. The chain agreed to the idea and to letting him build it, and in December 1962, he broke ground on a 13,500-square-foot supermarket there. It cost $125,000—just over a million in today's dollars—but the combined rents of Acme and the Sports Mate Diner covered Dad's mortgage on the land and buildings.

That gave him a lot of breathing room, though you wouldn't have guessed it from the way he continued to fret about going broke. He'd devised and executed a virtually fail-safe plan to finance his business, but he always saw himself as close to the cliff's edge. And one way or another, everyone around him got to share in his discomfort.

CHAPTER 3

# "THIS IS WHAT PUTS FOOD ON THE TABLE"

In the early years at 345 Court Street, Dick's was a boys' club. Everyone who worked the sales floor was male, and just about everything it sold was geared to male customers. This was before Title IX, and the public schools in the Southern Tier didn't field many girls' teams, as they do today; soccer and lacrosse hadn't yet jumped the gender barrier to a significant degree, and field hockey hadn't established a foothold. Aside from tennis, women's sports in general were afterthoughts.

But then, Dick's wasn't big on supplying a full range of equipment for men's and boys' team sports, either. When I started playing Little League baseball at age nine, and continuing all the way through high school, I couldn't buy cleats at my dad's store, because he didn't stock them; you could buy a glove or a bat, but that was about it—and even then, the selection was narrow. For baseball shoes, I had to shop at one of Dad's competitors, Irv's Champion.

Dick's was an old-school sporting goods store, true to its origins in fishing tackle and hunting. The guys who worked there were old-school enthusiasts themselves. They had a lot in common with my dad—it was a fast, loose, foul-mouthed, rough bunch. Everyone smoked, and back then they smoked in the store, which might seem incongruous with a place devoted to sports; at the time, however, even pro athletes smoked in public. It wasn't unusual to see my dad, who went through three packs of Pall Malls per day, with a cigarette between his fingers as he roamed the floor, and the same went for everyone else.

The sales staff was led by my dad when he was there, and otherwise by his second-in-command, a stocky, fair-haired, baby-faced former marine named Bob Aiken. He was a no-bullshit guy, gruff at times, who strove to do right, and he was the linchpin of the store's smooth operation. Fishing was overseen by Ira Foote—tall and bony, an Ichabod Crane character who knew his stuff. He lived across the state line in Pennsylvania and drove twenty-five miles each way to the store. Ira was sweet natured and uncomplaining; he kept his head down and his mouth shut, except when he was sharing his deep knowledge with customers.

My cousin Denny handled hunting. Dave Polosky ran golf and tennis. And Conrad DeLuca, a.k.a. Cootzie, a self-described ladies' man, was a generalist who bounced among the store's departments.

Others worked there—a local tennis pro would drop in to string rackets, and an older guy, George Palmer, a.k.a. "Uncle George," sat out in the warehouse repairing fishing reels—but this was the full-time, core staff. The amazing thing about them, in retrospect, is that they made working at this little independent store their careers. These were family men: all were married with kids, owned houses, drove late-model cars, and in general enjoyed a middle-class lifestyle. Ira had a cottage at Page Lake not far from ours.

It wasn't as if they had time to moonlight. My dad didn't work his staff in shifts; if you had a job with him, you worked every day the store was open, morning to close. You'd get an hour for lunch and another for dinner, so a typical workday ran ten hours, spread out over twelve. Saturdays we closed at six, so everyone headed home after eight hours. The total: forty-eight hours on the clock per week. I don't know what Dad paid his staff, but evidently it was enough, because most stayed for twenty years or more. It helped that he paid them cash bonuses at the end of the year. He made a real effort to take care of them.

The guys who ran the various departments considered themselves more than coworkers. They were friends on and off the clock, perhaps because they didn't have much time to broaden their social circles. Most of them golfed, including my dad, and they usually did it together; Dick's was closed Sundays and Mondays, and for years the guys at the store would gather Monday mornings to play a local course.

The only women at Dick's worked in the office. One was a young bookkeeper, Donna LaBarre. Donna was petite and pretty, with dark hair trimmed short and a stylish wardrobe. She was three years out of high school. Kind. Playful. Warm.

My parents' divorce, in August 1965, probably shouldn't have surprised anyone. Afterward, my mom reportedly had second thoughts and talked about contesting the new arrangement. My dad nipped that by remarrying in December.

At twenty-one, Donna was fifteen years younger than my dad. My dad moved out, handing over 16 Ardsley Road to my mom, who dated a little but never remarried. Every year, my mom would take all of us kids to a studio to get our picture taken, and always give us a copy to present to my dad at Christmas. Every year he got that picture, my dad would cry, despite knowing it was coming. Dad could show kindness to her, too. Each Christmas he'd tell my sister Kim to pick out something nice for Mom, to serve as a present from us kids.

But what Mom chose to show us most often was a deep bitterness and savage animosity toward him. And most often, Dad wasn't any nicer to her. Each of our parents would send messages to the other through their kids, which put us in the middle of their hostile back-and-forth. Early on, Kim and I were the only two old enough to grasp what had happened—I was ten, she was eight, and the others were still really little. That worked against us. We understood that the world had turned upside down. I was lucky to have baseball.

Mom went to work as an aide in the cafeteria at our school. She got alimony and child support from my dad, but even so, she worried constantly about money, and it wore on her. She wasn't always easy to be around, having to carry the load of caring for five kids. We always had clean clothes and plenty to eat, though. She came to all of my Little League games and school functions. When I needed what she couldn't provide, I only had to cut through a couple of yards to see my grandfather.

Meanwhile, my dad and Donna lived in an apartment for a while, then bought a lot on a wooded hilltop south of the Susquehanna. In the winter, when the leaves were gone, you could see across the river to 345 Court Street. On that lot he built a brick ranch, a nice place big enough to accommodate all of us kids on weekends.

That was the setup. My mom kept us during the week. We stayed with my dad and our stepmom on weekends. As rough as the divorce was for all of us in the early going, it really turned out pretty well. We saw Dad at least as much as we had when he lived at home, because we were with him Friday evenings and all day Saturday and Sunday, plus Monday in the summer. I saw him more, because he never missed a baseball or football game.

The other reason it worked out was Donna. I could not have written this while my mom was alive—none of us could so much as mention Donna's name without sending her into a rage—but my stepmom made the best of a difficult situation and threw herself into her new role.

She wasn't the least bit moody or hotheaded; her steady warmth calmed my father, grounded him, and her gentle persistence could (at least some of the time) smooth his rough edges. She was vibrant, full of energy, and seemed to love playing with us kids. I never saw her lose her temper, and she never tried to discipline us. She told Kim years later that when she'd informed her mother she was going to marry my dad, her mother had said:

"If you do this, you need to remember that he had those five kids before he had you, and they'll always come first." She took that to heart.

Donna was one of eleven children raised on a farm southeast of town, and she'd take us there sometimes. It was a lot of fun crawling around on the hay bales and watching the cows. I think farm life must have given her an enormous capacity for work, because she seemed tireless. She kept a spotless house and prepared wonderful meals while continuing to keep the books at the company.

My dad seemed much happier in his new life. He and Donna continued his ritual trips to Florida each winter, at first staying aboard a Chris-Craft cabin cruiser that he bought, the *Fun Seekers*, and later in a condo. He had the cottage at Page Lake, too, and we went there almost every weekend. It was there that I spent the most uninterrupted time with my younger brothers and sisters. We were far apart in age—Nancy was just two when my folks split—but with all of us crowded under the roof, along with our friends, the cottage was a busy place. My dad got a boat, and we water-skied, three of us at a time, on lines cut to different lengths, my dad keeping the lines straight as we ducked under each other. In the winter we raced around on snowmobiles. Weekends there were great fun. The only thing that would tear us away was Little League or peewee football. We always drove back into Binghamton for my games.

I was among thousands of kids who played in Binghamton's Little League over the years, and for that experience I have my dad to thank. In the early sixties, the city was home to just four teams, one on each of its east, west, north, and south sides. The city's population at the time was about seventy thousand, and the surrounding suburbs ballooned that number considerably. Binghamton's Little League provided play for maybe sixty boys, ages nine to twelve.

My dad thought that was disgraceful. His own athletic past had made a huge difference in his life—if he hadn't had baseball and fishing to occupy his time and quiet his teenage mind, there's no telling what might have happened to him. He thought it vital that other kids have a shot at the transformative experiences he'd had. Plus, he recognized that a kid engaged in baseball is too busy to get into trouble.

So my dad talked to his friends who ran businesses in Binghamton—insurance agents, car dealers, plumbers, a local pharmacy, restaurants—and he convinced them to underwrite an expansion of the league to sixteen teams, four from each neighborhood. They also created a developmental farm league for kids who wanted to play organized ball. In place of sixty kids, there was now room for two hundred forty to play Little League, and another two hundred to play on the farm teams.

He made one stipulation: the teams created through his efforts couldn't buy their uniforms or gear from Dick's. He wanted no one thinking that he'd spearheaded the expansion just to make money. I'm sure he earned a lot of goodwill, and that surely translated into some families making a point of shopping at the store. But in terms of direct benefits to my dad and his business, there were none.

As you'll see later in this story, Dick's makes a priority of fostering opportunities for young people to compete in both team and individual sports, and if you were to trace that effort back to its earliest incarnation, this is where you'd end up—in Binghamton in the early to midsixties, and my dad's solicitation of support for the baseball expansion. That kind of community involvement is built into our corporate DNA.

It would be interesting to find out just how many kids in my hometown have benefited from the program he started. This is certain: their lives have been changed for the better, all because my dad recognized that sports matter. I did not immediately benefit. I was a decent student in elementary school, but one semester I got a D in handwriting because I hadn't mastered cursive script. Dad forced me to spend half of that summer—the summer I was due to start Little League—on the front porch, practicing my handwriting. I had to write letters to my grandmothers, one of whom lived three hundred yards away, and the other just across town. I wrote to my aunt Rosemary, my father's sister, who lived in Texas. I wrote scores of letters to people all over the country, to satisfy my dad that I'd mastered cursive. He finally released me to play baseball with four weeks left of the season.

I played briefly in the farm league, then moved up to Little League. I loved every minute of it. My favorite part of catching came when an opposing player tried to steal second or third. My dad's drills had included "hot potato," in which I'd try to get the ball out of my glove and back to him as quickly as possible, and in games I enjoyed the payoff, getting the ball out and firing it to second. Sometimes, the ball got there before the runner—sometimes it didn't. Unfortunately, as good as I was behind the plate, I couldn't hit worth a lick—I treated every pitch as a potential home run and swung at it with all my might, which is rarely a formula for success in the batter's box.

The games were a big deal in Binghamton. The newspaper ran box scores. Playoffs earned bona fide coverage by real reporters and stories in the sports section. The stands were always packed. Dad, Mom, Gramp, and my grandmother never missed seeing me play.

After our games, if we won—and often when we didn't—one of the team parents would give the coach a few bucks to take us to the Tastee Freez on Court Street. The ice cream tasted even better when I got to eat it in uniform with my teammates, on those hot, muggy nights in Binghamton.

Let's jump ahead four years to 1968, when I was thirteen. Playing ball was all I cared about, and that would remain the case for years to come. School was a distraction. I did well enough to earn C's and the occasional B, but classwork didn't interest me, and it didn't seem terribly important to my parents. I regret it now, but I didn't apply myself.

I'd graduated from Little League to muni league teenage baseball by then and was the catcher for the Cortese Restaurant team. Of all the things I miss in Binghamton, that restaurant is near the top—a little hole-in-the-wall, family-run place a couple of blocks from the store, with food that is still out of this world.

Anyway, I was playing for Cortese's, and we were good. Not great, but solid. Among my teammates was Tim Myers, another kid who lived on the East Side. He was a year behind me in school and played shortstop and first base. We played summer baseball together, starting when he was nine and I was ten, as well as for Binghamton North High School. He was almost as bad a hitter as I was. We became great friends.

Baseball wasn't my sole obsession. From about the time I started Little League, I'd played pickup football on the sprawling grounds of a state mental hospital at the end of Ardsley Road. It was full-tackle play; we'd wear helmets and shoulder pads over shorts and sneakers. I loved the physicality of football, the tackling, the hits. I loved running the ball and throwing passes.

I'd started playing peewee football when I was twelve, and I can still picture details of my first game. I played linebacker. When the first whistle blew I was sure that I was about to be killed. In the third or fourth play I got hit. A play later, I hit somebody. And I recall thinking: *Hey, this is cool. I'm going to like this.*

So by that summer of 1968, I was looking forward to a joyful sixteen games of muni league baseball, followed without pause by football training camp in August. I was torn between the two sports and didn't know which I loved more. My dreams were no longer restricted to making it into the big leagues to play catcher for the Yankees. Now I pictured myself as the starting quarterback for the New York Giants.

That's where my head was when, with school just ended and the summer stretching languidly ahead, my dad made an announcement at dinner one night. "You're thirteen," he said.

"It's time for you to get some responsibility. Be at the store at eight thirty tomorrow. You're going to work."

The next morning I rode my bike from Ardsley Road to Dick's. I'd never ridden on Court Street; to get to school or any points west of home, I was required to take quiet, two-lane Robinson Street, which ran parallel to Court. But that would have taken me out of the way, and my dad had made it clear that I'd better not be late. Court Street was four lanes wide and jammed with traffic, and I remember thinking as cars whizzed by that I probably shouldn't be there. I survived, needless to say, and made it to the store on time, and that ride became my summertime ritual for years.

My assignment was to unload trucks and stash the arriving merchandise in a little prefab metal warehouse my dad had erected behind the store a couple of years before. It was connected by an intercom to the sales floor, and if Dick's sold the last of an item, or something too big to have on regular display, the staff would call over: "I need a Eureka twelve-by-twelve tent," or whatever the item was. I or one of the other warehouse guys would hunt it down and carry it across the back parking lot into the store, or position it out front for easy loading by the customer. It was hot, hard, manual labor, and I freaking hated it—not because it was uncomfortable, but because I knew that Tim Myers and all of my other buddies were at Fairview Park, playing baseball. I worked from eight thirty a.m. to one p.m., Tuesday through Saturday. One o'clock couldn't arrive fast enough.

I made no secret of the fact that I didn't want to be there, but that didn't dissuade my dad from keeping me on. On the contrary, sometimes he got annoyed that I was leaving at one. When I broached the idea that maybe working a kid through the summer was unjust, and that it was limiting my athletic development, he shut me down. "This is the family business," he said, "which makes it your business. This is what puts food on the table. This is how you're able to eat, and sleep with a roof over your head."

The implicit message was "Toughen up." The explicit message

was "No." I knew better than to raise the subject twice. And two summers later, Dad rewarded my lack of enthusiasm by extending my hours to full time: I now worked twelve hours a day, like everyone else.

I showed up before the store opened to move all the outdoor displays onto the sidewalk out front—Coleman coolers, canoes and johnboats, lawn furniture—and was stuck until it was time to move all the stuff back in after we closed. It was torture. None of my friends worked such hours, and I knew they were all shagging flies while I was trapped indoors, moving boxes around or applying price tags. The days seemed as if they'd never end. I couldn't bear to be there.

I wasn't off the hook with the end of summer. My dad put me to work through the Christmas break, as well, when my friends were out sledding and ice-skating or just enjoying a respite from school. Dick's had a tradition each hunting season of weighing the deer shot by locals, keeping track of the weights, and awarding a prize at season's end to the hunter who'd bagged the biggest buck. On the sidewalk outside the front doors was the contraption used to weigh the carcasses—a glorified engine hoist with a scale inserted between its boom and the straps from which the deer were suspended. Throughout the days during the season, guys would pull up outside with dead deer roped to their roofs or in the beds of their pickups, and we'd help muscle their prizes to the hoist and crank them off the ground.

No one liked the duty, as even sunny December days were cold in the Southern Tier, so if I was working, it was left to me to do it. The deer would bleed buckets while suspended on the device. We spread sawdust on the sidewalk to soak it up, or at least prevent people from slipping in the gore on their way into and out of the store. By the end of the day, the sidewalk would be heaped with sodden wood chips, which it was my sad duty to clean up.

One day I brought something in from the warehouse and saw a man in the golf department, looking at golf clubs. No one was helping him, so I walked over and asked if there was anything

I could do for him. He looked askance at me for a moment— remember, I was then a skinny kid of fifteen—before saying he was looking for clubs but wasn't sure what he wanted. We got to talking. I walked him through his options. Afterward he nodded, said he needed to think on it, and left.

A couple of days later I was back in the store, dropping something off that I'd lugged from the warehouse, and the man walked back in and headed for the golf department. My dad intercepted him and asked if he could help. The guy spotted me walking toward the back of the store and said: "Actually, I'd like to talk to that young man right there about these clubs."

My dad, following his gaze, turned to find me standing there and let out a startled laugh. I walked over. "Yes," I told him, "I remember." And within minutes, the man walked out with a set of Wilson Black Heather golf clubs, retailing for $119.

Two things happened at that moment. I realized, with a thrill, that, holy *smokes*, I could sell—and I liked it. And my dad and the guys on the sales floor all realized that, holy *shit*, this fifteen-year-old kid could sell. "You're going to stay on the sales floor now," my dad told me. "Tomorrow, when you come in, you're working on the floor."

## CHAPTER 4

# "GO PLAY BASEBALL— STAY OUT OF TROUBLE"

Though the store had always been a major presence in my life, until I started working the sales floor I had only a vague notion of what my dad did and whether he was good at it. The only thing I knew firsthand was that he had an almost paranormal awareness of what was on the shelves. Back when I'd been in fifth or sixth grade, Kim and I were assigned to help with the annual summer inventory. Dad would put us in the fishing tackle, where we were to count how many of each little item—lures, hooks, swivels, packets of line, and such—hung from each peg. We were to write down the tally, making sure that we didn't mix different hook sizes, etc. As the day went on, it was tempting to eyeball a peg and guesstimate a number. If we did, he'd know it. "You wrote down 'twelve," he'd say, "and there are fourteen of those." How did he know that? To this day, I have no idea.

Now I saw him in action every day. First observation: my dad's management style was not by-the-book. In fact, it was a textbook lesson in how not to handle your employees. He played each of the guys against the others. One week, he'd buddy up to one, saying that his hard work had made him an obvious choice to lead the staff in my dad's absence. A week later, it would be another guy who got the boss's approval.

The result was a constant hum of tension in the store, with

each employee jockeying for my dad's attention and favor. Today we'd call it a toxic work environment. I'm betting the place might have blown apart at the seams had my dad not been spending months at a time in Florida, which gave everyone else a chance to settle down. Finally, he formalized Bob Aiken's status as his number two. Bob's level head and straightforward leadership were an antidote to the craziness.

Another insight of mine, which would be bolstered many times, was just how effective a salesman my dad was. He was the quintessential Irishman—jovial, a back slapper, full of . . . well, an ability to shoot the breeze. Sometimes I'd watch him from across the store, laughing with people. He could banter and bargain with anyone, and I could see that his customers enjoyed the exchange. He knew a lot about the merchandise, and that came through when he talked about it. He believed in what he was selling. He was also an expert at going for the added sale—if a customer bought a pair of sneakers, he made sure to push a pair of socks. This wasn't a mere cash grab. He considered it a disservice to that shopper to have him leave the store without everything he needed to get the best possible results from his purchase.

He roamed the floor through the day, visiting with customers, making sure that each one felt, every minute he was in the store, that he was looked after. The moment the front door opened, we were to be on hand to greet the guy walking in and be ready to answer his questions or show him around. Treat him as you would a guest at your house, I remember him telling me: "If you had a visitor there, you wouldn't keep doing what you're doing. You'd drop it to say hello and make him feel at home."

That was a lesson that stayed with me. You can have the greatest merchandise in town, but if you don't throw your energy into customer service, you won't keep people coming back. To this day, nothing annoys me more than to walk into a store unacknowledged. I hate having to roam the aisles looking for help. At 345 Court Street, that never happened.

Another lesson that stuck: never judge a customer by his

looks—the way he's dressed, the way he carries himself, whether his fingernails are clean. "He might be a farmer," my dad told me, "and this might be the one day of the year he's come into town to do his shopping." Great point. To see it played out in everyday terms, look around you the next time you're at a gym, and try to pick out who among the sweaty people around you showed up in a suit.

How good a salesman was my dad? Before I started working for him, he was in New York City for a sporting goods show at the old New York Coliseum. One evening he and some other guys were going to dinner at the Cattleman. The restaurant was a fair distance away, and it was raining, and they had zero luck hailing a cab. They're standing at the curb, getting soaked, when a taxi pulls up and the driver climbs out and crosses the sidewalk, on his way into a corner grocery. My dad asked him, "Hey, could you give us a ride to the Cattleman?"

"Forget it," the guy said. "I'm off duty." Unnecessarily nasty.

My dad looked in the cab and saw the keys in the ignition, so he hustled everyone into the vehicle, climbed behind the wheel, and hit the gas. I'm not sure how far they got before they were pulled over, but soon enough, cops were all over them. And you know what? Dad talked his way out of it. Charmed the cops and even the cabbie to the point where he and his friends were allowed to go on their way, no charges pressed. They ate steak that night.

Now that I reflect on it, that's probably a cautionary tale about alcohol, too, because I can't imagine my dad would have stolen that cab without artificial courage. Still, when he laid on the charm, the guy could talk his way into or out of anything.

Over the course of many years, Dad inspired in me a building aversion to drink, but there were a few key moments that cemented it. It must have been in the late summer of 1968, the same year I started working in the warehouse, that we held a Stack family reunion at my dad's house, and a lot of my paternal aunts, uncles, and cousins came. Among them was my favorite, Uncle Ed. Of all my father's relatives, he was probably the best to me, and I'd bet my siblings and cousins felt the same way. He could make anyone he was with feel like the most important person around. Each of us thought we were his favorite.

Uncle Ed was a wild man, however—he liked to drink, to a degree my dad never approached. Ed was a happy drinker but a dangerous one. So, this reunion lasted all day, until the warm afternoon turned cool and darkness was coming on, by which time Uncle Ed had thrown down quite a few. We walked him out to his car, watched as he headed down the hill, and were strolling back into the house when we heard an enormous crash. The sound of it was catastrophic—it was so loud, and so violent, that it seemed a sure bet someone had just been killed.

Automobile travel hadn't been good to the Stacks. My grandfather had died in that 1935 car accident. My cousin Diane was eighteen when she, too, collided with a truck, in 1961. Another cousin had been hit by a car and gravely injured, and my own brother Rick had been hurt by a runaway car in a parking lot earlier that year—a vehicle left unattended with the motor running. The car had shaken itself out of park and rolled over Rick, breaking his leg and causing other injuries that put him in a full-body cast for months.

So when we heard this explosive bang down the hill, my father fell to his knees screaming, "Oh, my God! Not my brother now, too!" I took off like a shot toward the sound, fearing the worst. I was sure I'd find my uncle's car mangled and smoking, and his lifeless body inside.

But, no. I was shocked to discover that Uncle Ed was unhurt. He'd plowed into a parked car, then careened into the woods. He was trying to back his car out of the trees when I reached him, my dad pulling up just behind me in a stripped-down green van. He'd bought it after Rick's accident, because wearing that full-body cast, my brother wouldn't fit in my dad's car.

We loaded Uncle Ed into the van and drove him home. On our

way back, my dad said, "Listen. I know you love your uncle, that you think he's a great guy—and he is. But he drinks too much, and someday he's going to break all of our hearts. We're going to get a phone call that he's killed himself in a car accident.

"I just want you to be ready for it," he said, "because it's going to happen."

You're allowed to raise an eyebrow here over my dad's commenting on someone else's drinking. But he was right. In May 1969, when I was fourteen, my uncle was driving home drunk after a round of golf, went off the road, and hit a tree. My dad called me with the news that he might not make it. At the least, he'd be paralyzed from the neck down.

Uncle Ed spent a long time in a local hospital before he was transferred to a Veterans Administration center in Beacon, New York, 140 miles away. I went to see him there a few months later. I remember the horror I felt when I walked into his room: He was held fast by braces and straps, and by a huge iron halo bolted to his head. He couldn't speak. I must have worn my shock on my face, because when he saw my reaction, tears streamed down his cheeks.

He'd been a bigger-than-life presence—a war veteran, a successful businessman, and a loving and lovable mentor. It was a terrible moment.

He died at the VA fourteen months after the accident.

A second episode contributed to my development as a lightweight drinker: When I was seventeen, Dave Polosky, the golf guy, convinced my dad to hold a one-day springtime sale of golf clubs and equipment away from the store, and to advertise the daylights out of it. They called it Golf-A-Thon. That first year they held it at an American Legion post, but for several years after it took place at St. Michael's Hall, the community center attached to a Russian Orthodox church on the West Side, about three miles from Dick's. We'd clear out the golf department and buy a pile of additional merchandise, truck it over to St. Michael's, and open for a few hours on a Sunday in late March or early April. Golf-A-Thon became a huge event. Customers would swarm in. One year in the early seventies, we did $75,000 in sales. For an operation the size of Dick's, that was a very big day.

Anyway, after Golf-A-Thon ended, the staff packed everything up and hauled it back to the store. Once it was all put away, my dad would take everyone out to dinner at Cortese's. One year my father was drinking, maybe more than usual, and somebody made a remark, or something got under his skin, and the evening ended with his firing everybody. The whole staff, every last man.

The next morning he was sleeping it off when the phone rang. Donna answered. It was a customer down at the store, reporting that the doors were locked and the lights were off, and asking why. Donna called a couple of the staff, who told her they'd been fired.

Aw, no, she told them. Dick didn't mean that.

Oh, he meant it, they assured her. You should have seen him.

She pleaded until a couple of the guys agreed to go in and open for the day. Later, my dad apologized to the staff. Everyone stayed, and normalcy—or Dick's version of it—returned, as if nothing had happened.

Third and final episode: One hot and humid summer day before the start of my senior year, I followed up a brutal football practice by joining a bunch of friends bound for a nearby lake. Our high school had sororities and fraternities back then, and the girls of one sorority had a cottage up there. The gathering was unsupervised. No parents would be around. On the way, we stopped for some beer.

Now, you have to bear in mind that although I played quarterback on the football team, wearing 14, the number of my Giants idol, Y. A. Tittle, and although I played catcher on the varsity baseball team, I was no big man on campus. I was never one of the cool kids at Binghamton North. In retrospect, I lived too much on the straight-and-narrow, overly mindful of my dad's warnings that anything I did reflected on the family business. I didn't party like the popular kids. And I had no idea what I was doing when it came to beer.

We football players hadn't had anything to eat since practice, and as hydration wasn't the priority it is today, I doubt we'd had nearly enough water. I drank a six-pack of beer on an empty stomach, chugging one after another. I remember trying to walk and toppling sideways to the ground. Then I got sick and stayed that way.

A classmate, bless her, looked after me. The next morning, I hiked with the others to another classmate's family cabin, where his mom offered me breakfast with a knowing smile and the words, "Ed, you're not very hungry this morning, eh?" She knew that I'd crashed and burned as a beer drinker.

I sat in the back of a pickup truck on the ride home, just to get fresh air. What my father and my uncle Ed had started, that experience finished: I was never much interested in alcohol after that. As I got older, my dad would make fun of me for not drinking or smoking. "You're a ham-and-egger," he used to say. That's an old boxing expression, used to describe a fighter who doesn't have a lot of fight in him, who's in it just for a meal. Not sure how that applied to my abstinence, but that's what he called me. "Lighten up," he'd say. "Every man drinks. You need to drink." That only encouraged me to dig in my heels. I won't say I never have a drink, but my friends say they love going out to dinner with me, because when I order a glass of wine they know I'll take two sips and hand the glass to them.


In March 1971, when I was sixteen, my dad made an unexpected move: he opened a second location. Fifteen years had passed since the Hillcrest disaster, and he remained conservative in his approach to business: he wasn't interested in expanding our range of products or the customers we drew. But a guy who ran a small chain of groceries west of town also owned a little sporting goods store, called Sports Unlimited, on Main Street in Vestal, a village across the Susquehanna from Endicott. He offered the store to my dad at a great price, and my dad couldn't let the deal pass.

When I say it was small, I mean it—2,800 square feet, or roughly half the size of the store in Binghamton. With that addition, the company's payroll grew to about twenty people.

The Vestal store did solid business from the start. That was great for Dick's, and ultimately for my family, but it did nothing to lift me from the depths of misery I felt whenever I was stuck working at the Court Street store. I enjoyed working with customers and liked the guys on the staff; in fact, it was exciting to be a teenager among those older, more worldly guys, and to listen to them talk about women, nightclubs, and other grown-up stuff. But my days on the sales floor remained torture. While I marked time, the summers raced by without me. I hated being there in my mid-to-late teens even more than I had early on, because now it took me away from the serious business of getting ready for the big leagues.

The only place where I was able to find clarity during my high school years was on the field. Whatever my shortcomings in retail sales or the classroom, I made up for them with the enthusiasm I showed my teams. They were everything to me. I remember vividly walking home in the rain with Tim Myers. Baseball practice had been canceled, and I was heartsick about it. What were we going to do? What *was* there to do? The day was ruined. We stopped at Al's Market and got cream-filled cupcakes and a Coke—then, as now, I had a fierce sweet tooth—and the weather cleared, and the sun came out, and I thought: *I wonder if we can go back.*

We couldn't, but that's typical of the single-minded devotion I had for the game. I lived for baseball. And if it's possible, that might have gone double for football. I tried to be the first at football practice, which in August amounted to "three-a-days," or three hard-core training sessions: in the morning, in full pads; after lunch, in helmets but without pads; and in the late afternoon, back to full pads. I wanted more. I stayed late with classmates Gary Dombroski and Joe Hein, who ran routes while I threw passes to them. When I was a junior and senior, the whole team went away to weeklong training camps. I gave them my all, and I wished they lasted longer.

It paid off. Despite my size, I held my own on the gridiron. I remember one of my football coaches saying, with surprise: "You can throw that ball with some serious zip." The first game of my junior year, when the starting quarterback wasn't playing well, I was sent in with orders to throw the ball "all over the field," to get things moving. It was my first game as a varsity QB: I'd moved up from the JV team late the year before but hadn't come off the bench, and I joined the huddle both excited and scared to death. When I took the first snap, all my fear evaporated. I played for four minutes, during which I went four-for-four and passed for two touchdowns, and we beat Chenango Forks High School. The following year, I was the starter and co-captain of the team. I loved every minute of every practice and game.

So I had some gifts, one being a willingness to outwork my innately more talented competition. If life were fair, that would have been enough, and you'd be reading the memoir of a retired New York Giants legend who also won a few World Series rings with the Yankees. God knows, I wanted it.

But making it as a pro athlete requires a huge helping of God-given ability. We lesser mortals can learn technique, and with practice we can get better—a lot better. We can more or less perfect the tools we have. But in the end, a top-tier athlete needs to have size, speed, and quickness. You can't learn to be fast if you're born slow. As they say in basketball, you can't coach height.

Still, every kid dreams. That's something we keep in mind at Dick's today. When a parent comes in to buy his or her kid a baseball glove or soccer cleats, we're selling them a dream of greatness for that child. I saw my dad demonstrate his understanding of just how important sports can be to a kid when I was fifteen or sixteen, working the sales floor. One day a little kid walked in and wandered over to the baseball section, then bolted for the door with a glove. Someone in the store nabbed him as he reached the parking lot and brought him back inside. He was yelling at the thief when my dad saw what was going on and walked over.

He looked the little boy up and down and laid a hand lightly

on his shoulder. It was clear this kid came from a family with no money—the ragged way he was dressed signaled as much. "Why'd you steal the glove?" my dad asked.

The kid, about nine years old, looked up, eyes as big as saucers. Tears streamed down his cheeks. "I just want to play baseball."

My dad nodded. "You can't steal," he said. "No matter how bad you want something, you cannot steal it. I want you to promise me you're not going to do this again."

"Yes, sir," the kid said.

"Okay," my dad said. Then he walked him over to the baseball section of the store and had the kid pick out a ball and a bat to go with the glove. "You go play baseball," he told him. "Stay out of trouble."

I think my dad figured out early on that I wouldn't have a career in sports. He recognized that I was too small for football and too poor a hitter to make it as a baseball prospect. But he was encouraging. He urged me on. Reality dawned on me slowly. I noticed that no college was scouting me in either baseball or football, for starters, and by my junior year in high school, I understood enough about how both games worked to know that didn't bode well. With my average grades, I'd need an athletic scholarship to win admission to any big conference school. That seemed a more distant possibility with each passing month.

When it came to football, I needed only to look in the mirror for an explanation. I stood five-ten and weighed 160 pounds. If I were going to be a realistic prospect as a college quarterback, I needed to wake up one morning four or five inches taller and fifty pounds heavier.

Coming to terms with my limitations in baseball was harder to take, in some ways, because my physical size wasn't a deal-breaker. I had my first glimmer that I wouldn't play for a living when I went out for the one local Legion team, composed of boys sixteen and older. As always, my fielding was good. My hitting, unfortunately, was no better than it ever had been.

I remember a scene during tryouts when I was in the batter's box and finally ripped a line drive over the shortstop. On my way to first I passed the coaches, all making notes, and overheard one say: "Huh. Just when you make your mind up about somebody, they surprise you." Still, that hit came too late, and I didn't make the team. When I got cut, I remember thinking: *Well, Stack, maybe you're not as good as you wish you were.*

Then, in the spring of my senior year, I lost my place as Binghamton North's starting catcher. Joe Hein, my football teammate, beat me out. It came as a surprise. That's understating it. It stung *bad*. I lay awake in bed the night I got the news, confused and hurt and determined to work harder. I lifted weights, tried to build up my strength, stayed late to take extra batting practice.

For a while we went back and forth—he'd catch some games, I'd catch some—but eventually I had to admit to myself that Joe was better. Not by much, but enough: we were both good behind the plate, but he could hit. He was a more complete player. And with that came a final, sad epiphany. If I couldn't beat out Joe for a spot on our high school team, I couldn't very well beat out seventeen million guys hungry to make a living in baseball.

Had Dick Stack been the sort of dad to offer me encouragement at such times, he might have shared his insights into the lasting value of athletics, having been an athlete himself—might have told me that playing the game is its own reward, for example. That I'd be a better man for the triumphs and disappointments I'd had on the field. That making the big leagues wasn't the point. He wasn't that kind of dad, however, at least not then. I came upon my insights on my own, and they've grown clearer to me in the years since I played.

What I learned on the field, as part of a team, transcended athletics. How to work hard, for starters: you have to commit—to practice, to improving, to making an effort. There were always people on our teams who were doggers, who didn't go all-out in practice and didn't give all they had in games. As an adult, I've come to see that there are people like that in any organization.

At the same time, you learn that a team is only as strong as its component parts, and that if one of those parts fails, the whole team has a problem. If your left tackle lines up offsides and gets called for it, on the next play the whole team lines up five yards back. Successful plays work the same way: they inspire the whole team to reach farther. I've seen that many times at Dick's.

You learn that the team is more important than you are, that you're part of a greater good. That can be humbling; it can mean taking a demotion or an unwanted reassignment for the good of the group. That willingness to sacrifice is key to teamwork, and to success in any collective effort.

You learn how to win and lose, and how to be a good sport. When you win, you don't rub your opponent's nose in it, and likewise, you don't resent it when he beats you. You take that lesson into whatever you do for the rest of your life. I've certainly applied it in my career. We've had our share of losses, along with wins.

Individual sports are a little different. Everything hangs on how you, and only you, answer the call. In golf, wrestling, skiing, and singles tennis, you're on an island. I think it takes a lot of guts to play those solo sports. But they share one important lesson with team sports, which is that what you get out of any endeavor is directly proportional to the effort you put into it.

My life would be very different if I hadn't played sports. Though I had grand ambitions as a player, it was the journey, not those dreams, that changed me. Being on a team focused me. It gave me specific goals. It gave me a community. And not least, it occupied my time; if it hadn't been for baseball and football, I think I could have gotten into trouble. I wasn't an engaged student, which put me at risk. I might well have ended up smoking, loitering, or worse with my uninspired classmates outside the Wigwam, a convenience store and hangout near the high school. And there's no telling where, if anywhere, I would have gone from there.

The latter-day revelations about the risks in some sports don't cool my enthusiasm for them. Football, in particular, has come under scrutiny. At Dick's, we've seen our youth football business nosedive in the last few years, as evidence mounts that a hard hit can cause a concussion, leaving lasting damage to a player's brain. The decline has been especially big in equipment for pee-wee football—the younger the players, the bigger the drop in our sales. Parents are deciding the game's risks are overwhelming.

I can't blame them. The concern is long overdue, and I can foresee the day coming, and soon, when top athletes no longer choose to play football, but take their skills to other, lower-impact sports. I can't imagine that schools will be able to defend football without changes to the game that alter its very character. Then again, maybe guys good enough to play college ball will decide that its glories outweigh its risks.

Would I have played, knowing of the dangers as I do now?

No doubt about it. I loved every minute. Nothing could have kept me away.

I say that as somebody who suffered his own share of injuries. Once, playing quarterback in a game against Union-Endicott, I was scrambling down the field when two opposing players sandwiched me. When I got up, my whole body felt like it was asleep, all pins and needles. Pretty clearly, I had a concussion. If it happened today, I'd be rightly subjected to a strict set of protocols to minimize the effects of the injury.

But those were different times, and the prescription for most injuries was to play through them. To complain was to show weakness. "Rub some dirt on it," you'd be told. "Suck it up." You'd be mocked even for telling the coach you needed water. I remember mine scowling as he baby-talked to a player: "Aw, do you need a gwass of water?"

In that game against Union-Endicott, I sat out for a couple of plays, until the coach asked, "Can you play?" I answered, "Absolutely." He sent me back in.

While we were in the huddle, the ref ran over. "Are you all right?" he asked me.

"Yes," I replied.

"Well, son," he said, "you have to be wearing a helmet to play this game." I hadn't realized I wasn't wearing one. He went over to the coach and recommended that I stay on the sidelines the rest of the game. Luckily, I did.

Baseball was no kinder to my body: at various times I dislocated a finger, had a bat crash into my head, and stopped a wild pitch with my groin. Would I encourage my own kids to play, despite these injuries?

Sure, I would. Of course.

I wouldn't trade my experiences on the field, with those teams, for anything. They were key to what I've done with my life. They helped make me who I am.

## CHAPTER 5

# "I LOVE YOU"

As I began my senior year, the question of college loomed. I wanted to go. I wanted to go because I wanted nothing to do with my dad's business. I'd had it shoved down my throat for five years. I'd sacrificed my summers and, really, a whole lot of what it means to be a teenager to the store, and it would have been okay with me if I never entered Dick's again.

My father wasn't eager to send me away for more schooling. His view was that I didn't need college, that I could stay in Binghamton and learn from him. He'd teach me all I needed to know—certainly more than I'd learn sitting in class. We struggled over it for months. He didn't appear to be budging until Donna finally got through to him. I'm guessing she told him that if he didn't let me go, he'd lose me—I'd leave home, leave the store, and leave him behind. "Fine," he said at the dinner table one night. "You can go to college. But I'm not going to pay for all of it." We struck a deal: I'd work during holidays and summers, and save a thousand dollars or more per year toward my expenses. He'd cover the rest.

The decision didn't suddenly transform me into the greatest of college prospects, however. Decades later, my daughter Katie was preparing to take the SATs and asked me whether I scored higher in the test's math or verbal section. I answered accurately: "Sports, honey."

One high school course I did enjoy, and that had a tremendous impact on me, was a public speaking class taught by a mild-mannered guy named Lawrence Feltham. Had it not been for him, and for what I learned in that class, I don't know that I'd be able to do what I do today, because speaking in front of an audience is part of leading any big company. One of my favorite movies is *Mr. Holland's Opus*, about a teacher who devotes his life to teaching in a public high school and leaves a mark on generations of students. Whenever I see it, I think of Mr. Feltham. I suspect he had no idea how much he affected me.

Many of my courses didn't go so well. I was taking a lot of New York Regents classes—something like today's advanced placement—but not bringing glory to the family name in any. So I knew I wouldn't be going to Notre Dame, Penn, or Syracuse. I applied to smaller schools and was accepted by Moravian College in Bethlehem, Pennsylvania—not too far away, but far enough, and I could play football there; by Widener College, just south of Philadelphia; and by St. John Fisher, a small, private liberal arts college outside Rochester.

I was struggling in French, among other subjects, while I mulled these choices. My French teacher was a young woman named Katie Madigan, whose dad had been good friends with my uncle Ed. She recognized that I had more scholastic potential than my grades let on, but she was also realistic. She pulled me aside after class one day. "You're never going to pass the French Regents final," she told me.

"Ms. Madigan, I know," I said. Understood was that if I didn't pass French, I wouldn't have enough credits for a Regents Diploma.

"I'm going to help you out here," she said. "I want you to write me a paper on a French author, French artist, French philosopher—I don't care which. Just write me three pages on any one of these, and I'll excuse you from the final. Under one condition."

That sounded great to me. "What's the condition?" I asked.

She answered: "That you promise to never take another French class."

In another conversation, she asked where I wanted to go to college. I hemmed and hawed. "You should go to St. John Fisher," she declared. Her brother, Freddie, was a student there. Her sister, Mary, went to Nazareth College, which was more or less a sister school to St. John Fisher. They both liked Rochester. "Go up there," she said, "and spend a weekend with Freddie. See what it's like."

I did. I had a wonderful weekend at the school and fell hard for her sister. Mary Madigan was a year ahead of me, and gorgeous, and went out of her way to be nice to me. In retrospect, her sister probably told her to be, but I didn't think that at the time. I chose to attend St. John Fisher because I was interested in Mary Madigan. I'm sure there are worse reasons to pick a college. It's possible that there are better ones, too.

As my senior year ended, I faced a dilemma. Binghamton North doled out four graduation tickets for each member of the class; without a ticket, you didn't get in. I invited my mom and my dad, and there was no way I wasn't inviting Gramp and my grandmother, but that left out Donna. I didn't know what to do. My dad lost his mind that I was even thinking about leaving her out, but he didn't have any ideas about how to get out of the dilemma. I decided the ceremony wasn't worth the anguish it was causing everyone and announced I wouldn't attend my graduation.

As it happened, I ended up going. My dad skipped it.

That summer I again worked at Dick's for twelve hours a day. My only comfort was that I no longer imagined Tim Myers out having fun while I was stuck inside. My dad asked me one day whether I had any friends who might want to work at the store, and when I asked Tim, he said sure, he'd love a job there. So while I worked the floor, helping customers, Tim was now across the back parking lot in the warehouse.

Spoiler alert: he kept working for Dick's. He still works for the company. He's never worked anywhere else. Besides me, he might be our most senior employee, with forty-five years on the job and counting.

I couldn't wait for the summer to end. My plan was to spend a year at St. John Fisher, work my tail off, then transfer to Notre Dame, where I'd decided I really wanted to be. I wouldn't go out for any intercollegiate sports; I had no future in the pros, so I had to get serious about my studies—not only because that might help me get to South Bend, but because I'd have to get a real job once I graduated.

I'll give away how that turned out right now: I did not go to Notre Dame. At Fisher, I pulled something like a 2.75 grade-point average. In business courses, I managed a little north of 3.0. Not bad, but not setting the world on fire. A fellow student once remarked to me that "retail and real estate are the C student's best friends," and I have to say he was probably right.

At long last came the day when my dad and Donna drove me to Rochester and helped me carry my few belongings into the dorms. I remember watching as they drove off, the paraphrased words of Dr. Martin Luther King ringing in my head: "Free at last, free at last, thank God almighty, I'm free at last." I'd never have to work at Dick's again. I was beyond happy.

St. John Fisher was a young school, founded in 1948. It occupied a tree-shaded campus with brown-brick dorms and classroom buildings, neither modern nor old-fashioned, on 150-odd acres of rolling hills in the southeast Rochester suburbs, an area of town largely given over to golf courses. Originally a Catholic college led by the Basilian Fathers, it had gone independent of the church five years before I arrived; still, priests accounted for a good share of the faculty and administration. The school had also started accepting women in the recent past, though the student body remained overwhelmingly male. All-female Nazareth College, and Mary Madigan, were a mile away. Each school served as the dating pool for the other.

Another spoiler: I got absolutely nowhere with Mary. She was unfailingly kind but had no romantic interest in me whatsoever. Instead, I dated a couple of her fellow Nazareth students. One taught me how to play the piano.

My first weeks in college introduced me to friends who'd be part of my life for years to come: great guys like Mark Muench, from Syracuse, and Bill Colombo, from Brooklyn, who'd later become a major part of Dick's. My decision not to attempt a transfer to Notre Dame had little to do with my grades and everything to do with these friendships, and with the charms of Rochester, and with the relationships I had with my professors at Fisher. I quickly fell in love with the place.

Halfway through my freshman year I'd forged an outline for my future. I'd be a business lawyer. I'd major in accounting and learn everything I needed to know to properly manage a company's books. Then I'd go to law school and pass the bar. The combination of business acumen and legal know-how would make me attractive to any business. I'd be sitting on a corporate board someday, or leading a meaningful company.

I finished my freshman year excited. I'd written a letter to a law firm in Binghamton and landed a summer job as a clerk there. I was proud and full of myself, and went to tell my dad of this first success on my road to becoming a lawyer. He didn't want to hear about it. "You're not going to work there," he said.

"Sure I am," I said. "I got the job. They've said yes."

"No," he said. "This business has put food on the table since you were a kid. It's what's helping you go to college. You're going to get your ass down to the store, and that's all there is to it." Knowing that I couldn't continue college without him, I did as I was told. I rubbed some dirt on the hurt and sucked it up. But my disdain for working at the store in high school was kid's stuff next to my hatred for it now.

The one bright spot in my life that summer was a new game. I'd been in my midteens when Gramp first advised me to take up golf, and he'd kept up the pitch ever since. I hadn't been uninterested. I'd watched a lot of golf on TV with him, and I'd been riveted by some big coffee-table books he had that showed off golf holes located around the world. The colors of those fairways and greens reminded me of my almost overwhelming first glimpse of Yankee Stadium as a kid. So I'd been receptive; in fact, in high school I'd often doodled golf courses—drew doglegging fairways and diabolical water hazards and sand traps when I should have been paying attention to the teacher. What with baseball and football, though, I'd never had time for the game.

That now changed. Between my semesters away and my schedule at the store, I didn't see Gramp nearly as often, and I missed our time together. So beginning that summer, I started playing golf with him on my Mondays off. I learned immediately that he was a very good player. I was not, but I learned the game from a quiet and patient teacher.

He usually had a simple solution to problems on and off the course. Once, I was hitting balls off the practice tee and complained, "Gramp, everything I'm hitting is going left."

"Well, Eddie," he responded, "aim a little more to the right."

Another day we were playing at En-Joie Golf Club—its "E-J" abbreviation is a clue that it was developed by Endicott Johnson for the company's employees, back in the 1920s—and on the third tee I hit a bad drive. I was steamed about it as we walked the fairway, and as he strode past me Gramp slapped me on the back. "Hey, Eddie," he said, "who you mad at?" He kept walking, and I realized I'd been ticked off at the golf course, and my clubs, and the weather, and the fates, when of course none of those were to blame for that lousy shot. I was being a jerk, and he made me laugh at myself. I hollered after him: "I got it!"

He downplayed his own skills. He made nine holes-in-one, all after he'd turned fifty, but I didn't learn that from him—I read it in the newspaper. The same went for his most remarkable achievement. Beginning at age seventy-one, he shot his age for nineteen years straight; in other words, when he was seventy-one, he shot a seventy-one or lower. More often than not, he did it several times per year. If you're not a golfer, let me assure you, that's a big deal.

If you said anything about how amazing it was, he'd wave off the compliment. "It gets easier every year," he said, "because I get one more shot to play with."

When he was seventy-four, he felt a stabbing pain in his back while playing a round in Florida and underwent spinal disc surgery a short time later. It kept him away from the game for three months. He was pretty sure he managed to shoot a seventy-three that year, regardless, but admitted that he might have snapped his string. Otherwise, the feat was amply documented.

Gramp never stopped offering me insight into a life well lived. When he was halfway through his eighties, he and my grandmother came home from one of their regular trips to Las Vegas, during which they held themselves to a few hard-and-fast rules. They went out every night. They never returned to their room before eleven and never stayed out past two. This time, Grandma arrived back in Binghamton with her arm in a cast. "What happened?" I asked her.

"I broke my arm," she said.

"How'd you do that?"

"We were doing the Bump," she said. That was a disco dance popular at the time in which dancers bumped butts. "And your grampa missed."

Bottom line, so to speak: that summer Gramp rescued me, as he had so often in my childhood. He salvaged what otherwise would have been three months spent stewing in purgatory and plotting my escape. As it was, I still thought a lot about my future. Three more years of school, and I'd be done with Dick's, and Binghamton, and my mercurial father.

My stay in the dorms ended after two years. There was this kid—I won't mention his name, but let's call him "Ralph"—who hung around with us. We couldn't figure out why, because we had nothing in common. One day in February of my sophomore year, a few of us in the dorm decided it would be a good idea to grab Ralph while he took a shower, wrap him up in the shower curtain, carry him to the elevator, and send him down to the lobby.

Streaking was the big rage at the time, and at St. John Fisher this prank had become a sidebar to the wider craze. It wasn't my idea to subject Ralph to it, and I certainly wasn't the ringleader, but I joined in on the plan once it was already hatched. The mission was a failure: we never got Ralph into the elevator.

Unfortunately, he called his father, just the same, and his father called the school. We were in big trouble. We were summoned to the dean of student housing. I was the last to walk in, and when I did the dean looked me in the eye and muttered, "Fucking Stack. I should have known." I have no idea why he said that.

There was talk of suspending us, which eventually was dropped—the administration came to see that we were all decent students and had merely been playing a prank. But the matter wasn't finished. Father Joe Dorsey, the dean of students, taught English, and I was taking a class with him. I loved the guy. Father Dorsey was kind and smart, and the glue that held Fisher together. After a class in late April, near the end of the semester, he asked me, "Mr. Stack, can I see you in my office?"

I took up a position in front of his desk. He looked at me over his half glasses and asked, "Ed, have you and your friends ever thought of moving off campus?"

"You know what, Father? We have," I answered. "We've been thinking about it."

He nodded. "My son, I would strongly suggest that." He paused before continuing: "There is no on-campus housing for you and the other boys next semester."

My buddies and I had to convince our parents that we were moving off campus because it was the mature thing to do—we'd learn how to cook, clean, pay bills, run a real household. We didn't mention that we had no choice. The only place we could afford was a rambling two-and-a-half-story wood-frame house on what was, at the time, a rough street in one of the rougher neighborhoods in Rochester. Put it this way: a candidate for city office campaigned on cleaning up the area.

So there, in a Rochester battle zone, is where I spent my nights for the second half of my time in college. Despite numerous distractions, most self-inflicted, I did all right. Accounting is a tough major, but I found I had an affinity for numbers, and I was able to stay sharp by applying what I learned at Dick's over the summer.

My college years coincided with high interest rates in the United States. The prime was 10 percent the month I started classes, rose as high as 12 percent in July 1974, and was still bouncing around 10 percent the following January. It would get a lot higher a few years later, but at the time, those rates seemed ruinous, and they did a number on consumer spending. Business was terrible. My dad, still scarred by his long-ago brush with disaster, was so depressed that on some mornings he didn't get out of bed. I'd come home and he'd ask what we'd posted in sales for the day, and when I told him he'd groan that the end was near.

But my summers home revealed that the prime rate was a minor concern next to some in-house challenges at Dick's. Remember how, when I was a kid, our garage was always stuffed with overstock? I saw now that one reason for that was that my dad played his hunches when buying merchandise. If he liked a product and believed it would sell well, he simply bought a lot of it. Following his gut usually paid off, but sometimes the only way to get rid of all the overstock was to discount it to the point where we made little, if any, money from its sale. My dad, I came to see, didn't have any real buying strategy or program in place. He wasn't financially disciplined. We could limp along by the seat of our pants for only so long.

His lack of basic planning was never more apparent than during our annual inventory, which he conducted each July, just after the June 30 close of the store's fiscal year. It took a week or so to go through the store, tallying up everything we had and figuring out what we had sold. It wasn't until we did that, and extended the inventory into dollars and cents, that my dad knew whether he'd made money during the year. He had no idea. He used a line of credit from the bank to buy merchandise, pay out salaries, and cover the stores' utilities, and all the while didn't know until the end of the year whether he'd break even. As I got deeper into my education in accounting, this flying-blind approach to running a business seemed ever more dangerous. It invited failure.

I worked part-time jobs in Rochester that opened my eyes to how well-run companies behaved. I was a gofer at Xerox for a semester, a secretary's secretary, given odd jobs and numbers to crunch—the smallest of cogs in a huge machine. Even so, it was clear that the machine was well designed and oiled. I worked at Wegmans, a grocery store. I held a job at the Oak Hill Country Club near campus. The bosses at all of these enterprises, I was sure, knew whether they were making money.

My dad's weaknesses as an administrator only stiffened my resolve to find a career of my own. I wanted no part of the family business. As soon as I graduated, I'd be gone.

Then one day my dad's doctor, Peter Zayac, was in the store and spotted my dad walking up the stairs to the office. He was dragging a leg. Get yourself to the hospital, the doctor ordered.


Dad's illness was all but inevitable. Dick Stack had plenty of habits that weren't good for his heart. He'd smoked a lot of cigarettes every day since his teens, and if you suggested he might want to cut back, he'd say: "Anybody can quit smoking. It takes a real man to die of lung cancer." He didn't exercise. He guzzled those Manhattans. He ate badly—toast, coffee, and Pall Malls for breakfast, next to nothing at lunch, and dinner late in the night. He ate a bowl of ice cream in bed before turning off the light.

Now, though he was only forty-seven, he required a double bypass—today all but routine, but in 1976 a major operation, with no sure prospect of success. A lot of people died on the table during heart surgery. It's a measure of how serious it was that he

70

was having the procedure at Massachusetts General Hospital in Boston, one of the leading centers for surgery in the East.

I went home for the holiday break with this operation looming. As always, I worked at the store. Toward the end of my time home, I decided to drive up to Rochester to spend a weekend with my girlfriend. I asked Bob Aiken if I could have Saturday off. He said it would be no problem. But it was—for my dad. He was at home, restricted to bed rest in anticipation of the surgery, but he found out about my conversation with Bob. "You're not taking Saturday off," he told me. "We're open. You're staying here."

"No," I said. "I'm going. Bob said I could go, and I'm going."

"You're not going," he growled back.

For the first time in my life, I stood my ground. "Yeah, I am," I said. I felt like I had nothing to lose. If he fired me, he'd be doing me a favor. And besides, nothing was going to keep me from my girlfriend that weekend. With that, I drove up to Rochester.

A week later, I was leaving Binghamton to return to school for the spring semester. My father was in his room, sitting in bed. His operation was scheduled for a few days later. I paused outside his door. I wasn't sure I'd ever see him again. "Dad," I said, "good luck with your operation. And I just want you to know that I love you." That was radical talk in the Stack household. My dad had never once told me he loved me. I half-expected that he might say it now. Instead, he grumped: "If you loved me, you wouldn't have taken last Saturday off."

A few days later he went under the knife. In the recovery room after the surgery, he started bleeding, so they wheeled him back into the operating room. His heart stopped. They revived him. But he never returned to his old self after that. He went back to work and remained nominally in charge, but my dad never made it all the way back, emotionally or physically, from that close call.

Seventeen months later I graduated, having not gone on a single job interview during my last semester in school. I loved Rochester and would have loved to stay there, and I felt confident that I could find work with an accounting firm in the city. But all of that was trumped by the reality of what was going on back in Binghamton. My father was sick. I was the oldest kid. I had to go to work in the family business.

At nine on the Tuesday morning after graduation, I opened the store.

## CHAPTER 6

# "WE'D BE DOING A LOT BETTER IF WE WEREN'T GETTING DICKED TO DEATH"

So it was that at age twenty-two I assumed my place at Dick's. In the wake of his surgery, my dad was operating at well under 100 percent and spent more time in Florida—he bought a house in Jupiter and was down there for more than half the year now, from October to May, with a brief visit home around Christmas—so running the business was pretty much up to Bob Aiken and me.

I already knew that in terms of record keeping, the stores were a mess. Now I looked around and saw more room for improvement. In fiscal 1977, the company did $2,090,000 in business. Before taxes, it cleared $100,000, which was a very thin profit, indeed. I realized that with a few small changes we could improve our sales, our margins, and our merchandising. I went through our financial statements and found ways we could trim expenses. I studied our advertising, compared it to the advertising other stores did, and dreamed up different approaches.

Bob could be gruff, as I said earlier. Example: A few years before, I'd worked at the store during spring break. Golf-A-Thon was happening across town. "Youngblood," Bob said, using his nickname for me. "Take this truck over to St. Michael's." He pointed to a truck outside that was loaded with merchandise. It had a manual transmission. "Bob," I told him, "I've never driven a stick."

"You better learn fast," he replied. "Get that damn truck over to St. Michael's." It wasn't pretty, but I jerked and stalled my way across town and delivered the goods, as ordered.

Now, years later, the boss's kid was suggesting changes to a guy accustomed to running the business while my dad was away. Another man might have resented my arrival and ignored my input. Bob welcomed it. "Youngblood," he'd say when I pointed out how we might improve the bottom line, "let's do it." He didn't hesitate to share the organization's leadership. So arriving at the store each morning didn't promise a long day of drudgery. Rather, it offered interesting problems to solve. And of all the surprises I've experienced in my life, perhaps the biggest unfolded over my first several months back at Dick's. I fell in love with the place.

On his visits home, my dad reminded me that he was still the boss, and he didn't do it gently. I was up in the office doing some paperwork one quiet afternoon when he stomped in, irritated that I wasn't helping customers. "Get your ass down on that floor," he snarled. I knew that the sales floor was everything to him and did what I was told. I'll give you another example of his warm and loving style. It involved a kid named Jay Mininger who, one wintry day, walked in the store to apply for a job. He was sixteen years old and a tennis player; one look told you he was an athlete. "What are you doing now?" I asked him.

"I work up at the Hess gas station," he said, adding: "It's cold."

We hired him. Jay would be an integral part of the company for decades. Early on, he wasn't my protégé, exactly, but I took him under my wing on a variety of tasks. We got a lot done together. At one point, after careful study and lengthy debate, Jay and I decided it was time for Dick's to go into the cross-country-ski business. There was usually snow in town for months each winter, and cross-country skiing had grown in popularity over the past couple of years, so the timing felt right. We went out and bought cross-country skis, boots, and poles, and built a big display of them stretching thirty feet across the back wall.

It looked great. We were excited about it. At that point, in walked my dad. He was headed to Florida the next day and had stopped by for a last look around. He glared at the ski display for a moment before walking to a set of skis at one end and throwing it into the next set over. The entire display toppled like dominos. He shot me a glance and said, "Get these the hell out of here," then stalked out.

Poor Jay was rattled. "Oh my God," he whispered. "What are we going to do?"

"Let's pick up the skis and put them back up," I said. "He's leaving tomorrow, and we'll sell them all before he gets back." Which is what happened—not only did we sell all the ski gear, we sold a lot more coats, hats, and gloves to go with it. The episode encouraged what became my strategy for introducing new products and ideas: unless I was pretty sure my dad would agree, I'd wait until he left town. Otherwise, I got nowhere, because he'd block me or simply blow me off.

I wanted badly to get into the athletic footwear business. All through my teens, I'd been shopping at Irv's Champion for my cleats because Dick's didn't carry the Puma and Adidas shoes that every kid wanted to wear. The only cleats we carried were old-fashioned, heavy leather Riddells. If you bought those, you might as well wear a leather helmet. Puma and Adidas made cool, modern sneakers, too. We carried canvas Converse high-tops and P.F. Flyers—not cool. We should be carrying the new stuff, I'd tell my dad. It's what everyone wants.

He didn't want to hear it. He was comfortable in the outdoor category, augmented by a little golf and baseball. Why change? His mantra was, "This is what we do, and this is how we've done it." Whatever its roots, his resistance to change was a gift to me. It forced me to think through my proposals to him, to really analyze the positives and negatives of an idea, to make it bulletproof. And it reinforced a truth that has been demonstrated to me time and again, which is that the moment a business stops evolving, the moment its leaders sit back and think, *Everything's good*, that's when it starts to fail.

Maybe that's especially true for retail. Change has to be a constant. Improvement can never end. You have to stay fresh to your customers, and to do that you have to be perpetually rethinking everything you do, questioning your every assumption. You have to be willing to sometimes blow up everything in the name of staying focused, and exciting, and better—and ahead of your competition.

So dealing with my dad was a constant struggle, but it was always interesting. Many of the battles I won, I won by not fighting—I just didn't ask ahead of time. Most head-on disagreements I lost. I loved the business a little less on those occasions, but the good days outnumbered the bad.

That said, I came close to quitting a year after I graduated. In the summer of 1978, Mark Muench, who'd become my best friend while at St. John Fisher, was getting married in Rochester. He asked me to be in his wedding. So a week out I went to Bob Aiken, to let him know I'd be away for a weekend. "Bob, I'd like to leave Friday around noon," I told him. "I'm in my buddy's wedding on Saturday. It's a three-hour drive and the rehearsal dinner is Friday night."

"Sure," Bob said. "No problem."

My dad, home for the summer, caught wind of my plan and approached me in the store. "You're not going to that wedding," he said. "The store is open, so you're working."

"What do you mean, I'm working?" I asked him. "It's Muenchy's wedding. He's my best friend. I'm *in* the wedding."

"I don't give a shit," he said. "You're working. End of conversation."

"I'm going," I said. It seemed a repeat of our argument when I'd left town to see my girlfriend. "I'm going to the wedding."

"If you go," he said, "don't come back on Tuesday."

I should have told him to pound salt. With the advantage of

hindsight, I suspect he might have respected that. I could have pointed out that he'd have to be stupid to fire me, because he'd have wasted the decade he'd already spent grooming me to take over someday. That might have shut him up. Then again, he was a hothead and used to getting his way. He might have canned me on the spot. I might be a lawyer in Syracuse today. Whatever the case, I caved. I called Muenchy with the news that I couldn't come. "What do you mean, you're not coming?" he asked.

"My father won't give me the day off," I said.

He was not happy. But Muenchy was not one to hold grudges. We'd stay great friends for forty years, until his death from a brain tumor at fifty-eight. Over all that time, I can count on one hand the number of times I saw him visibly upset and without a smile on his face. He was one of the most naturally upbeat and generous people I've ever known.

So he got over it. I did not. I was angry with my dad and furious at myself. It was a defining moment. I wanted to stay at Dick's, had come around to loving the business, but I saw that I couldn't work for my father indefinitely. I was twenty-three, and it was clear that he and I were coming to a day of reckoning.

I've spent some time reflecting on why my dad seemed so hell-bent on busting my stones every chance he got. I used to be angry about it. Now I'm merely curious—it's a puzzle that I'd like to solve. Playing armchair shrink, I've considered a wide range of possible answers. An obvious starting point is that he had no idea what he was doing as a father: his own dad was killed when he was seven, and he had no male role model besides my uncle Ed, whose example wasn't reliably positive. He was twenty-five but still an unfinished kid when he married my mother, and eleven months later, I showed up to steal away all of my mom's focus. Two years later, there was another baby, and suddenly he was twenty-seven years old and a father twice over, without a clue about how to handle the situation.

My mom's theory was that he was jealous of me—that he saw I was smarter than he was and a better athlete, too. But my mom was an iffy source when it came to my dad, and besides, he started in on me long before I displayed an aptitude for anything at all, so that explanation doesn't wash. A simpler idea is that I happened to come along first, and his idea of rearing a boy (shared by many of his generation) was to toughen me up, above all else. To make a man of me. Can't do that by coddling, he might have thought. Can't do that by showing love.

And maybe my response to that toughness was to become the serious, stoic, duty-bound youngster I was—and the very sort of straitlaced kid my dad hadn't liked in his own youth. He wasn't nearly as hard on my brothers, but they'd get into trouble now and then, and I think that he could relate to them more. I was a mystery to him. I did what I was supposed to do, when I was supposed to do it.

I know this much for sure—I'm my father's creation. We're all products of our DNA, so there's that, but in addition, I'm confident that had he not been tough on me, I wouldn't be the same person today. I suppose I owe him thanks. But I'll tell you what: when it comes to parenting my own kids, I'm different from my dad. I tell my kids I love them every chance I get. I've tried to support them, and reassure them, and leave no doubt that I'm proud of them and want them to be happy.

True, none of them can make a perfect Canadian Club Manhattan. Otherwise, though, they've turned out pretty well.


Following a serious romantic relationship that didn't end well, I wound up sharing an apartment with a good friend of mine, Ronnie Saul, whose family owned a men's clothing store in downtown Binghamton. He, too, was in the process of taking charge of his family business. The apartment was on the South Side, on McNamara Avenue, just a few doors down from my dad's mom, Nana. I'd drop in to see her from time to time. She loved it.

Tim Myers and I were at a nightclub one night, and I couldn't take my eyes off a young woman at the bar. Now, I wasn't afraid of much in this world. But one thing that did scare me was a pretty woman. I was shy, tongue-tied. I had no game. This night was pretty typical. I stared. She eventually crossed the room to our table. "Are you just going to stare at me all night," she asked, while wearing a big, confident smile, "or are you going to ask me to dance?"

"Would you like to dance?" I asked.

"I'd love to," she answered.

That was Gail. We dated on and off for years.

Meanwhile, my growing role at the store was introducing me to aspects of the business I'd never learned in school. One was the way we got our merchandise. A few brands, such as Woolrich, dealt with us directly. Most hired reps who'd handle goods produced by several companies; a rep might have both McGregor golf clubs and Timberland boots, for instance. They'd swing through Binghamton, show off the products, offer us a price, discuss the terms.

A price listed in their paperwork wasn't necessarily what they expected to get for an item, so negotiation was a big piece of the ritual. My dad's long-standing rule was that you never met with a rep during business hours—it would distract you from your focus on the customer—so these meetings with the reps happened early in the morning or fairly late in the evening. The reps never complained. And in truth, these off-hours meetings might have been fairly standard among sporting goods retailers at the time, because we were part of a small, fragmented industry. No big players dominated the market; most were like us, with a store or two. Off the top of my head, I can think of just a couple regional chains that had more than a half-dozen stores in the seventies and early eighties—Oshman's, out of Houston, and Herman's World of Sporting Goods in New York.

A meeting with a product rep usually took place at a local motel, where he'd get two adjoining rooms and use one to set up his merchandise. I'd had no training before my first try at buying. About all I knew for certain was that we made a lot more money on clothes than we did on guns and tackle.

One day in February, which is when we did the bulk of our buying for the fall, Bob Aiken said to me, "Youngblood, Paul Grossman's over at the Holiday Inn. He'll be expecting you at nine thirty to look at next year's Raven and Comfy lines." Raven and Comfy were winter jackets. Bob handed me a two-page order sheet that reflected our buying for the previous year. "Here's what we bought last time," he said. "Go over there and see what they've got for next year."

So I went to the Holiday Inn and met Paul, who was considerably older than me and a big, bearish guy with jet-black hair and a kind, patient manner. He had samples of his new clothing lines laid out on the beds and hanging on portable racks. I looked over the jackets. "What do you think?" he asked.

I pointed out a jacket I liked. "Let's start with this one," I said. "I'll take it in black. I'll take two small, four medium, four large, two extra-large." He nodded okay. I moved on to other colors, ordering a similar selection of each, then another jacket. "I like this one, too," I said. "In blue. I'll take two small, four medium, four large, two extra-large." We moved on to a third style, and as I listed what I wanted, he looked over his glasses at me and said, "Son, you don't have enough money to buy all the stuff you're trying to buy. Let me help you."

With that, he went through his lines and helped me pare down my list to a reasonable size. He didn't have to do that. He could have figured, *Hey, this is the boss's son, and I have a chance to take these guys to the cleaners.* But he was honorable and smart, and valued the relationship he'd forged over years of working with us. He spent a long time with me that night, walking me through how to place the order. We stayed friends. He was a guy I always trusted.

Others helped educate me, too. Mike Rich of Woolrich, our single biggest vendor back in those days, was one—he wouldn't let me get too far out over my skis. I met with him at the Holiday Inn for years, and once a year I drove a large truck down to Woolrich's Pennsylvania headquarters to buy closeouts. I'd meet with him and go over shirts and jackets that hadn't sold or that they'd overproduced, and haggle out discounted prices on the stuff. He'd say, "This was originally forty dollars, but we'll sell it to you for twenty." And I'd respond, "Mike, you know what? I'll take all you have left for fifteen apiece." As often as not, he'd go along with me.

We both enjoyed those meetings. I think he often agreed to drop his price simply to help us out. It wasn't going to make a big difference to his bottom line, but he knew it would make an impact on ours, and I suspect he enjoyed giving us a little push. After we'd finished, his crew would load up the truck and I'd make the three-hour drive back to Binghamton. We'd either sell it at the end of the season or pack it away for the next year.

Those meetings helped establish a pattern that we've followed ever since: we forged personal relationships with our vendors. Sometimes, as I've described, our close ties prompted them to steer us away from trouble or to give us a hand when we needed it. In some cases, we were able to help them when they were new at the game and needed outlets, or were having trouble with a line of merchandise and needed a push.

In a few instances, we partnered with unknown brands that later blew up into major players, and they did it with our help. But they didn't need to be big to earn our attention. We always agreed to meet with a vendor, always took the time to talk with and get to know the people. We tried to show respect to both the reps and their product. And in return, they always respected us.

In the beginning, we needed the brands a lot more than they needed us. That shifted over time. But from the beginning, we always tried to treat them as partners. If you go into a deal looking at it as a partnership, it almost always works out.

• • •

With my dad back in Florida, I made my first stabs at broadening the array of merchandise at Dick's. As I mentioned, I wanted to carry Puma and Adidas, the two hot brands of the day. They were both German companies, started by brothers who'd been in business together before they had a falling-out after World War II. By the late seventies, they were at the center of a sneaker-as-fashion craze that continues today in the United States. The Adidas Superstar and the Puma Clyde, named for NBA star Walt "Clyde" Frazier, were among America's most popular basketball shoes, and sought after by status-conscious high schoolers. People came into Dick's asking for these shoes. It was obvious we'd sell as many as we could get our hands on.

Sporting goods vendors displayed their wares at two big trade shows each year, in New York in October and in Chicago every January or February. We'd go see the new products, talk to the management teams at each of the brands, buy some closeouts, and sometimes place orders. Starting in 1978, I sought out the Puma and Adidas booths and asked them to sell to us, or "open us up," as we say in retail.

I couldn't get either company interested. They were already selling to other stores in Binghamton—Irv's Champion, of course, and Allen's, a combination sporting goods store and jeweler that was our fiercest competition—and they wanted to protect these retail partners with whom they had long-standing relationships. Plus, they saw Dick's strictly as an outdoors store, which they considered a weird fit. We went back and forth with them for three years. Between shows, I'd call them on the phone. More often than not, I didn't get a call back. When I did, they still said no. We couldn't get the slightest bit of traction.

Meanwhile, we had better luck with a newer company. Nike had been around for a while as a distributor for a Japanese brand before it started making its own shoes in 1971. Bob Aiken bought some basketball shoes from them while I was still in school; they were building a distribution network, and they were happy to sell to us. Here was an example of a vendor that was virtually unknown when we partnered with it. In 1978, I added their running shoes to the mix. We put them on the shelves and they sold great. We ordered more and sold those. In no time we were selling a *lot* of Nikes, and those sales were moving the needle on our overall business. By 1980, Nike had swallowed up half of the US market for athletic footwear, and we rode that wave with them.

It was at that point, with Nike ascendant, that a conversation with Puma's rep took an unexpected turn. When I asked him again to open us up, he said: "I think we can do that now." Stunned, I made my way to the distributor's Adidas rep. "You know," I told him, "Puma's going to sell to us."

"Really?"

"Yeah." I showed him the Puma rep's business card.

"Well," he said, "if they'll sell you, we'll sell you."

I went back to Puma. We wrote a small order for Puma shoes. I returned to the Adidas rep, showed him the order, and with that, Adidas opened us up. With a catch. When this rep came to Binghamton to take our first order. Jay Mininger was with me in the office overlooking the Court Street store as we listed the shoes we wanted to buy. "What about apparel?" the rep asked.

I'd always sought just footwear from Adidas—sneakers, baseball cleats, football cleats. We had no room in the store for their clothing line. "We're not really interested in apparel," I told him.

He shut his folders and packed up to leave. "If you're not buying apparel," he said, "we're not giving you shoes." It was a heavy-handed way to handle the situation, and it ticked me off. It was also clear that if I didn't agree, three years of legwork had been for naught. "Okay," I told him. "We'll buy some apparel."

I was still annoyed after he left. "Someday," I said to Jay, "those guys are going to be *begging* us to buy from them."

You know what? That apparel blew out of the store. Running was becoming a national passion, and runners needed shorts, shirts, and socks to go along with their shoes. We sold a ton of Adidas apparel, even more of Nike apparel, and the margins on such sportswear were far higher than they were on fishing, hunting, and camping gear. The clothes made Dick's a much more profitable company. So the Adidas rep did us a favor. He helped create the Dick's we'd become. And in the process, he helped bring about the scenario I predicted. Because today, next to Foot Locker, we're Adidas's biggest account in North America.

That's getting ahead of the story, though. The immediate fallout of having apparel in the store was that my dad wasn't happy about it. Fortunately, he did most of his yelling over the phone, from Florida. By this time, Bob was deferring to me in many aspects of the business. "Youngblood," he'd say, "you do what you think you should do."

My dad really lost his mind when I made some changes in our advertising. Dick's had always bought space in the Binghamton paper. My dad had taken out display ads to announce sales since the 1950s, and he had been pretty clever about attracting customers with special events, too. "Are you puzzled about the many conflicting claims about insulated underwear?" he'd written in a come-on for a two-day "insulated underwear clinic" in November 1959. "You hear that one is so much superior or less expensive than another. Now is your opportunity to learn from factory representatives all that you should know when you go to buy your insulated underwear." Not sure how many people turned out for the clinic, but it lasted eighteen hours.

These ads weren't small. Many occupied a half page, and some a full page. Dick's maintained a regular presence in the classified section of the paper, too. My dad advertised there mostly for guns. "Need money for your vacation?" one typical example from June 1964 read. "We need 100 Used Guns and will pay CASH NOW! Don't delay—Take advantage of this opportunity to convert 'Old Betsy' into Vacation Cash." Regardless of their size, the ads were always rendered in black and white, and always ran in the sports section. Back in the days when Dick's catered strictly to men, that made sense, but no longer. Now our ads were unseen by a lot of female readers, a significant percentage of the market.

With my dad away, I oversaw the stores' ads myself, and I wasn't satisfied with the results. I noticed that a few retailers had bumped up their presence in the paper with eight-to-twelve-page, tabloid-size inserts. Many were in full color. They definitely caught your attention, and you didn't have to wade through the sports pages to find them. I decided we needed to try this. I built our first tabloid ad myself—laid it out, with stick figures and primitive renditions of the products we wanted to feature—then turned it over to the advertising department at the Binghamton *Press and Sun-Bulletin*. They took my layouts and photos I brought in of the clothes I wanted the figures to wear, and turned my scrawls into a crisp, colorful, eight-page tab. From the moment the first one ran, our business went through the roof.

I realized that, because these tabs were very expensive, we needed a strategy for them. Some focused on hunting. Some targeted back-to-school shoppers with eight pages of sneakers, cleats, jackets. Jerry Harper, who was Bill Colombo's brother-in-law, was our Nike rep. I worked with him on ads that emphasized our footwear, and we did tremendous back-to-school sales. We added radio and TV to our marketing, too, and the combined effect of this blitz was so good that when Jerry walked into Irv's Champion and asked a kid working there how back-to-school business was going, he answered: "It'd be a lot better if we weren't getting Dicked to death."

This success came at a cost—to run a tab every couple of weeks boosted our annual ad budget from $40,000 to $100,000—but the increased traffic more than made up for it. We scrambled to secure enough inventory to meet the new demand. I knew there'd be hell to pay when my dad returned from Florida. Sure enough, it wasn't long before he reviewed our expense statements and flipped out when he saw that I'd boosted our ad spending by sixty grand. "What the *hell* are you doing?" he asked me.

His accountant and friend Bill Humston interceded on my

behalf. Look, Dick, he told him. Yes, Eddie spent more, but the sales—check out the sales.

We'd done just over $2.7 million in business the year before. Now we were pulling in $3.1 million. We'd doubled our net earnings. "They spent a lot of money," Bill told him, "but they made a lot more. The kid is onto something." My dad was stubborn and averse to change, but he couldn't argue with the numbers.

The storm quickly passed, though he still bitched at me about the tabs. But his complaints were so half-hearted that I took them as a compliment. And in the months that followed, my dad backed away from the regular operation of the stores, even when he was in town. He remained the owner of Dick's, but at twenty-six, I was running the business.

CHAPTER 7

# "WHO DO I THANK FOR THE DRINK?"

When I say that I was running the business, I mean that I didn't have to run most things past my dad before I did them. I do *not* mean that he didn't get in my face on a regular basis or block me outright from the more ambitious changes I wanted to make. My dad and I had very different views of the company's future. He remained pretty conservative and was content to imagine Dick's as a two-store venture for the rest of his life. He considered it an almost mystical success story as it was. "Where else but America," he was fond of saying, "can a dumb kid who got out of high school by the skin of his teeth make it like this?"

I wasn't at all satisfied with things as they were. Since I'd graduated from Fisher I'd read everything I could get my hands on about business success—by or about Sam Walton, John DeLorean, and other captains of industry. And one lesson that came through in such books was that fortune favors those who aren't satisfied with the status quo—those who are hungry, who have a vision for where they'd like to be and the confidence to get there. You might say that the recipe is boldness mixed with a healthy dose of caution.

Having had a taste of success, I was feeling hungry. I wanted to do more—add more product, increase sales, and ultimately, open more stores. I thought that with care, we could grow the company far beyond Binghamton. There was more than just blind ambition at work. I was paranoid, too: Big national retailers had started to materialize across the country. Small department stores were the first local businesses they steamrolled. Soon, local lumberyards were gone, too, replaced by big-box hardware chains, and mom-and-pop pharmacies were under siege from chain drugstores that multiplied at major intersections. It was only a matter of time before the same thing happened in sporting goods.

Whenever I raised the subject with my dad, however, he got worked up. You could see his anxiety in his body language, hear it in his voice—the ghost of Hillcrest haunted him as powerfully as ever. One thing I suggested was that we try a store in Cortland, a town about forty miles up Interstate 81. The location made sense to me: we'd have no competition there, for one thing. It was close to Ithaca and its college students, as well as to Syracuse. It was in the heart of upstate New York's hunting and fishing country, too. None of that swayed my dad. He shut me down. He wanted nothing to do with the idea. If I pushed the matter, his Irish temper would surface, and he'd start sputtering in incomplete sentences and one-syllable words.

Still, he got his point across: he wouldn't allow it. He was scared to death that any new venture would fail and take everything down with it. I sympathized with him, but I also believed that if we didn't take on this risk, it was only a matter of time before someone else would. It was eat or be eaten.

We went back and forth on the Cortland idea for months, until finally, completely exasperated with me, he stopped in the middle of one of our spirited conversations and said, "If you think you're such a goddamn smart son of a bitch, go down to the bank and get your own line of credit and buy me out."

So . . . I did. As I've said, I was a dutiful son. I went to the First City National Bank in Binghamton and talked to the lenders about buying Dick's. They studied the numbers, figured what it would take to complete the transaction, and told me that yes, they'd finance it. We didn't prepare any formal papers; we simply shook hands, and they verbally committed to a credit line. I went back to my dad. "We're ready to go," I said.

"What do you mean, 'We're ready to go'?" he asked.

I can get the line of credit, I told him. I've talked with the bank, and they'll back me up. I can buy you out. At which point I learned in no uncertain terms that no, I could *not* buy him out. That would not be happening that day or any time soon. He was surprised I'd called his bluff—very surprised. And he was indignant. "This is *my* business," he said, "and it's going to stay my business."

In part, he wasn't ready to retire because he didn't think I was ready to take over. "Do you really think you can buy all the product we need to keep this business going?" he asked. Well, yes, as a matter of fact, I did. I was already buying pretty much everything but guns and fishing tackle, and I had plenty of help with that.

My feeling was that if he hadn't meant it, he shouldn't have said it.

While I struggled with my dad over every little thing, changes were coming to some of the other Stacks that would eventually ripple into the store. The most profound involved my sister Kim. Maybe because we were our parents' first two kids and came along before there were so many others in the house that keeping the peace was a job in itself, Kim and I had been held to a different standard than our younger siblings, and we'd both turned out serious and ambitious. And while the drinking in our house turned me away from any real relationship with alcohol, it had an even more profound effect on Kim: she's never had a drink in her life.

We'd been close since we were little kids. Gramp and my grandmother liked to tell the story about the day I ran away from home at age five or six. I told Kim I was leaving and asked if she wanted to come. She said yes, so I put her in my red wagon, along with a few of my toys. The belongings of hers we packed: one shoe. We set off.

My mom watched us leave, then called over to my grandparents. "Eddie's on his way over," she said. "He's run away. He has Kim with him." Gramp and my grandmother met us at the door and told us they were in the middle of dinner, and that we'd have to wait outside until they finished. They apparently savored every bite, because it seemed that hours passed. Running away lost a lot of its appeal, so I pulled Kim home.

As we got older, Kim would sometimes play sports with me and my friends. She even attempted to play football with us once: I can still picture her in a yellow helmet, no chin strap, getting submarined by a couple of guys as she carried the ball; that was her first and only day as a running back. Mostly, she put up with a lot of the teasing you'd expect from teenage boys. She finished at Binghamton North two years after I did and attended a couple of junior colleges before enrolling at the State University of New York at Cortland, a.k.a. Cortland State, with plans to be a schoolteacher.

After graduation, she returned to Binghamton for the summer and started spending time with Tim Myers. Over the seven years that he'd been with the company, Tim had gone from the warehouse to the sales floor, where he specialized in archery. He'd done some buying, and then, in his early twenties, had been named manager of the Vestal store. We remained great friends.

They'd been circling each other for years. Kim had long counseled Tim on his various girlfriends, and while she was at Cortland State they'd see each other when he came up on weekends to ski; she and her roommates let him crash on their sofa. My dad detected early on that there might be more to their friendship than met the eye. "What's going on with you two?" he'd ask her.

"Nothing, Dad," she'd say. "We're just friends." And she probably meant it. But she wasn't speaking for both of them.

At a party after her graduation, a singing telegram showed up. The guy sang a song about Kim and her achievement, and when Kim asked who'd sent him, he answered that it was anonymous. A few minutes later, Kim was wondering aloud about who might have sent the telegram when a friend—Carol Hillis, whose kids Kim had babysat—blurted out: "It's the person who loves you so much he can't even stand it!"

"Who?" Kim asked, mystified.

"Oh my God," Carol moaned. "It's Tim Myers!"

Kim had accepted a teaching job in Denver even before she left school, and at summer's end, just as their romance was getting into gear, she left for Colorado. They stayed in constant touch by phone and letter. My dad thought a lot of Tim (actually, of his whole family, because once Tim's dad retired from the US Postal Service he came to work for Dick's, drilling bowling balls and repairing fishing rods). Now Tim and my dad commiserated on how to get Kim back home, and in the process became a lot tighter.

One day at the store I noticed Tim wasn't around and asked the other guys if they'd seen him. They all looked at me weirdly, until I demanded to know what was going on. "He's in Denver," one said.

"Denver? Why's he in Denver?" I asked. It took a few seconds for me to realize that this relationship was a lot more serious than I'd thought. I wasn't displeased that one of my oldest buddies was dating my sister, though it violated the age-old Guys' Code that says you don't do that. But I sure was surprised, and even more so when I learned that Tim had already asked Kim several times to marry him. She'd put him off, but while he was in Colorado she finally told him yes. She moved back to Binghamton in March. They married five months later.

• • •

Okay: so my dad wasn't going to sell out to me any time soon, and until he did, there seemed little chance that he'd let me open any new stores. The one thing we could do in the meantime was grow the stores we had, so I suggested expanding the Vestal store to him. It was still a minuscule 2,800 square feet, in a suburb that had grown up fast around it. We had a lot of customers out that way and simply couldn't serve them well with a store we couldn't cram any fuller.

He was in Florida when we talked about it on the phone, and he didn't seem dead set against it, which was about as much as I could hope for with any of my proposals. Over the next few months I had a friend of his draw up plans to boost the store's size to 7,500 square feet. We were ready to break ground when I sent the plans down to him.

Kim and Tim had just had their first child, Timmy, and were visiting Dad at the time. A few days after I mailed the plans, I got a frantic call from my sister. "Dad's lost his mind over the Vestal store," she told me. Tim got on the phone. "Your father's locked himself in his room," he said. "He's really pissed, and he says he's not coming out until you get your ass down here."

The next day I got on a plane and flew down to Florida. He was mad as hell with me, wanting to know why I thought I could nearly triple the size of the Vestal store when it was doing just fine the way it was. "Dad," I told him, "we have to do this. It's not fine the way it is." Vestal wasn't the little, out-of-the-way town it had been when he bought the store. It was the epicenter of the population growth in the Triple Cities. In other words, I said, this isn't like Hillcrest. This is nothing like Hillcrest. We've got the customers there to support a much bigger store.

He calmed down. We expanded the store. Business took off immediately, and Vestal was soon outperforming 345 Court Street, which none of us had seen coming. That was a signal that it was long past time to expand our original store, too. The Sports Mate Diner had moved out, which had opened up some floor space, but we'd already filled it. We needed more room; five thousand square feet was just too tight for all the merchandise I wanted to carry. My dad went along with that expansion. We knocked out the back wall and boosted the store's area to ten thousand square feet. Business exploded.

The relationship between my father and me was one of constant push and pull. I was bothered, for example, that some of our inventory would sit unsold on the shelves for years. That's no exaggeration. We had a pile of blue Levi's corduroy pants that occupied a couple feet of shelf space when I was in college, and when I graduated, and that were still there four years after that. They'd fallen completely out of fashion, and we were asking way too much for them. This was a twofold problem. First, we had capital tied up in inventory we weren't selling. And two, this stuff was taking up space that we could better use displaying stuff that *would* sell.

My dad didn't mind that those cords and equally ancient merchandise were gathering dust. He didn't want to lose money on them; by his way of thinking, he had to sell them for at least as much as he'd paid. But the value of inventory drops with time, and keeps dropping until it's virtually worthless. You have to keep it moving. So without talking to him first, I put together a warehouse sale, piled those cords and a variety of other dated merchandise on tables out in the parking lot, and slashed the price on all of it. People showed up in droves to take it off our hands. The sale was under way when my dad pulled up in his car and barked at me, "What the hell are you doing?"

"We have to get rid of this stuff," I told him.

He looked like his head might explode. "I can't believe you did this," he said, and sped off. At day's end we'd sold almost everything, including the cords. I phoned him to report how we'd done. The numbers cooled his jets so much that starting then, we set clothes aside at the end of each season and augmented the pile with the closeouts I bought from Woolrich. We rented a closed-down grocery store not far from Dick's for the month of January and held a fire sale for ten days, with everything marked down by half. It was a huge hit.

The bigger stores and special events, along with the bigger margins we made on apparel, translated into big increases in the bottom line. Our sales climbed from $2.5 million to $3.1 million, then to $4 million and beyond. Those are big jumps. We still spent most of the year in debt to the bank and our vendors, but cash crunches came far less often.

In 1984, the Acme next door to 345 Court Street closed, and we moved Dick's into that space, increasing our square footage by more than a third, to 13,500. My dad was okay with that, especially when sales again jumped. We posted earnings of $1 million on those sales—ten times what we'd been earning when I graduated from college.

We still have that store, by the way. If you look at our sales reports, you'll see that old Acme building that my father built is listed as Store Number 1. We'll never close it. It's a direct connection to our past, a constant reminder of where we started.

One weekend in January 1983 I went skiing in Vermont with Tim and a couple of other friends. We were staying at a Holiday Inn and were talking in the bar when I noticed a young woman a few feet away, her back to me. What I could see looked great; she had lovely, long dark hair. I glanced her way time and again, hoping she'd turn around. I was still seeing Gail on and off, in roughly equal portions, and at the time we were off. I told the guys at the table I was going to ask this girl to dance.

They scoffed at me. "You're not going to ask her," my buddy Dave Ziebarth said. "You never do that." I replied that I just might surprise them. But for the moment, I remained in my chair—until someone elsewhere in the bar sent drinks to this young woman and her aunt, who was sitting with her, and she turned around to face us. And holy smokes, she was drop-dead gorgeous: big brown eyes, dark complexion, and a smile that would light all the Southern Tier. She was the most beautiful creature I'd ever seen. "Who do I thank for this drink?" she asked.

None of us had sent it, but I realized I had to move—if I didn't ask her to dance, I'd be kicking myself for years to come. That face would haunt me. So I worked up my courage and asked her, and she said yes.

Her name was Denise. We danced a couple of fast dances, followed by a slow one, then sat and talked. I had a rare few drinks that night, and the time flew; too soon, the bar closed. Denise was staying in the hotel with her family, and it turned out we were all staying on the same floor, so we rode the elevator together, then said good night. As I watched her walk down the hall, I turned to Dave Ziebarth. "Z," I told him, "I'm in love."

I didn't know it at the time, but she heard me. The next morning, Z found a note slipped under our door. "My name is Denise Prenosil," it read. "This is my address. If you ever get to Boston, look me up." As soon as we got back to Binghamton, I wrote her a letter. By week's end she'd written back. Through the rest of January, into February and March, our letters grew longer and more frequent. I learned that she was twenty-three, had grown up in western Massachusetts, and had graduated magna cum laude from Boston College, with a dual degree in accounting and marketing. She was smart and had big plans: she was working at a drugstore, learning the business on the sales floor, but saw herself rising through the ranks into high-level retail and living in a penthouse apartment overlooking New York. For now, she lived with a couple of roommates.

We kept exchanging letters until, in late May, I phoned her to say that I was coming to see her. On Friday, June 3, I stepped off a puddle jumper with a long-stemmed red rose in my hand, and there she was, waiting on the tarmac in a pink dress. I had never even imagined so beautiful a woman. We spent a fantastic weekend together, exploring Boston and talking for hours. When Ronnie Saul picked me up at the airport back in Binghamton, I told him: "I'm going to marry that girl."

I went back the following month, and she came to Binghamton in August. I couldn't pick her up—work interfered—so she took a cab to the apartment Ronnie and I shared on McNamara Avenue. Ronnie opened the door to find an absolute knockout standing before him. "Please," he blurted, "tell me your name is not Denise."

After that, I flew to Boston every Friday night and back to Binghamton late on Sunday. I knew I'd found the One. She mentioned one evening at dinner that her career was important to her and she wasn't sure she ever wanted to marry. I wasn't dissuaded. Another time she told me that if she did marry, she wasn't sure she wanted kids. I was undeterred. In yet another conversation, she said that she could see herself chickening out of marriage as she walked down the aisle. I didn't care. I wanted to marry her, and she knew it, but she needed time. I was patient.

Still, I had my limits. After months of being put off, I called her one day while she was at work. "If my love for you is so strong that I can be there in ten minutes, will you promise that you'll marry me?" I asked.

"What?"

"If my love is so strong that I can magically appear before you in ten minutes," I repeated, "will you marry me?"

"Fine," she said. It goes without saying that I'd flown to Boston and was standing at a pay phone outside the drugstore. I walked in and found her in an aisle, stocking shelves. She about died when she saw me. She did not commit, however. That November, she was headed to West Springfield to spend Thanksgiving with her family and agreed to detour to Pittsfield to meet me. There, finally, we talked in concrete terms about getting married, and over the holiday she told her parents she thought she'd say yes. I talked to her father. A week later I was back in Boston to propose.

Meanwhile, I was still playing golf every Monday with Gramp. One event we never missed was a spring fund-raiser for the American Heart Association, the Golf Fore Your Heart Tournament, held in Binghamton. My grandfather loved playing in it, and I was always partnered with him. As my wedding to Denise approached, I broke the news to him that the ceremony was going to take place the same weekend as the tournament, and we wouldn't be able to play.

"Well," he said, "can the date be changed?"

"Gramp, I don't think so," I replied. "I mean, the tournament has reserved the golf course, and everything's set."

He squinted at me. "I'm not talking about the golf tournament."

"I don't think so, Gramp," I said. "We're kind of committed to this date."

Spring came, and Denise walked to the altar on her father's arm, smiling—my nickname for her was Sunshine, because that smile brightened any room she entered. I'm not sure I looked so ecstatic. I was scared to death that she'd bolt.

She didn't.

I'd bought a house a while before, a little contemporary with multiple levels. Ronnie moved out, and we brought Denise's stuff down from Boston in a U-Haul. The realities of living in a small-ish, out-of-the-way city hit her while we were unloading. She went missing, and when I went looking for her I was alarmed to hear the sound of her crying. I found her in the bedroom, distraught. She looked up at me with tears streaming down her cheeks and asked, "Do you think that they'll ever build any big buildings in Binghamton?"

"Honey, I don't," I told her.

"Will you promise," she asked, "that we'll move to a big city someday?"

"Yes," I said. "I promise."


I think that it was about this time that my uncle Joe, along with my dad's accountant and other friends who had his ear, started telling him that maybe it was time for him to step aside. I doubt that's the way they put it—I think my uncle probably convinced him that, given his continuing poor health, he needed to do some succession planning, and the conversation went from there.

My dad was fifty-five and had been running the family business for thirty-six years. Though I know he still considered it his baby and took great satisfaction from its success, I think he was ready to slow down and was sick of arguing with me. I was making changes in the business that I don't think he much enjoyed, aimed at professionalizing how Dick's intersected with the world. I remember inviting him to join me on a business meeting—to a vendor, or perhaps the bank; I no longer remember with whom—and telling him he had to wear a tie and a sport coat.

Dick Stack was not a fan of neckties, and I doubt he owned a suit. He was the salt of the earth, as unpretentious in his appearance as a man can be. He stepped out of his house wearing an old burgundy sport coat—his favorite—and a white, three-button golf shirt. A clip-on tie was hooked to the throat. "Dad, you can't wear that," I said. "You have to wear a dress shirt."

"The hell you mean, I have to wear a dress shirt?" he grumbled. "This looks fine."

"You have to wear a dress shirt," I insisted. He went back inside and put on a dress shirt.

Anyway, my uncle Joe helped convince my dad that it was time to sell the company to his kids, and after a great deal of back-and-forth, my dad agreed—with specific conditions that would keep him at least peripherally involved in Dick's for years to come, and with a pretty big income stream, to boot.

First: He owned the Court Street and Vestal stores. We'd lease them from him for twenty-five years, at a rent much higher than the market, and we could not terminate the leases without his consent. Second: He'd sell us the business itself for $1.25 million. No cash would change hands at the time of the sale; instead, we'd make monthly payments at 12 percent interest per year, for twenty years. We could not pay off the note early, either. The arrangement would give him a comfortable income for the rest of his life.

All of us kids would be equity owners of the company, with an equal piece, but because Uncle Joe argued that someone had to be in charge, my dad created two classes of stock and gave me 51 percent of the voting stock. My uncle introduced us to an up-and-coming young Binghamton lawyer named Larry Schorr to put the deal together. He was about my age and an impressively smart guy. He'd been to law school, as I'd wanted to do, and was enjoying the career I'd wanted to have. We met at the Vestal Steakhouse to discuss the business's transfer. As I understand it, it was Larry who suggested the arrangement that gave me effective control of the company.

So it was that in the summer of 1984, I married Denise and took over Dick's. It was a crazy, whirlwind few months. I was twenty-nine.

I was committed to setting the company on a new course but first had to address an urgent need. The little prefab metal warehouse out back of Court Street was bulging at the seams. It had been crowded when I'd started working there at thirteen; in the nearly seventeen years since, we'd tripled the size of our stores and broadened the goods we stocked. We used the old store at 345 Court Street to store the overflow of merchandise, but our growth outpaced our capacity. Storage was now a crisis.

Knowing that we'd continue to grow, we rented our first bona fide distribution center about ten minutes from the Court Street store. It was tiny—twenty thousand square feet for both warehouse space and a small suite of offices. We set up our bookkeeping, accounts payable, and other financial functions there. I had an office, and so did our buyers: Bob Aiken handled hunting, fishing, and camping gear; Jay Mininger bought footwear and apparel. Tim went to work as our first technology officer, though that's stretching the term, because in the mid-1980s, computers were slow and stupid next to a smartphone of today. Denise served as our first human resources officer and organized our record-keeping on payroll, employee benefits, and insurance.

My dad lost his mind that we weren't going to be in the stores whenever they were open. A retailer should be in the store! Everything happens in the store! How the hell can you know what's going on, sitting on your ass at a desk? He thought it marked the end of days. He believed we were doomed.

We squeezed into our new space, which felt overcrowded almost as soon as we moved in, and started plotting our growth between phone tirades from Florida. But I have to admit, I found it weird not being able to walk five steps from my office to the sales floor or across the parking lot to the warehouse.

So I made it a point to spend a lot of time at Court Street. Those visits were the beginning of a habit I've followed since. My dad was right: You can't run a retail operation remotely. You have to spend time meeting with customers and listening to your sales staff. That's where you find out what's working and what isn't, what sells and what doesn't. That's where you get ideas for how to improve. That's where your business thrives or dies.

Besides, you have to keep close to your customers and associates if you're to have any authenticity with either. It was with that in mind that I was working the floor one Christmas Eve when a woman walked in about two hours before close. She came up to me and said: "I need a gift for my sister-in-law."

"Okay," I said. "Let me help you." I took her to a table piled with Woolrich sweaters. "We've got these," I said. "Woolrich makes a really nice sweater, and we've just marked them down."

She scanned the sweaters, then looked back at me. "Those are the ugliest sweaters I've ever seen."

I chuckled a little. "Yeah," I admitted, "they're pretty ugly. That's why we marked them down." I pointed across the store. "Let me show you some other things over here."

I took a few steps that way and noticed she wasn't following. She was still at the table, and as I watched she picked up a sweater, gave it a close, disapproving once-over, then said: "On second thought, I'll take this. My sister-in-law is the biggest bitch I've ever known."

It always feels good to help a customer find just what she's looking for. I rang her up, and off she went. Merry Christmas!

## CHAPTER 8

# "THEY'RE REALLY NOT QUITE AS SMART AS THEY THINK THEY ARE"

I'd worked for Dick's for seventeen years when we took control of the company. I'd worked full-time in the stores for eight years and had led the business in my dad's lengthening absences for six. So I'd had an unusually long apprenticeship, which had versed me in virtually every aspect of running a small retail operation.

But when I turned thirty, I woke up feeling old and worthless. All those years of work hadn't taken me to where I wanted to be. My twenties had been a blur of lookalike days—walking into the Court Street store at eight fifteen a.m., closing up at nine, counting cash deposits and loading up the night deposit bag, and finally getting home at ten. I got to spend only a couple of hours with Denise before we'd have to turn in so that I could get up to do it again. It felt as if my life were passing me by. I was on the shot clock. And one action I felt a pressing need to take was to push the business beyond Binghamton.

I didn't know a thing about growing the much bigger company I wanted Dick's to become. I knew I needed advice on how to do that—my only experience in running a bigger and expanding chain of stores was that I'd *imagined* it happening and argued a thousand times about it with my dad. So among my first executive decisions as the new president of Dick's was to assemble a board of directors.

Its members wouldn't actually have a vote in the management of the company; they'd serve strictly as a source of advice. I wanted people whom I trusted and admired, who were smart and strategic in their thinking. So I chose Larry Schorr, the young lawyer who'd put together the buyout. Larry and I were beginning what has proven to be a long and wonderful friendship. He's been my confidant and my trusted adviser, and he's been instrumental in helping me and Dick's get out of tight spots for thirty-five years.

Another guy I asked to be on the board was Monty Pinker, one of my closest friends, who ran three TV stations in the region and had a deep background in advertising and marketing. I also asked my uncle Joe, my dad's brother, a really smart guy who'd owned a couple of businesses that did very well; one of them, Chenango Industries, assembled electronic components for IBM. And I asked Charlie Murray, the president of Endicott Johnson. I didn't know him well but felt he'd lend the board gravitas.

Finally, I asked Tim Myers, who knew me about as well as anybody, and who, now that he was part of the family as well as the company, was as invested in our success as I was. From their first quarterly meeting, the board members were a huge help to me. They talked me out of a lot of bad ideas. They encouraged me in my good ones. They were always generous with their time and frank in their views.

My dad served as an adviser, too. His standard advice, no matter the question, was "Don't do it." And the one ambition of mine that scared him the most was opening new stores. He remained convinced that any new venture would fail, which would not only wipe out the company but end his retirement before he'd learned to relax. His age-old nightmare of going broke would come to pass.

Sometimes he offered concrete arguments against proceeding. "You don't have the capital to expand," he'd tell me. "You don't have the systems." Now and then he'd deliver his advice as if he thought he was still the boss. "As long as that's my name on the front of the building," he said many times, "I can do as I damn well please." As often as not, he pleaded. "It's too risky," he'd tell me. "You should enjoy what you have. It was good for me; it should be good for you." And: "Rome wasn't built in a day. Cool your jets, Eddie."

But I was committed to the idea of expansion. I was thirty. I was convinced we should be further along. The board backed the idea of opening a third store. My stepmom, Donna, calmed my dad down as much as she could.

Syracuse. The first store outside of Binghamton, Tim and I decided, would be in Syracuse—three times the size of Binghamton, with a major university, a lot of hunters and fishermen, and heavy snow every winter, all of which promised to be good for us. Tim Myers and I drove the seventy miles up to Syracuse one Sunday to have a look around. We saw a bunch of real estate signs on open properties, all advertising the same broker, which is how we met Mary Claire Cod. She took us to Erie Boulevard East, where a piece of property was for sale near the big ShoppingTown Mall.

We looked at the property, eyed its proximity to the mall, and said, "Yeah, that looks great. We could build a store here." We had no idea what we were doing. We didn't know what this store would look like or how big it would be. We knew nothing about the economics of expansion and whether it made more sense to buy or lease. But we were excited by this tangible piece of the puzzle, this weedy plot, and before you knew it, we'd signed some papers.

Tim and I were driving home when he looked over at me and said, "Did we just buy a piece of land?"

Suddenly I was horrified. "I think we did," I said.

"What are we going to do with it?"

With deepening buyer's remorse, I answered, "I don't really know."

Over the course of the drive, we asked each other several times, "What are we doing?" By the time we got home we'd worked ourselves into a panic. We'd gotten way out ahead of ourselves. We needed to figure out what we'd build in Syracuse before we picked out where we'd put it—how big it should be, what we'd put in it, what its economics would look like. We called Mary Claire and told her we couldn't do the deal. We needed time to figure things out.

She was wonderful. "I understand," she told us. "No problem."

We thus dodged a bullet that could have undone us before we even got started. Later, when we were a little better educated, we took another trip up there. A strip shopping center was under construction off Erie Boulevard, not far from the place we'd nearly bought. Its anchor, a big Hechinger home improvement store, was taking shape, and work was under way on a lot of smaller shops. We talked to the folks developing the center, and they said they'd let us put a twenty-thousand-square-foot store there. Larry Schorr handled the lease negotiations and contracts.

With that, we figured we were in business. We had detailed plans for the store's interior, which would be unlike any sporting goods store anywhere: departments arranged almost like stand-alone boutiques, and a traffic pattern designed to encourage shoppers through all of them. A profusion of eye-grabbing displays on columns and slat walls—ball gloves, canoes, ski jackets, football gear—so that the second you stepped in you were dazzled by the variety of cool stuff we had for sale. We'd hired a designer to put it together and spent a lot of time working with him on it so that it maximized flexibility. With the change of seasons, we'd be able to easily move the departments around.

We handed off the plans to the shopping center's developer and waited with excitement for the store to take form. And waited. And we'd be waiting still, except that we had a conversation with the contractor handling the construction, which at that point consisted of the store's exterior walls and utilities. When we asked about his timetable for laying the tile floor and carpet, and putting up the slat walls, he squinted at us. "What are you talking about?" It turned out that he wasn't going to do any of that. He was contracted to provide us with an empty shell—a "vanilla box."

"Wait," we said. "You guys were supposed to build us a store."

"Yeah," he said. "We're building you a vanilla box." All of the interior was our responsibility. Not only did we not have anyone on deck to build out the place, we hadn't ordered any of the slat walls, fittings, lights, shelving, and a million other components of the store we'd envisioned. We were due to open in a matter of weeks.

He saved us. He had us order the fittings, and he agreed to do the construction. He was up front that the job would run into more money, because the work had not been in our contract, so it cost us. I suspect he gouged us a bit, but he proved to be worth every penny, because he finished on time and the store looked beautiful. I firmly believe that you learn more from your mistakes than you do from your successes, and that first store in Syracuse is a prime example. We were pretty damn well educated in how to open a store after that, and especially how *not* to do it. We'd narrowly avoided disaster.


My dad, meanwhile, remained vociferously opposed to this new adventure. While our work on the Syracuse store raced along, he woke one morning feeling sick and drove himself to see Dr. Peter Zayac, who'd saved his life years before. He'd made no changes in his habits after that close call—he still smoked dozens of Pall Malls a day, drank far too much, and continued to eat poorly.

A nurse at Dr. Zayac's office looked him over. His skin was the color of cigarette ash, and his belly was distended. You need to get to the hospital, she told him. With that, he passed out. A short time later, in the emergency room, doctors discovered that his bypass had blown out, and he was gushing blood internally. Fortunately, the hardware from the bypass had lodged in a muscle in his back, which, as I understand it, blocked some of the flow. Had that not happened, he would have bled out on the drive to the doctor's office.

Kim, Marty, and I raced to the hospital. We weren't allowed to see him, but from a room away we could hear my dad screaming in pain. It was a shocking sound, bloodcurdling, and it scared the hell out of all of us. They rushed him into surgery.

It lasted more than twelve hours. We knew a lot of people at the hospital, and they told us later that a bed had been prepared for him in Intensive Care but that nobody in the operating room thought he'd need it. But stubborn as always, Dick Stack survived the operation. When I went in to see him the next day, he was connected to a spray of tubes and so pumped full of fluids he looked like he weighed three hundred pounds. I thought for a moment I'd walked into the wrong room. He was unconscious for the next forty-eight hours. When he came around and was able to talk, he grabbed my arm. "You finky kids," he rasped. "I can't believe what you've done."

"Why? What have we done?" I asked.

"You bought this hospital," he said. "Why the hell did you do that? We don't need a hospital."

"We didn't buy the hospital," I told him, fighting the urge to laugh.

"Yes, you did," he said. "And you shouldn't have. We don't need a damn hospital."

For the record, we didn't buy the hospital. We had our hands full running a sporting goods business, thank you. When my dad was still hospitalized but feeling a little better, he called over to Court Street. A young manager answered the phone. "Listen, it's Dick," my dad said. "I want you to go to Cortese's and get me an order of spaghetti, and go to the store and get me a carton of Pall Malls."

The manager was paralyzed. He called Jay Mininger. "I'm

screwed," he told him. "I don't know what to do. If I don't take him the Pall Malls, Dick will fire me. If I do take them, Ed will fire me."

I heard about the request before the manager had to worry for long. My dad might have gotten his Pall Malls, but he didn't get them from anyone at Dick's.

Despite all of our missteps, the opening in Syracuse was a great success. We moved people up from Binghamton to manage the store, among them my sister Nancy, and ran help-wanted ads in the Syracuse paper to fill out the staff—we set up a table in the place as the construction crews hurried to finish their work, and hundreds of people lined up to apply.

Our advertising campaign started weeks beforehand. The first newspaper ads we took out read simply: "The biggest sporting event in Syracuse starts on August 3." That got people talking around town. In later ads, we revealed little by little what was coming. We did a soft opening, for which we unlocked the doors, welcomed customers, and had everyone in place but didn't announce we were open—just to get everything running smoothly. Then came the grand opening.

The response was overwhelming. We had reps from a lot of the major sports brands there, and even they were shocked by the crowds that pushed into the new Dick's that day. My dad had recovered enough to attend with Donna and the rest of the family. Tim and Donna had to skim the registers and take piles of cash in a bag to Nancy's apartment, just to have somewhere safe to put all the money we took in. It was crazy.

About a year later, Dad was recovering from an illness, and I was trying to get him out of the house. We were having a meeting in Syracuse with Nike, and after a lot of negotiation I got him to agree to come with me. By this time, the store was well on the way to doing $8.3 million in sales in its first year. We'd knocked the cover off the ball. With that one opening, we doubled the size of the company.

We got to the store and were exchanging pleasantries with Gary DeStefano, Nike's regional manager, when Gary turned to my dad. "Dick, you must be really proud of these kids," he said. "The store looks fantastic. They've done such a great job."

My dad nodded. "The store looks great. They're doing a great job," he said. "But these kids did twenty-five percent more business than they thought they would. So you know what? They're really not quite as smart as they think they are."

I took it as a compliment.

That first Syracuse store was a comfortable leap for us because it was little more than an hour's drive from Court Street. I went up there a couple of times a week to check on the operation and make sure the team there had everything it needed. Shuttling merchandise between Binghamton and Syracuse was easy and fast on Interstate 81. The new store's operation went so smoothly that we almost immediately thought about opening a second store up that way. The site we chose this time was on the north side of town, twelve miles from the first store. We were excited. We expected it would do every bit as well as the first had, that between them we'd be racking up more than $16 million in sales.

But again, we were new to the business of running multiple locations, and while the construction of the second Syracuse store went off without a hitch, its operation still brought surprises because there was much we had yet to learn. We opened in 1988, and at the end of the year hadn't pulled in $8.3 million—the new store did about $7 million, and what's more, sales at the first store sagged to about $8 million. Now, by just about any yardstick, those were incredible numbers, but they weren't what we'd projected, and the reason is a phenomenon that retailers call *cannibalization*. With one Dick's in town, our customers came from all over Syracuse—north of town, the west side, down south. They came from many miles away to reach that one store on the east side of the city.

With a second store, a lot of the customers who'd faced a long drive to reach us had a store closer by, and their business peeled away from the original location in favor of the new place. We drew a lot of customers we'd never had before to that second store, but we also cannibalized the first store for some of that business. It taught us that when we located multiple stores in the same market, one plus one didn't necessarily equal two—it might instead equal 1.75. Expensive lesson. From then on, we knew we had to be incredibly careful about where we located, to minimize the impact of one store on another.

Even so, the two Syracuse stores were wildly profitable, enough so that we were eager to expand into a new market. We set our sights on Rochester, an even bigger city about eighty miles west of Syracuse, on the shore of Lake Ontario—another town with lots of college students, an active population, and a ton of snow, all pluses for Dick's. I knew Rochester from my college years and couldn't wait to open there. A local car dealer was building a shopping center anchored by a Toys "R" Us, directly across the street from the big Marketplace Mall in Henrietta, and it looked to be a good spot for us. We told him we thought we could do $8 million in sales in his plaza, and after reviewing our tax returns and sales at our Syracuse stores, he welcomed us in.

By now, building out a store was almost routine. We went a little bigger, at twenty-five thousand square feet, but the construction and build-out went smoothly and when we opened, people just crammed the aisles, wowed by all they found inside—which included, to their disbelief, a *driving range* where they could test golf clubs before buying them. The store took off like a rocket. We did $10.3 million in sales in our first year.

It was in the midst of these first stabs at expansion that the savings and loan crisis rocked the country's financial sector. As hundreds of savings and loans failed, bank regulators tightened their policing of not only S & Ls but banks across America. Dick's had always relied on debt, from the company's earliest days—we couldn't have supplied our stores with inventory, or made payroll, or kept the lights on if we hadn't had a credit line that we were able to carry for most of the year. We'd never missed a payment. We'd always done what we were supposed to do. We were a good account. And one of the ways you demonstrated that was that each year you had to clear your credit line to a zero balance for thirty consecutive days. We did it every year after Christmas.

But it was a new world during the S & L crisis, and so it was that regulators reviewing the First City National Bank's books told them that they'd have to dispose of one of their accounts— us. The bank informed us we had sixty days to find a new lender. This wasn't an easy time to go looking for a fresh source of money. We'd been searching for weeks without success when Larry Schorr told me about a guy he knew at Binghamton Savings Bank, the head of the lending department there, named Glenn Small. "I'll introduce you," he said. "He might be able to help."

I met with Glenn, told him about our business, showed him all of our figures. "I think we can do this," Glenn said. "We need to go through the Credit Committee, but I think we'll be fine."

I didn't understand the whole regulatory process at the time. I sold socks and jocks for a living, you know? But I recognized that had it not been for Glenn Small, we might have gone out of business right then, just as we were starting to grow as a company. Despite the fact that we'd always been a good credit risk, some artificial metrics in a bank regulation could have strangled us. If we hadn't found a new credit line with Glenn and Binghamton Savings Bank, we'd have had nothing to sell.

I've thanked Glenn many times for saving us. He's a humble guy and invariably comes back with, "I didn't do it—you did." As we got bigger, and for as long as Glenn was with Binghamton Savings Bank, I made sure we kept it in our consortium of lenders. Our bigger banks didn't want to have such a small bank involved, but we insisted that it get a piece of the action.

There was a lesson in our near-failure: you have to be prepared for the unexpected, have to build yourself a cushion so that you're able to survive challenges, those both within and outside your control. I'm not saying we took that lesson to heart right away. Unfortunately, we'd have it hammered home to us again before it stuck. But still, the lesson's a good one.

It was not long after that that we experienced a short-term cash crunch. A lot of our bills came due in early November and December, and while I knew we were doing well, and we'd be fine once Christmas was behind us, we were bumping against our credit limit. To pay the bills I borrowed $100,000 from my dad. He worried about that loan from the second he made it, and I was sitting in my office on my birthday two days after Christmas when he called and screamed at me that he wanted his $100,000 back, and he wanted it back that very day.

Hillcrest had again ballooned in his mind to blot out everything else. A couple of days later, with the Christmas receipts in, we repaid his loan. I never asked him for another.


Another big development from that period was much happier. For a few years after college, I'd fallen out of touch with my friend Bill Colombo. This was long before the Internet made connections easier to maintain, and we were both busy with our careers, but I thought about him now and then and wondered what he was up to. Bill was from Brooklyn, but even so had apparently lived a sheltered life before we ended up in the same dorm at St. John Fisher, and on arriving there he'd gone hog wild in the style of 1973—bong hits, hippie chicks, long hair, loud drums, howling at the moon. He was a tremendous amount of fun. Beneath all that wildness, he was smart, compassionate, loyal, and trustworthy. I thought the world of him.

Bill had settled down as a senior and gone to work at J. C. Penney shortly after he graduated, first as a management trainee. It was his first brush with retail, and it surprised him that there was real science behind running stores. That was especially true at Penney, which had developed sophisticated systems and a unique structure. At the time J. C. Penney was one of the most well-respected and well-run companies. Its stores operated semi-independently, each handling its own buying, marketing, and hiring, while staying within the boundaries of an overall corporate program. The arrangement enabled a store to groom its selection of products to its community, and it encouraged middle managers to become merchandisers. At the same time, a J. C. Penney store had to meet corporate objectives for income, salary cost control, shrinkage, and a host of other measures of performance, and those filtered down to department heads and, ultimately, everyone in the company. It was an enormously disciplined operation. The former wild man thrived in that environment.

Penney moved him every two years, through jobs in merchandising, human resources, and systems. He'd worked in Utica and Syracuse, and was now in Buffalo. He was on a fast track, and by about the time we'd opened our second Syracuse store, it was apparent that the company was considering him for a big promotion to the regional office in Pittsburgh. He didn't want to go. The aspiration of everyone at Penney in the 1970s was to run a store, and he knew that if he went to the regional office before they gave him his first store, he might end up somewhere he didn't want to be.

That's about when we reconnected. We at Dick's had ambitions to expand further, and faster, and I knew I needed help. And of all the people I'd met in my life, Bill was about the smartest, and most serious, and most capable. Ten years had passed since graduation. One day when I was talking with his brother-in-law, Jerry Harper—who happened to be our Nike rep—I asked, "Do you think Bill would ever come work for us?" Jerry replied that I could ask him, but he doubted it because Bill was rising fast through the ranks at Penney.

I called him anyway, told him what we were doing, and nosed around about whether he'd want to be part of it. "We can talk," Bill said. Looking back, he said that only because we were friends. He didn't want to tell a buddy from college to hit the bricks. We talked by phone again and set a date to meet in Buffalo. That face-to-face conversation made it clear to me that Bill had little interest in joining our business; he was playing in the big leagues, and we were Double-A. I offered him a great salary and a piece of the company, but I just couldn't get him over the hump. Finally, I said: "Billy, what else can I do? Why won't you do this?"

He smiled. "I understand your plan," he said, "but it's such a small company. I'll be a divisional president someday at Penney. I'm on the fast track. I don't know that there'd be enough for me to do at Dick's."

It took a lot more talking—altogether, this courtship went on for more than six months—but I eventually convinced him that there'd be plenty for him to do. He told me later that he spoke to his brother, who asked him, "Do you think Dick's is going somewhere? And if it doesn't, could you get another job?" He answered yes to both questions. His brother said, "Then why *wouldn't* you do it?" He called one day to say he'd come aboard and started at Dick's in June 1988, shortly before we opened in Rochester.

We started him as a district manager to get his feet on the ground, but it was just a few months later that he became our director of stores. Bill brought the discipline he'd experienced at Penney to our seat-of-the-pants operation; until he came along, we hadn't developed any systems for buying or much of anything else—our style, though a bit more grounded in reality than my dad's had been, was still *have a hunch, buy a bunch.* He changed our in-store product presentation and signage. He was an expert at store operations. But more than that, he would serve as my partner in guiding the company's growth. I trusted him completely, and we complemented each other. I was the visionary; Bill was the executor. I could get emotional at times, could be a bit of a hothead; Bill could calm me down and play the intermediary when I needed one.

He stayed plenty busy. Over the years to come I'd stop by his office, and I'd always ask, "You got enough to do in here?" To which he'd always respond: "Fuck you." It always made me laugh.

• • •

I wish I could tell you that our every move was intentional and that we were thinking strategically as we opened each of these new stores. Fact is, we didn't think strategically at all. Tim and I would drive around a new town, counting swing sets in people's yards, and if we figured an area had lots of kids, we were good to go. We picked the specific locations for our stores based on what space was available and what other retailers were nearby. We bumped up the square footage to twenty-five thousand because we were always cramped for space for apparel. We were lucky that we had only so much money in those early days and couldn't get too far ahead of ourselves. As undisciplined and excited as we were, we could have worked ourselves into trouble.

As it was, these new, bigger stores presented challenges that we didn't see coming. They required much bigger staffs than we'd had on Court Street and in Vestal, and the employee turnover was higher: people weren't taking up careers in retail as they had just a few years before. Plus, the size of the stores meant more aisles to walk, more customers to help, and more merchandise to keep track of. That last part required some education because in these bigger cities we found that a lot more of our merchandise vanished. We got beat up pretty badly on "shrink," the retail term for stuff that leaves a store unpurchased. The biggest source of shrink is theft.

Our shoplifters didn't limit themselves to clothes. They stole athletic shoes, baseball gloves, even golf clubs. Graphite-shafted clubs had entered the market and created a sensation, but despite the hoopla, the value wasn't in the shafts, it was in the club heads. Thieves would loiter in the golf department until no one was looking, then take a razor blade to the graphite shafts, stuff their pockets full of heads, and walk out. Then they'd go get the heads reshafted—in essence, they'd put a $25 shaft on a $200 club and sell it on the black market.

Our expansion to Syracuse and Rochester saw our shrink numbers balloon to 2 percent of total sales. But Bill put a special loss-prevention group to work. It nipped the problem. In eighteen months, Bill and the group cut our shrink number by more than half.


It was in one of these new, big stores that I had an experience that remains vivid and important to me thirty years later. My dad was living almost full-time in Florida when this happened, enjoying his life in the sun, and he hadn't seen the changes we'd made to our layouts after that first store in Syracuse. I called him and said, "Look, we're opening this store, and it's really something. Why don't you come up to the grand opening? You haven't seen anything like this."

"No," he said. "Too expensive." He had plenty in the bank, but he still worried that it could disappear at any time and that he wouldn't know where to scrounge his next meal.

"We'll pay for your flight and the hotel," I told him. "Why don't you come up?"

Without missing a beat, he said, "Love to be there."

So I picked him up at the airport at dusk, and we drove to the new store. Snow was falling gently as we got out of the car. His name shone enormous above the doors and cast a glow on the snow one hundred yards away. I could see he was surprised and moved by the sight.

Then we stepped inside, to a new design we would use as a model for the next several years. It was a wonderland for someone who loved sports, and I could see he was getting choked up. I walked him into the driving range, closed the door, and he burst into tears. His little store, transformed into such an incredible place. His humble beginnings, memorialized with his name in lights ten feet tall out front. He cried like a six-year-old.

And in that moment, I realized that for all of his hard-ass ways, his stubbornness and the hot temper that he'd directed my way over the years, he was my father, and I loved him. I'd wanted to please him since I was a kid, and his opinion still counted with me.

And though he didn't say so, I'd just made him awfully proud.

## CHAPTER 9

# "IF YOU TEE OFF ON NUMBER ONE, YOU PUTT OUT ON EIGHTEEN"

Two years after Rochester, we set our sights on New York State's second-biggest city, Buffalo. Located in the far northwest corner of the state at the eastern tip of Lake Erie, it was a long way from Binghamton. But like Syracuse and Rochester, it was just off Interstate 90—the New York State Thruway—which simplified the logistics of getting merchandise into a store there. Plus, Buffalo was home to a vibrant fishing community on Lake Erie, and a lot of hunters, and had some of the coldest, snowiest winters in the Lower Forty-Eight. All of that made it our kind of town.

This time, our build-out did not go as planned. A developer out of Syracuse was building the new Walden Galleria Mall just off the interstate, and we struck a deal to put a forty-thousand-square-foot store in the development. Construction got under way. We didn't see much going on where our store was supposed to be. We checked with the developers to make sure everything was in place. Yeah, yeah, they said. No problems. Still, there didn't seem to be much progress. We checked again with the builders.

They told us everything was fine. They weren't being straight with us. It wasn't long before we learned they'd leased our planned location to a clothing retailer, the Limited.

They evidently figured that little Dick's Sporting Goods, with five stores in its portfolio, didn't have the stones to make an issue of it. We met with the developers and made it clear that we wanted that space. Sorry, they replied. Can't do it. Well, we countered, that's a problem, because we have a signed lease. They basically dismissed us with a "So what?"

We didn't have a lot of available cash at the time. We were undercapitalized, all of our money tied up in inventory. My own house, and Kim and Tim's, too, was pledged as collateral to the banks. But I was pissed and didn't feel I could let the situation stand. I have never been litigious, but the breach of contract demanded we fight. I went back to the board and spoke with my uncle Joe and Larry Schorr. "We have to sue these guys," I told them. "We have to make them perform on this lease."

My uncle Joe, in sharp contrast to most of the Stack bloodline, never lost his cool. "Look," he said, "they're going to offer you a check to walk away from this. And I know you're upset, and you have every right to be, but if they offer you half a million dollars, don't you dare turn them down." With that advice in my pocket, I returned to the developers and met with one of their decision-makers. Listen, we're not going to build your store, he told me. We're sorry about that. But we're willing to offer the Ed Stack Children's College Fund $300,000.

That sounds like a bribe, I told him. That's not going to work. After a couple more conversations, they apparently realized I wasn't going to back down and offered a half million. Per Uncle Joe's instructions, I had to say yes. They wrote us a check for $500,000, and we opened a forty-thousand-square-foot store across the street. It was a huge success—Buffalo had never seen anything like it, and half the city seemed to squeeze through the doors the day we opened. I remember standing in the footwear department on our second day, bone tired, watching the front doors as customers just kept pouring in, and thinking: *I know we want people to come, but please, just give us a break. Just ten minutes of rest.* It never came. More customers did.

The store had a display of baseball gloves that stretched across thirty feet of wall, and I was standing near it when this little boy and his mom approached. The kid, maybe nine years old, was wide-eyed as he took in this wall of gloves, looked at his mom, then looked back at the wall. "Mom," he gasped, "I've waited for a store like this my whole life." A thrill ran through me, hearing that. I smiled as I thought about what a great commercial the scene would make. As it turned out, much of Buffalo felt the same way that little boy did, because we did $12 million in sales our first year there.

With six stores up and running, we were starting to make some money. We still went deep into debt for our inventory, but we were feeling pretty excited about the way things were going. Our run continued, because we then got an unexpected offer from Wegmans, the Rochester-based chain of high-end grocery stores, where I'd worked briefly while in college. Their head of real estate, Ralph Uterro, called to say that he had an opening in a shopping center they owned in Greece, a neighborhood on Rochester's northwest side, clear across the city from our store there. Wegmans owned a chain of home improvement and gardening stores called Chase Pitkin, and one of these stores occupied about forty thousand square feet in a strip shopping center in Greece. We're relocating the Chase Pitkin, Uterro told me. We don't want the space to sit empty. We'd like to make a deal with you.

More as a courtesy to him than anything else, I drove up to Rochester to have a look. It was a nice space, and far enough away from our first Rochester store that he didn't think there'd be much cannibalization. Problem was, we were already stretched thin, from a cash standpoint. We'd opened four stores in five years, all significantly bigger than Court Street, and we needed to take a year off, take a deep breath, and reduce our debt. "We can't do it," I told Ralph. "I wish we could, but we're undercapitalized. We can't make it work. It would be too risky."

He pressed. "What would it take for you to say yes?" he asked.

What it would take was well beyond what I thought he'd agree to, and I told him so. He wanted to hear our terms. "Ralph," I said, "you'd have to build out the store for us. You'd have to buy all the fixtures for us. And on top of that, you'd have to loan us more than a million dollars for inventory."

"Ah," he said with a smile. He was a good guy, and I liked him. "Well, we can't do that."

"I understand," I told him. "That's no problem. I hope we can do business together at another time." We parted on friendly terms.

Two days later he called me. "I talked to Mr. Wegman," he said. "We'll do it."

With that, Wegmans built out the store, bought about $200,000 in fixtures, and lent us $1 million for inventory. Besides that, they were wonderful landlords. The store did well—not as well as our other Rochester store, but then, we had virtually no skin in it, so it didn't have to break any records. What it did do was solidify our presence in Rochester.

We'd long since outgrown our Binghamton headquarters and warehouse—we couldn't take in all the merchandise we needed to service our new and larger stores, and now we had a group of full-time buyers, a team of accounts-payable clerks, accountants, and all the other people who kept the stores full of product and customers. Shortly after Bill Colombo moved down, we built a new distribution center in Conklin, a small town just above the Pennsylvania line. It seemed vast—sixty thousand square feet of warehouse receiving and storage, along with twenty thousand square feet of office space.

We remained a fairly unsophisticated operation, however. None of our merchandise went directly from the manufacturer to our stores, which is a process called drop-shipping; it all came into our warehouse, where we did "splits," parceling out the contents of each crate to our various locations. We did many of the splits by hand. It was time-consuming, tedious work.

Still, now we had two stores in Rochester, two in Syracuse, one in Buffalo, and the original two in the Binghamton area. We were feeling pretty good about ourselves.

As I mentioned a while back, in my first years out of college I'd read a lot of business books. All had lessons to offer, but none resonated quite like the story of Sam Walton—how the owner of a Ben Franklin five-and-dime franchise in rural Arkansas grew that one small store into the retail juggernaut that is Walmart today. One of the principles that guided Walton was to grow his business quietly, unobtrusively, to stay below the radar so that his competition didn't notice him. He did it by expanding his geographic reach in concentric circles, radiating out from his launching point in tiny Bentonville.

We replicated Sam Walton's strategy. From Binghamton, our expansion had come in small, outward steps—to Syracuse, then Rochester, then Buffalo. From there we moved in the early nineties to Albany, New York, about 130 miles northeast of Binghamton; put a second store in Buffalo; then opened another ninety miles to the southwest in Erie, Pennsylvania. After that we slid eastward to Springfield, Massachusetts, eighty miles from Albany, and Hartford, Connecticut, twenty-five miles south of Springfield.

These were small or medium-sized markets, which gave us a shot at customers without having to worry too much about a bigger, better-capitalized competitor moving in on us. The modest geographic area we controlled made distribution pretty simple—the stores were located on a handful of principal highways, so that one truck could service several on a single trip. Most important, they were all in cold-weather markets, and in hunting country, so we understood their customers' needs. Winter outerwear for hunters and skiers remained an important piece of our sales mix.

For a while, our low-key, small-market strategy worked. We had only local competition, and we were accustomed to dealing with that. Let me tell you a story about the kind of competition I mean. Back in the day, you could only hunt deer in the Southern Tier with a shotgun, the preferred ammunition being solid lead or copper slugs. Two weeks before hunting season began, one of our competitors, Philadelphia Sales, would offer their shotgun slugs cheap, as a loss leader, and I remember my dad taking cash out of the register and sending us kids over there to buy up their inventory. They caught on after a while and set a five-box limit, but my dad had a lot of kids.

By the time I was running the store, we competed with both Philadelphia Sales and the local Kmart for our hunting business, and we'd undercut their prices on ammo in our ads. When they dropped their prices to match ours, we'd ratchet ours down again. I was standing behind the gun counter one day when in walked a guy from Kmart. He was dressed like a New York lawyer in a suit and tie, and though I was twenty-three or twenty-four, I was baby faced and often mistaken for a teenager. The Kmart fellow, apparently figuring he could intimidate us, stopped on the other side of the counter and said, "You people need to stop this price war."

"What do you mean?" I asked.

"You have to tell the boss you need to stop this price war," he said, "or we'll put you out of business."

"Okay," I told him. "I'll make sure he knows." As he walked away, I thought: *What an asshole*. In our next ad, we knocked another ten cents off the price. They matched us. I sent my brother Marty over to Kmart, and he cleaned them out. He filled an entire shopping cart with shotgun slugs, case upon case of them. We added them to our inventory, and once the season started, we had a pile of slugs that we'd bought for less than we would have paid Remington or Winchester. They drove a lot of traffic into the store.

All of which is to say that in the early going, competition had been something we looked forward to, that we had fun with. It was a game we were good at, and we enjoyed playing it. Because we were willing to be aggressive, we usually beat the other guy.

Now, however, came bigger and far more dangerous adversaries. Our first real threat came from Herman's World of Sporting Goods, the industry's apex predator on the East Coast during the 1970s and 1980s. Based in Carteret, New Jersey, the company dated to 1916, and for a long time was centered just in the New York metropolitan area. But in the early 1980s it began an aggressive expansion, and one of the markets in its sights was Binghamton.

We were alike in many ways. They catered to a wide variety of sports-minded customers, with a good selection of team sports and camping equipment, fishing tackle, golf gear, footwear, and apparel. Their arrival had us worried. They dwarfed us, and they had a reputation as good operators. Defending ourselves meant understanding how they did business, so we took a field trip to New York and looked over their stores. We also researched their past advertising, which was instructive, because retailers are creatures of habit. They follow a schedule that doesn't change much from year to year—back-to-school happens at the end of every summer, and hunting season starts the same time in the fall, and Christmas always comes on December 25. Sports retailers advertise pretty much the same sales at the same time every year, always pushing the same sort of products, because that's the merchandise that drives their business.

Our research into Herman's advertising revealed that, sure enough, they took out newspaper insert advertising that was as predictable as the earth rotating on its axis. Their modus operandi was to run their inserts in the Sunday papers. We, on the other hand, usually ran our inserts on Wednesdays—that was the traditional day that supermarkets ran their ads and papers published their food sections, and it drove a lot of readership. It also gave us the ability to give our customers a heads-up about what we'd have on sale during the coming weekend.

They opened at the Oakdale Mall in Johnson City, apparently unconcerned about the small-town stores already in the market. We had a pretty good idea what they'd be advertising each week and prepared our own inserts to push the same items, only at lower prices. When their insert came out each Sunday, we had about twenty-four hours to fine-tune our own Wednesday insert. And week after week, we just beat their brains in. They were so big that for a long while they didn't even know they were getting pummeled.

When we opened in Albany, they were already there, and we did the same thing. I'll tell you a story that's embarrassing about our face-off with them there. Albany marked the first place outside of Binghamton in which we tangled with Herman's, so Tim Myers and I went up there the Monday after Thanksgiving to see how they'd arranged their store for the holidays, so we'd know what to do to compete with them the following year. We walked in and found that it looked okay but fell far short of great. Tim and I grabbed dinner, during which I idly mentioned that I'd really like to know how their business had been over the Thanksgiving weekend. "Buy me another beer," Tim said, laughing, "and I'll find out."

I bought him another beer, and we went back to the Hampton Inn, where we were staying. Tim called the Herman's store, which we could see across the parking lot. The manager came on the line, and Tim said, "This is Bob Corliss. How you doing?" Bob Corliss was the CEO of Herman's.

"Good, Mr. Corliss," the manager replied. "How are you?"

"I'm calling around," Tim said, "to see how business was over the Thanksgiving Day weekend."

I wasn't entirely comfortable with the stunt, but it was too late to stop it now. The manager told him what categories had sold well, what hadn't. He spoke in generalities, but that was all we wanted to know. Then Tim surprised me by saying: "Well, the reason your business might not have been so good is that I was in your store, and it's really a mess. I'm going to be back there tomorrow morning at nine thirty, and it better look different."

We were expecting Jay Mininger, who was driving in from Syracuse, so we went out to meet him. We had a drink, talked for a while, then drove back to the hotel at about eleven. Every light was on over at Herman's. The parking lot was full. I'm sure there was nothing but asses and elbows in that store through the night.

I am not advocating that kind of behavior. To this day, I feel bad that we did it. My only defense is that we were young. The stunt made no difference in our struggle with Herman's, and it made life miserable for some folks who didn't deserve a sleepless and anxious night. Moreover, we've been on the receiving end of corporate subterfuge, and I can attest that it doesn't feel good.

In the interest of staying on subject, I'll tell you about that episode now, though it happened more than twenty years later, in 2014. One day that February, Mitch Modell of Modell's Sporting Goods, a prominent retailer in New York, walked into our store in Princeton, New Jersey, with a female companion, and told our manager that he was a Dick's senior vice president gathering information for an upcoming meeting with me. He asked the manager to walk him through the store and tell him what was selling, what wasn't. He asked to see the back room.

Our manager did as he was asked. He took him into the back room and gave him a look at the stock. Business was so-so, he reported. Footwear was doing okay, but some categories had been disappointing. He didn't offer up sales figures, but still, he passed on proprietary information we didn't want a competitor to have. And the back room is sacred ground. You never let a competitor into your back room.

Once Mitch left, the manager began to feel the whole visit had been sketchy and called his district manager. It was then he learned that no senior vice president had been down his way. A look at our security camera footage identified the imposter. I knew Mitch pretty well, and liked him, but let me tell you, I was *pissed*. Modell's had a store just down the street, and I saw this as underhanded, a far greater violation than we'd pulled on Herman's. I called our general counsel and told him—though, as I mentioned before, I'm not a litigious guy—that I wanted to sue Mitch. He didn't think we could. I insisted that we should. "Okay," he said. "If you really want me to do it, I'll get started."

We filed suit in New Jersey superior court, and in no time the press was on it. Mitch had done an episode of the TV show *Undercover Boss*, which made the story irresistible to the media, and he got crucified—here was a corporate CEO taking the whole "undercover" thing a little too far. For weeks the story built, until one morning, as I was getting ready for work, I caught a segment about the affair on ABC's *Good Morning America*, in which he was absolutely flayed. And I realized it had gone on long enough: he'd done more than enough penance for his sin.

At the office I called our general counsel and told him we needed to settle. He told me that Mitch's people had just called, looking to settle, too. "I'm sure they'd write us a check for half a million dollars," he said. "We might be able to get a million." I suggested he call Mitch's lawyers and tell them we'd settle for one dollar, on the condition that Mitch never do it again. So that's what we did: we settled for one buck. I didn't want to take half a million dollars from Mitch. I just wanted to encourage him not to play dirty again.

The situation reminded me of another story. Back when I was playing Little League baseball, one of my teammates was a kid from a big family that barely scraped by. We were at Tastee Freez after a game, and my dad went to pay for the team's order when the kid's dad said, "No, Dick. I've got it this time." My dad stepped aside and let him pay. Kim, who was about ten, was there with us, and she whispered: "Dad, why did you let him pay? You know they don't have much money." To which my dad said, "Kim, you have to understand—you never want to take away a man's dignity."

At times when I'd be ready to write off my dad for his flaws as a parent and businessman, moments like that intruded, forcing me to admit that he'd displayed moments of grace and compassion. The example he set that particular day has stayed with me, when as an adult I've found myself facing competitors whom I intended to drive out of business, or haggling with a vendor over the price of a big order. It's fine to play tough, but you have to be fair. You have to let the other guy walk away with his dignity intact.

Back to Herman's. We were small, and nimble, and far more maneuverable than they were. In the end, they weren't in any shape for a fight: they were bought by a British supermarket chain that didn't understand retail in the States, and by the early 1990s they were in retreat. Among the first markets they pulled out of were the ones they shared with us.

All through the company's early growth, I spent a lot of time on the road or in the office. I'm not sure whether I'd be classified as a workaholic, but like my dad, I had something to prove. I wouldn't play at Yankee Stadium, but I wanted to run our sporting goods business like I was competing for the Cy Young Award. Besides, I had a wife and a baby son, Michael, and a mortgage, and employees who depended on me. Failure was not an option.

But no matter how busy I was, I viewed four hours each week as sacred: my Monday round of golf with my grandfather.

When Gramp was eighty-seven, we played the American Heart Association tournament, as usual, at Endwell Greens outside Binghamton. It was a cold and drizzly day, which was on my mind because at that point in his life, my grandfather was susceptible to colds, and I knew that my very protective grandmother wouldn't approve of his being out in such inclement weather. We weren't playing well, had no chance of winning, and the weather was turning worse, so as we teed off on the sixteenth hole, which was right beside the clubhouse, I said, "Hey, Gramp. We have no chance to win this. It's nasty out here, and if you get sick, Grandma is going to be upset with me. Let's just pack it in."

He teed up his ball. "Eddie," he said, looking my way, "if you tee up on number one, you putt out on eighteen."

My buddy Dave Ziebarth, who was playing with us, chuckled. "Guess we're going to keep playing!"

A couple of days later, Gramp had come down with pneumonia. I went over to see him, and as I'd predicted, I was in hot water with my grandmother. "Why did you have to finish playing?" she hissed at me. "Now he's sick!"

He recovered and was back on the course a few weeks later. That year, he shot his age once again, and he did it again the next year, and the year after that. At eighty-nine, he played in the B.C. Open with my brother Marty and me. We were in a pro-am fivesome with PGA Tour pro Paul Azinger and watched Gramp smack tee shots down the middle of one fairway after another. Azinger, amazed, turned to us halfway through the round: "That's the smoothest swing I've ever seen."

But by that time, Gramp had developed a circulation problem in his legs that forced him to use a cart. Not long after, his doctors discovered cancer in one of his shoulders. That limited his play, and at ninety-two he missed playing the American Heart Association tournament for the first time. He came out and watched a few holes from the gallery.

Gramp was normally so upbeat all the time, so happy with his life, that it was hard to read just how quickly the cancer was progressing. We found out soon enough. His condition worsened until he was put into in-home hospice care and spent most of his days in a hospital bed in his living room. I went to see him often. One day I found him out of bed and sitting on the sofa, but it was clear the end was near. "You know, Gramp, you were always there for me," I told him. "At baseball games and football games and always. You were always the one I could count on. You were the best grandfather in the world."

He nodded, and smiled as if to say, "I hoped you felt that way." We sat quiet for a moment, then he looked at me. "Eddie, I'm ninety-three and I know I'm a goner," he said. He smiled again. "But I feel I could go out and play third base right now."

I'm so grateful that I had that conversation with him—not only because I had a chance to tell him how much he meant to me, which was a wonderful gift, but because his comment stands as one of the most inspiring demonstrations of positive attitude I've ever heard. I hope I can age as gracefully.

It was a couple days later, while he was lying in bed, that he called my grandmother over. "Annie, it's time for me to go now," he told her. "I'm going to go to sleep now." They talked for a few minutes, cried together, kissed, and held each other's hands. Then he went to sleep. My grandmother sat with him. An hour passed. His breathing grew shallow.

Suddenly his eyes opened. He looked at her and asked: "I'm still here? What the hell happened?"

He died the next day.


My grandfather's influence didn't end with his death. Years later, he prompted me to reverse a pretty big business decision. The Binghamton area had long hosted the B.C. Open ("B.C." standing for "Broome County" and for the *B.C.* comic strip—Johnny Hart, who drew it, was from Binghamton). It drew some of the biggest names on the tour and was a real point of pride in town. The first time I saw Arnold Palmer and Lee Trevino was at the tournament.

But the PGA Tour changed the schedule, and the B.C. Open lost its slot in 2007. The tour made it clear that if organizers could attract a title sponsor, they'd book a senior PGA event in town. A guy named Alex Alexander led the effort to find a sponsor, and he called me several times to ask that Dick's fill that role. I was sympathetic but couldn't see any economic sense in our being involved. I politely said no.

Alex, who'd been a friend of my grandfather's, did not give up. He called. He wrote. He was always a gentleman about it, but he was persistent. Time was getting short—Alex had less than a week to find a sponsor—when he wrote one last time. I was sitting at my desk as I read his note, which repeated some of the arguments he'd made earlier—that Binghamton needed a tournament, that it'd be great, and so on and so on. He ended the note with: "I can just hear what Dutch would say if you did this. He'd say, 'Hey, Alex. How 'bout that?' "

I read that and felt a chill go up my spine. It was exactly what Gramp would say. I found myself thinking: *Gramp is trying to tell me something.* I took the letter down to our head of marketing and told him, "Let's find a way to make this happen."

We've sponsored the Dick's Open for thirteen years now. The tournament has raised millions of dollars for Broome County charities. When I attend the tournament—which is held on a course where Gramp and I often played—I always make it a point to thank the army of volunteers who make it possible, and many respond with some variation on, "Are you kidding? I take my vacation to do this every year. I wouldn't miss it." Some of those volunteers have been out there working the tournament for a quarter century, dating way back to the B.C. Open days.

It's clearly important to my hometown. I feel good that we do it. But the fact is that the credit doesn't belong to me. It was all Gramp's doing.

CHAPTER 10

# "DID YOU EVER THINK ABOUT CHANGING THE NAME?"

From time to time in those first years of growth we'd hear from venture capitalists who wanted to invest in the company. We weren't interested. We didn't need their help. We were doing just fine on our own; we could plan and finance our growth ourselves and didn't want anyone looking over our shoulders. We were feeling pretty confident.

But over time, as they kept calling, we came to see that if we wanted to grow faster, we could use the extra equity and the stronger balance sheet they'd bring. I thought we'd benefit from their real-world experience with other, bigger retailers, too. We had a few stores turning a nice profit, but we were still, with the exception of Bill Colombo, the same green kids who'd started together in Binghamton. With the know-how of more worldly partners, we could accelerate our plans for growing Dick's and defend ourselves against a bigger player moving in to swallow us up.

The investors who came calling were interested in the flip side of the relationship. Venture capitalists invest in a company to make money, of course, and they do it by helping that company grow, in the process becoming more valuable—in which case the value of their stake balloons with the business. They typically seek a fairly short-term partnership. After securing a nice return for their own investors, they'll either cash out or help take the company public, which carries the prospect of further boosting the value of their shares.

So if we accepted outside investors, theoretically both sides stood to benefit. And to tell you the truth, I was also coming to believe that an infusion of new voices in the company could only help the Stack family, because we weren't getting along particularly well. My siblings were unhappy that I was in charge. My dad was ticked off at the pace of our expansion and doing his best to rile up my brothers and sisters.

Things came to a head when we experienced a short-term cash crunch and I clamped down on any buying until it passed. I told our buyers that I would have to sign off on every purchase order. My brother Marty had worked as an assistant manager in Syracuse and was now a buyer for the company. He wasn't happy about having to report to anyone, especially me, and forged my signature to a number of purchase orders. I asked him to leave the company. When my dad heard the news, he stopped talking to me for more than a year.

The upshot is that in 1991 we were more receptive to the idea of outside investors than we'd been in the past, and one day I got a call from Michael Barach, of Bessemer Venture Partners. He asked if he could talk to me about investing in Dick's. I said that I'd be happy to listen.

We had dinner. Some people in life you feel good about instantly, and Barach and I hit it off. He was a few years younger than me, intense and a little awkward, and a very smart guy: he'd gone to Amherst, where he'd graduated summa cum laude with a history degree, and had a joint law degree and MBA from Harvard. His dad had run U.S. Shoe Corporation, and Barach had himself worked in retail for six years; he'd both succeeded and failed at it, so he understood the opportunities and pitfalls.

We talked about what kind of investment he'd want to make. We didn't want to take quite as much money as he wanted to put in, but he spoke with my siblings and a couple of them sold some stock. He came aboard as a venture partner for about 10 percent of the company.

This was in the summer. Barach broached the idea of bringing in a couple of other venture groups, as well, and introduced me to Jerry Gallagher from Oak Investment Partners. Gallagher had worked in retail for two decades, including ten years at Dayton-Hudson, better known today as Target. He was a lanky navy submarine veteran about thirteen years older than me, and he'd already invested in, and helped grow, Office Depot and PetSmart, among other companies.

Barach also introduced me to Janet Hickey, of the Sprout Group, the venture capitalist firm of Donaldson, Lufkin & Jenrette of New York. We did a walk-through of our store in Buffalo. At the time, the Sports Authority was a rising power among sporting goods retailers, the darling of Wall Street, and as we toured the store Hickey asked, "Do you do everyday low prices, or are you promotional?"

"Promotional," I answered.

"I don't know if that will work," she said. "Sports Authority does everyday low prices."

We walked around a bit more and she asked, "Do you use central distribution or do you drop-ship to your stores?"

"We use central distribution," I told her.

"I don't think that works," she said. "The Sports Authority drop-ships to its stores."

As we walked on, she ticked off a number of other facets of our operation that she didn't like, all the while comparing us with the Sports Authority. *No problem*, I thought. *She won't invest. So what?* I liked how we compared with the Sports Authority, which ran warehouse-format stores and carried lower-end products.

Both Gallagher and Hickey decided not to jump into an investment until they saw how we did during the holidays. Venture capitalists have a reputation as risk takers, but they're really pretty risk-averse. They do a lot of research to guarantee themselves the highest chance of success. Fortunately, business late that year was terrific, and Gallagher, now very close to investing, came to see me in the course of doing his due diligence. He was a Princeton grad and a bit of a blue blood, and I found him a little pompous. Really smart, too, which I liked.

We went to dinner at the Vestal Steakhouse and afterward went to our new store up the street. In place of our old 7,500-square-foot operation, expanded from that tiny, 2,800-square-foot store my dad bought in 1971, we now had a 50,000-square-foot prototype for all the new Dick's stores we'd be building over the next couple of years.

Like its predecessors, this new Dick's was set up as an assortment of specialty shops under one roof, each with staff grounded in that department's sport and merchandise. It was a cold winter's night, and as we got out of the car the sign over our door glowed ten feet high: Dick's Sporting Goods. Jerry looked at the sign, then over at me. "Did you ever think about changing the name?"

I knew immediately what he was getting at—we'd heard it all before—but I decided to make him spell it out. "No, Jerry. I never did."

"Well, I was talking to my assistant," he said, "and she asked me, 'Did they ever think about changing the name?'"

I waited for him to go on. He did: "I talked to my wife, and she thought the same thing."

"Jerry, I don't understand," I replied. "I mean, it's Dick's Sporting Goods. That's what we are—we're a sporting goods retailer." I was starting to enjoy watching him squirm.

"Well," he said, "maybe Dick's isn't the best name."

He looked uncomfortable, as if he was worried he might have to explain what *dick* means. I let him wonder. I kept my mouth shut. "I mean, you know, *Dick's*," he said. "Like, guys' anatomy."

I looked over at him. "Jerry, that is what my grandmother named my father," I said, my tone indignant. "My grandmother was one of the sweetest and nicest people I ever met. My father started this business. The name of the company is Dick's Sporting Goods."

The subject did not come up again.

• • •

I was eager to have Jerry Gallagher as an investor. He impressed me. I'd done my research, and everything I'd heard about him had been glowing. I wasn't nearly so excited by the idea of having Janet Hickey aboard, and I said so to Barach and Gallagher, both. Barach said he didn't care one way or another, but Gallagher insisted that she had to be part of the deal. "I want her in," he told me. "I'm not saying I won't invest if she isn't part of this, but I might have to revisit whether I want to invest." When I asked why, he explained: "I really want some people with some dry powder around the table, in case we get into trouble."

At the time, I didn't think we'd be getting into trouble and didn't see what would be so great about having the Sprout Group at the table, dry powder or no. But he was persuasive, so I decided I'd try again to build a bridge with Janet. She made arrangements to fly into Binghamton, and I picked her up at the airport.

I am not a good poker player when it comes to people I don't care for—they pick up on it fast. The fact is, I didn't like Janet. She seemed arrogant to me. She clearly loved the Sports Authority and didn't think much of what we were doing. I wondered why she was even interested in us at all. So it wasn't surprising when, as we walked out of the Binghamton airport, she asked: "You don't like me very much, do you?"

I was straight with her: "No, Janet, I really don't." After a long moment of awkward silence I asked, "Do you still want to go to the store?"

"Yes," she said.

Our afternoon spent talking about the business did nothing to change my feelings about allowing Sprout into the deal. It would not have broken my heart if Hickey had decided to pass.

It turned out that both Gallagher and Hickey bought in. Altogether, the venture capitalists invested about $6 million. Everyone was happy, maybe my siblings more than anyone—they got a chunk of the incoming money by selling some of their shares. Selling stock wasn't an option for me. I didn't want to give up any shares, anyway, though I could have used the money: eight years after taking control, I was going to work in the family business every day but had no money in the bank. But our new friends wanted to keep me hungry. They had no use for a complacent CEO.

The most immediate change their arrival brought to Dick's might have been the professionalization of our board. Until now, I'd been guided by the advisory group I put together in 1984. The venture capitalists wanted a board of big-box-retail executives, an experienced group who'd done what we were hoping to do. Of the board's seven seats, our partners would fill two and I'd have five—and I'd have the power to remove and replace any one of my designees whenever I wanted.

Barach and Gallagher themselves took their two places on the panel. Jerry quickly grew into the role of lead director, years before that term became commonplace. He was the liaison between the venture group and me. He said to me once, "You need to understand that not all venture capital money is the same shade of green." By that he meant that some investors will introduce you to others who can help you and take a real hand in getting you through tough times. That's the kind of director Jerry Gallagher was. He was in it for more than just a check. The color of his money was definitely different from that of the other early investors.

To my board seats, I named Sam Parker, the CEO of PetSmart, and Dave Fuente, CEO of Office Depot, both of whom had worked with Gallagher in the past; I'd met both and liked them, especially Fuente. I also named Walter Rossi, who'd been vice chairman of the apparel giant Phillips–Van Heusen and CEO of Mervyn's, a California-based department store chain. Larry Schorr, our Binghamton attorney, who'd helped get us through every major transaction thus far, including helping to broker this venture capital buy-in, was the only old face that remained from our original board, besides mine.

I remember how promising the whole arrangement seemed, with

these experienced hands now guiding us. I felt that we were bound for glory. And in fact, the new board turned out to be a great help to Dick's. But I wonder whether, had I known then what I know now, I'd have welcomed our new venture partners into our lives.

It's a tough call, in the case of some of them. They unquestionably made us a tougher, more capable, smarter company. But that came at a steep price. I was to lose a lot of sleep in the years ahead.

It was at the same time they came aboard, in 1992—eight years after my dad left the company—that we started talking about moving Dick's out of the Southern Tier. One of the reasons it came up was that Denise and I wanted to get out of Binghamton. Aside from the time I'd spent at St. John Fisher, I'd lived there my entire life, and I was ready for a change. Denise couldn't wait to leave. And I'd made that promise to her years before, that someday we'd live in a big city.

Our marriage had seen plenty of challenges since. From the outside, little hinted that all wasn't right. We'd had four children—Brian, a year after Michael; Katie, three years after Brian; and Maggie, a year after Katie. The kids were beautiful, smart, and healthy. Both Denise and I loved being parents and threw ourselves into the roles. She and I were each other's best friend. Even so, we were drifting apart.

Still, I was true to my word, and it was time to get out of town. There was a strategic argument for a move, too. We had a hard time attracting talent to Binghamton, the kind of top talent we'd need to further grow the business. We had a few recruits in to talk with us, and they tended to love Dick's but balk at moving to our humble little city. On one occasion, we were trying to recruit a chief financial officer, and a guy from Frank's Nursery came in to discuss the job. We liked him a lot. He liked us. It seemed that we were about to make an important hire.

We were so close that he made another trip into town with

his wife and daughter. We had them over to the house for a little social hour with Bill and Sheila Colombo. Afterward, his daughter stayed with our kids and we all went out to dinner and had a wonderful time. They seemed excited to come to Binghamton. Then the sun came up. They went out looking at houses and the shopping in town, and his wife announced that she wouldn't move to Binghamton. He told me he couldn't take the job. "Is there any reasonable salary and equity that I can offer you," I asked, "that would make you change your mind?"

"There's not," he said. "My wife said that if I wanted the job, I could go to Binghamton, but that she and my daughter wouldn't be coming."

It was an *aha* moment. All doubt had been removed: we had to look for a new home. Boston was our first choice. Denise had gone to Boston College and had grown up in western Massachusetts, and I'd come to love the place. But a survey of real estate prices nixed the idea—we couldn't find a place to put the company, and housing would be beyond the reach of the staff we wanted to bring with us. Raising all those salaries so that our folks could replicate the homes they'd had in Binghamton was too big a hit. We just couldn't do it.

We looked at Hartford. Denise and I even found a house there that we absolutely loved. We couldn't find reasonably priced office space for the company, though, which forced us to move on. We thought seriously about Philadelphia, but in the midst of our explorations there, the evening news ran a story declaring Philly to be the murder capital of the United States. We had small children, and Denise laid down the law: "We are *not* going to Philadelphia."

Pittsburgh had been on our radar screen, too. After we opened the Erie store, we eyed Pittsburgh as the first big city we'd move into, and in the course of researching the market we saw that it had a lot to offer. It was in the geographic center of the area we thought we'd be expanding into next, with avid hunting and fishing populations, great sports traditions, lots of kids. It had a terrific airport, built as the central hub for USAir, which would make it easy for us to get out to see our vendors and easy for them to come to us. Its cost of living seemed a bargain compared to Boston. Not least, it had a Midwest feel to it. People there were warm and friendly.

Pittsburgh had something else going for it, too: the change of seasons. It was well south of Binghamton, but it shared similar weather, which in our business made it familiar territory. A close friend who handled our Nike account, Ed Haberle, pushed Pittsburgh relentlessly. He'd grown up there, and no one loved the city more—given the choice, Habes would have rather been mayor of "the Burgh" than CEO of Nike. If a story about Pittsburgh appeared in the paper, he'd clip it and send it to me. Eventually, he showed us around, then sealed the deal with a dinner up on Mount Washington, overlooking the city.

So early in 1994 we decided on Pittsburgh and started packing up our headquarters. We had fifty-one people working in the office in Conklin and invited all of them to make the move. One was Tommy McCauliff, who was part of our store operations group. He was pretty typical of the Dick's team at the time—he'd grown up near Fairview Park and had spent his whole life on the East Side of Binghamton. He'd also just married, and both he and his wife were worried about leaving town. "Tommy," I said, "why don't you and Mary go to Pittsburgh for the weekend? We'll pay for it. Go there, look around, and let me know what you think. We'd really love for you to join us."

We hadn't yet inked an office lease or committed ourselves publicly. The following Monday I saw Tommy in the office. "How did you like Pittsburgh?" I asked him.

"We loved it," he said. "I bought a house."

Pittsburgh had that kind of effect. Ultimately, forty-nine of our fifty-one office folks agreed to make the move, which excited all of us. We'd have a familiar team to join our exploration of this strange, new place and friends with whom to share our discoveries. The two folks who didn't want to move would remain at our distribution center, which stayed put in Conklin.

We entered the town with a splash: that March we opened three Dick's stores in and around Pittsburgh on the same day, bringing our total roster to twelve. They were bigger stores—while our new stores had averaged about forty thousand square feet until then, these followed the new Vestal model of about fifty thousand square feet. Pittsburgh reacted as if it had been waiting its entire history for just such a place. All three stores blew away our expectations.

That summer, we opened a new headquarters in rented space, in an office park on the west side of town, near the airport. This wasn't one of those cases you read about in which the city rolls out the red carpet and offers an incoming business tax deals and such. I doubt anyone in officialdom even knew we were coming. Dick's was still a small operation. We employed many more people at our three Pittsburgh stores than we did at our new company headquarters.

The Stacks left Binghamton on August 16, 1994. It was a wistful day. Binghamton had been the setting for not only my childhood but our kids'. My history and our history were inextricably tied up in this unassuming, unpretentious place. And while Dick's technically had been headquartered a short ways out of town for the last few years, this was ground zero. This was where my dad had made his mark, both as a businessman and through his community work. Court Street would always be Store Number 1. We were leaving home.

The moving vans were in front of our house as we loaded up our Toyota minivan. Our second-born, Brian—who'd turned six the day before—asked, "Dad, can I sit in the very back of the van?"

"Sure," I said. "But why do you want to sit back there?"

Brian was an empathetic kid. A few years before, he'd dressed as an Indian for Halloween and had earned the nickname Chief Make-Me-Smile. "Dad," he replied, a little teary, "I just want to look at our house for as long as I can as we drive away."

*Oh my God*, I thought. *Unpack the trucks*. I felt a sharp pang of doubt. Was this really a good idea? There's a fine line between balls and brains, and moving the company to a city to which we had no connection fell right on that line. It was way too late to second-guess the decision, but that didn't stop me from wondering.

It's a six-hour drive from Binghamton to Pittsburgh. It was dark when we rolled in on Interstate 376. Denise, riding shotgun and pregnant with our fifth child, Mary, couldn't have been happier. This wasn't Boston, but she was back in a big city.

It took me just a little longer to adjust. We moved into a rented house, and I felt my first pang of homesickness the morning after we settled in. I stepped into the yard, looked up and down the block, and realized I didn't know one of my neighbors. All my life I'd known everyone around me—and their families, and stories of their pasts, and how they fit into the mosaic of Binghamton life. I knew no one in Pittsburgh but Ed Haberle and the forty-nine families we'd moved down. It was an uncomfortable feeling. Within a few days the real estate company we'd rented our offices from called to invite me to play golf. I walked into the clubhouse locker room, as I'd done at courses in and around Binghamton since college. There must have been one hundred guys there, and I didn't know one. I was invisible.

But my discomfort passed quickly. Pittsburgh is, like I said, a welcoming place, and we made a lot of friends quickly. The city was loaded with culture—great restaurants, theater, music, museums—and neighborhoods that boasted history and character. Of course, we knew going in that it was fanatical about its sports teams, both college and pro.

Most important for me, Pittsburgh turned out to be a wonderful place to raise kids. We loved our neighborhood. The schools were terrific. And our new headquarters was a great base of operations for the company; the airport terminal was just minutes away. I could be in any of our stores in a matter of hours.

And yes, I became a Steelers fan. I still follow the Giants—that habit doesn't die easy—but my main fandom these days is reserved for the Steelers. It's interesting: Back in Binghamton, everyone followed either the Giants or the Bills. When we moved, those who'd followed the Giants became Steelers fans. Those who rooted for the Bills never did—they weren't about to back a conference rival.

I can't say I've switched allegiance to the Pirates, however. My relationship with the Yankees has run too deep for too long. That first glimpse of Yankee Stadium remains a seminal moment for me.

The three new Pittsburgh stores ushered a new phase of our long and close relationship with Nike. Since we first ordered the fledgling brand's shoes at Court Street, Nike had ballooned into an industry giant—it was, by now, the biggest brand with which we partnered. It had been key to our success, its footwear and apparel accounting for a large share of our revenue.

Nike's primary partner in footwear was then, and continues to be, Foot Locker. We'd always been a bit jealous of that partnership. Still, we believed we could build the business we did with Nike if we devoted more attention to their lines of apparel, which they were eager to market and which offered us high potential sales margins. Our thinking was that with the size of our stores, we could create a presence for their clothes that was bound to attract attention. The most dramatic way to do that might be with brand-specific shops within Dick's stores.

This wasn't a new idea. Department stores had built brand shops for years. I remember seeing my first one years before, in a department store in Syracuse—a Ralph Lauren shop, beautiful and compelling, filled with shirts, sweaters, jackets, and ties that all seemed coordinated, and that were presented in a wood-paneled, old money style distinct from the rest of the sales floor. My reaction had been, "How could we do something like this in *our* stores?"

At the time we had only four or five Dick's locations, but the idea had stayed with me, and when we were planning our three

Pittsburgh stores we approached Nike with the idea of creating Nike Shops within them. Nike liked the idea, so together we developed a small piece of each store that showcased the company's clothing. These Nike-specific shops took off—so much so that we rethought the way we displayed apparel throughout the chain. The result was our "power aisle" running up the middle of each store's sales area, lined with our top clothing brands. With those in place, our business took off.

Our partnership with Nike would continue to deepen in the years that followed the Pittsburgh innovations. This is jumping ahead a bit, but since I'm on the subject I'll tell you how it morphed. Around 2005, I went to Nike's headquarters to meet with two old friends—Gary DeStefano, the Nike rep who'd met my dad in our Syracuse store and who'd since become Nike's vice president and general manager for North America; and Ed Haberle, now the company's director of strategic accounts. I proposed that Dick's and Nike agree on a plan to double our business in three years. They came back with a concept that they called *Market Place Transform*. It called on us to redesign our sales floors by building a large Nike Shop up front, not far from the doors, with men's apparel on one side of the power aisle, women's on the other.

We tested the arrangement in a few cities and found it worked, so we installed these shops in all of our new stores and renovated many existing Dick's to include them. The public response was very enthusiastic. Our apparel sales took off, as did our margin rates. In three years, we more than doubled our Nike business. We then returned to Nike with the audacious suggestion that we double our business again over the next three years, and damn if we didn't pull it off.

We work well together. These days, Nike remains our most important strategic partner, accounting for roughly $1.5 billion of our annual revenue, or just under 20 percent of our business. I understand we're among their top five partners worldwide, and their biggest outside retailer of apparel.

I have to be honest, though: it still drives us nuts that at times we don't get access to some footwear styles that Foot Locker gets.

We were in the final stages of planning the company's move when we took on a second round of outside investment. The first buy-in by our venture capital partners had been very modest. They'd dipped in a toe, no more, just enough to enable my siblings to take some chips off the table and to give the company a little cash to use in planning new store openings. But fast as our growth so far had seemed to us, the investors were inclined to move things along at a much speedier clip. Opening a store or two a year, or even three at once, was in their minds a losing strategy, as others might establish a beachhead in markets before we got to them.

So now our existing investors wanted to inject more cash into the business to speed things up, and we invited in another big player. Denis Defforey was a French businessman who'd cofounded Carrefour, one of the world's largest retail chains. Carrefour (which is French for "crossroads") was among the innovators of the hypermarket, which combined a supermarket with a department store years before Walmart Supercenters began cropping up in the United States.

Defforey had led Carrefour until his retirement in 1990, and he now devoted himself to investing in entrepreneurial companies around the world, with a particular focus on retailers. Before he came to us, he'd already invested in Office Depot, Costco, PetSmart, and several other US chains. He wasn't looking for control; he seemed to just get a kick out of giving a boost to companies he liked.

I met him in roundabout fashion through Jerry Gallagher, who was an investor alongside Defforey in PetSmart and Office Depot. Gallagher introduced me to Defforey's investment banker, a guy named Steve Lebow, who came to see me in Binghamton with the news that Defforey was interested in investing in a sporting goods retailer. He didn't like the bigger American players in the industry but was intrigued by this smaller outfit that Gallagher seemed so excited about. If I was interested, he'd arrange for Defforey to visit.

Of course, I was interested. So Denis Defforey, one of the world's greatest retailers, flew into Binghamton to meet me. He was a generous, almost unbelievably humble man of few words—he didn't need to hear himself talk. When he did say something, however, it was worth listening to. In that respect, he reminded me of my grandfather. And I loved the guy from the first minute we talked. He convinced me that day that his sole interest was in seeing me, and the company, succeed to the greatest extent possible. Rarely have I met someone so instantly likeable. Even more rare, my initial impression never changed. Denis Defforey was a class act, a great man who also happened to be a great guy.

When I say he was humble, I mean it. "The one thing I'd like to do when I come to the United States," he told me, "is get a good steak." He had a favorite spot: LongHorn Steakhouse. I've eaten many steaks there with Denis. Whenever he later came to Pittsburgh, that's where we'd go.

Naturally, he wanted to see a typical Dick's in action, so we drove up to Syracuse together and visited the two stores there. He seemed to like what he saw. Back in Binghamton, we talked in my office. He was a gentleman throughout. I found myself, at age thirty-nine, thinking that he was the type of businessman I wanted to be.

Defforey committed to putting $10 million into Dick's, and he took a seat on the board. He was a great addition. He'd fly from Paris to JFK on the Concorde, catch a connecting flight to Pittsburgh for our meetings, and after we wrapped up, fly back home. He never once turned in an expense report for his travels. "You know, Denis," I said to him once, "we're happy to pay for your travel to these meetings."

"No," he said, "the company needs the money more than I do."

He was immensely respectful. I figure Denis might have spoken at half the meetings he attended. He'd always raise his hand. "Denis, did you want to say something?" I'd ask.

"Yes, if you don't mind," he'd say. "I'd like to share my opinion."

At about the same time that Denis came aboard, Lebow told me that Paul Allen wanted in, too. His Vulcan Northwest venture capital group out of Seattle was another investor in PetSmart. He was also cofounder of Microsoft, the owner of the Portland Trailblazers (and later the Seattle Seahawks), and among the country's great philanthropists. I was excited that he'd even heard of us, but I also knew we already had too many outsiders with a voice in how Dick's ran. "Steve," I told Lebow, "this deal is oversubscribed as it is. I don't want my family's stake in the business to be diluted any more." Lebow suggested I invite him to make a minimal investment—just $500,000. It wasn't much dilution, he pointed out, and he promised me that I wouldn't regret it.

We were still getting the paperwork together for this new round of investment when our chief financial officer walked into my office. "The strangest thing just happened," he said. "We just had ten million dollars turn up in our account. An extra ten million dollars."

We tracked it down and found that Denis Defforey had already sent in his stake, even before we'd signed anything with him. That's the kind of great shareholder he would demonstrate himself to be, time and again. And Steve Lebow was right—Paul Allen's Vulcan group was every bit as good. Both newcomers proved to be great friends to Dick's Sporting Goods.

Long after the fact, I learned from Jerry Gallagher that back in 1991 or 1992, when Gallagher had been conducting his initial research into Dick's, trying to determine whether we were a good investment, he'd called Jack Smith, the CEO of the aforementioned The Sports Authority. We're thinking of investing in Dick's, Gallagher told him, and I want to know what you think of them.

They're a little company in upstate New York, Smith replied. I don't think we're going to bother them very much. They're not a big deal.

Smith knew better. He knew we owned the markets we were

in because he'd been with Herman's before he moved to TSA. Our territory was familiar ground to him. I suspect it was his ego talking that day. But that's reportedly what he said, and with that, Jerry Gallagher put his money behind us. Jack Smith, destined to be one of our titanic competitors, made it happen.

Had Smith been more strategic in his reply, things might have turned out differently. He could have said he thought we were pretty good and that they'd eventually put a couple of stores in our markets to see just how good. I'm sure that would have been enough to scare off the risk-averse Jerry Gallagher. If he hadn't come aboard, he wouldn't have introduced me to Lebow, who in turn wouldn't have brought Defforey and Paul Allen into the company.

And without those two, we might be part of the industry's roadkill.

So here we were in 1994, settling into Pittsburgh, a chain of twelve high-performing stores that formed an arc up western Pennsylvania, across upstate New York, and into western Massachusetts and Connecticut. That made us a big operation by the measure of our past but barely a blip on the radar among the country's major-league sporting goods retailers. Herman's, though in trouble, was close to national in its reach. The Sports Authority was super-regional. Oshman's, based in Houston, controlled a sizeable piece of territory west of the Mississippi, especially sports-crazed Texas. A handful of big regionals that dwarfed us held lucrative markets all around the Lower Forty-Eight—Koenig's out of Cleveland, Chick's in California, Sportmart in Chicago.

We were in a viciously competitive business. The recently departed among sporting goods merchants already included some big names, and it would claim many others in the coming years. A dirty little secret of retailing is that there's really very little customer loyalty; customers will stick with you only until something better comes along—in other words, loyalty is simply the absence of an alternative. Which means that you have to constantly reinvent your product mix, your marketing plans, your style of doing business. You have to always assume you're under attack. If it's not true today, it will be tomorrow.

Not long after our new partners joined us, another big player in the sporting goods business moved in on our turf. Sports & Recreation Inc. was a publicly traded, Tampa-based outfit that ran big, warehouse-style stores. By that, I mean that their merchandise was displayed on the pallets that it had been trucked in on. They made little effort to emphasize the qualities of the products they sold or to have people on the floor who had expertise in the gear. But they were inexpensive and offered a wide selection of sporting goods.

The formula evidently worked for them, because Sports & Rec was growing fast in the early and mid-1990s, and eventually their expansion brought them into our territory. They opened a good-sized store in Syracuse and went after the same hunting, fishing, and camping business that we serviced. We were nervous about them, very nervous.

Our venture capitalists were even more so. Michael Barach was at a conference at which Sports & Rec was presenting, and during a question-and-answer session he raised his hand. "You guys are going into upstate New York," he said. "There's a little company called Dick's Sporting Goods there. What do you think of them?"

A Sports & Rec officer replied, "We're going to decimate them."

Barach came back to us all freaked out: "These guys say they're going to decimate us! What are we going to do?" I tried to calm him down. "They're going to be tough competition, but they're here," I told him. "Our only choice is to compete with them, and compete aggressively."

As any athlete will tell you, trash-talking the competition can work both ways. It can galvanize your team, get your fellow players pumped up. But it can also backfire on you and instill a resolve in the people you trash-talked. Now, in the boardroom at Dick's, and in the stockrooms and break rooms of our stores, and in our warehouse, "We're going to decimate them" became *our* battle cry.

We had some fun with it. In our newspaper inserts, we labeled our loss leaders "decimators"—every week, up in the top corners, our ads would showcase two or three decimators, with prices just plain stupid cheap to drive people into our stores. I doubt anyone at Sports & Rec picked up on the reference, but our people loved it.

The threat called for serious hardball, and that's what we played. We sent people into their stores every Saturday from one to three p.m., to casually take up positions from which they could see the registers and what their customers were buying. We'd keep track of all the transactions that took place during those two hours, then take sales readings of our own stores during the same period. We then took those comparisons and extrapolated their sales figures for the entire day and the surrounding week.

We found that as our attack with decimators and other loss leaders continued over months, their sales started to deteriorate. Their "comp sales"—that is, sales at stores that have been open for more than a year, which is the measure by which retail performance is judged—were sinking. As they fell, we amped up our attack. We cut prices further. We increased our number of decimators. Before long, *we* were decimating *them*.

One day I got a call from Stephen Bebis, who'd not long before taken over Sports & Rec. He said he'd love to have dinner. As a general rule, I'm always available to talk. If your competitor wants to sit down with you, you almost always want to accept the invitation. They'll invariably tell you more than you have to tell them, because they called the meeting. They usually have something interesting to say. I told him I'd be happy to have dinner.

Mike Hines, our chief financial officer, went with me. We met Bebis and his CFO at the Hyeholde Restaurant in Pittsburgh. They talked for a while about how the sporting goods industry needed to consolidate, how there were too many players running too many stores. Then Bebis got down to his point: What I'd like to do, he said, is buy your company.

I'd had a feeling that was coming. Sports & Rec was significantly bigger than we were. I couldn't imagine why else he'd have asked to meet. But I was proud of Dick's. I was proud of the niche we occupied as operators of specialty stores clustered under one roof. No one else in the business took that approach. I wasn't about to sell my family's company. "Stephen," I said, "I'm really flattered. But we're not for sale."

Well, again, he said, I think the industry needs to consolidate, and we'd like to buy you. I told him again that we weren't for sale. With that, the tenor of the meeting turned. "You do understand," he said, "that if you don't sell me your business, I'm going to put you *out* of business."

I didn't say what I was thinking, which was, *Fuck you.* Instead I said something like, "Well, we'll see what happens, and I wish you luck." I knew the right thing to do was take the high road. I also didn't want to do or say anything he could use to fire up his troops, the way his company had fired us up at Dick's. But as soon as Mike Hines and I were in the parking lot, we were both saying, "Fuck that guy."

We viewed the conversation as a declaration of war, even more overt than their promise to decimate us. We resolved at that point to take the fight to them. We doubled down on our price cuts and advertising in the markets we shared with Sports & Rec. And just as had happened with Herman's, when they started to have problems—which they ascribed to growing too fast—they closed their underperforming stores first, which happened to include those that competed directly with us. They attempted to rebrand themselves as Jumbo Sports, but they couldn't get any traction, and their business continued to erode until 1998, when they pulled the plug.

Like I said, there's plenty of roadkill in this category of retail. We were happy to see Sports & Rec go but knew we hadn't fought our last fight.

The original Dick's store at 453½ Court Street in Binghamton. By this point, it had grown into two storefronts and offered work clothes alongside its inventory of bait and tackle. Still, "nite walkers" and worms earned high billing.

Three women who left their imprint on Dick Stack and his company. At center is his mother, my Nana; standing to the right is Nana's mother; and at left is my father's paternal grandmother, Mamie, who bankrolled her grandson's first store.

It was from such a cookie jar that Mamie pulled $300 to finance Dad's start in business. These days, we award one to every employee who has reached twenty-five years of service. Inside is a symbolic $300.

My uncle Ed and Dad, right, show off the interior of the first store, a year or two after its 1948 debut. Though barely out of his teens, Dick Stack was already establishing himself as his city's go-to source for fishing gear and advice.

Fresh from his young company's failure at the Hillcrest Shopping Center, Dad poses for a 1956 newspaper ad showcasing the reborn Dick's. We've always respected the use of guns for hunting.

Here I am taking a break from catching for the Dick's Little League team, my planned first step on a fairy-tale trek to the major leagues.

That's me, suited up to play quarterback for Binghamton North High. By now I was dreaming of playing in the NFL, as well as the majors—but also learning that playing sports is its own reward, whatever the outcome.

Karl "Dutch" Krupitza, aka Gramp, an athlete throughout his life, a scratch golfer into his late eighties, and an inspiration to me in everything.

My dad at about the time I started working summers at Dick's, pictured with a new specialty that would be among our mainstays: golf equipment.

My mom, the former Mary Ann Boyle, attended the annual Dick's Open golf tournament with me in the early 2000s. Self-absorbed and high-strung in her youth, she eventually grew into a loving and generous matriarch to the Stack brood.

My sister Kim and I were a lot alike as kids. Ambitious, straitlaced, and dutiful, we were both pressed into service at Dick's as teenagers and remain close today.

It has been gratifying, seeing my kids pursue sports with gusto and enjoying the benefits. Here's the gang on a family ski trip to Snowmass, Colorado. Flanking me are Maggie, Brian, and Mary on the left, and Katie and Michael on the right.

Donna, Ryan, and I attend the US Open at the Oakmont Country Club in the Pittsburgh suburbs.

The Dick's management team rings the bell to open our first day as a public company in 2002. Beside me at the lectern is Bill Colombo, our president. The tall character beside him is our CFO, Mike Hines.

Nike's Ed Haberle, far left, joins a Dick's brain trust at Pebble Beach a few years ago. Moving right, there's me, Bill Colombo, Joe Schmidt, and my childhood friend, brother-in-law, and longtime Dick's exec Tim Myers.

LIVE ET
**abcNEWS EXCLUSIVE** 7:05 43°
**DICK'S** **MAJOR RETAILER BANNING SALE OF ASSAULT RIFLES** **GMA**
SPORTING GOODS DICK'S CEO CALLS FOR NATIONWIDE CRACKDOWN #GMA

February 28, 2018: Two weeks after the mass shooting in Parkland, Florida, I tell George Stephanopolous on ABC's *Good Morning America* that we're pulling assault-style rifles from all of our stores—and in so doing, touch off an eruption of praise and condemnation from coast to coast.

In all, Dick's destroyed $5 million in assault weapons, some of which were collected in this carton.

Our stand against military-style weapons and decision to raise the minimum age for other gun sales sparked editorials, TV debates, thousands of emails and tweets, and public displays criticizing and backing us. Here is a typical display in front of the White House. One thing we didn't provoke: action in Congress.

Up-and-coming Arizona ballplayers pose at a Sports Matter grant ceremony. The charitable campaign has pumped millions of dollars into community sports programs across America, exposing many thousands of young people to the transcendent benefits of competition.

The Dick's marketing team celebrates our Emmy for *We Could Be King*, our first venture into feature filmmaking. Judd Ehrlich, the movie's director, is holding the statuette. Frank Igrec and Ryan Eckel, both marketing execs, are to the left while Lauren Hobart, who was destined to become our president, stands on Ehrlich's other side. The film portrays two Philadelphia high schools that have been bitter rivals for decades until a budget crisis merges them, forcing the coaches to find ways to bring players together.

An all-star cast was on hand for the premiere of our second feature-length movie, *Keepers of the Game*, which chronicled the triumphs and heartbreaks of a Native American girls' lacrosse team. During the event, Ed presented the Dick's Sporting Goods Foundation Sports Matter Impact Award to NFL coach and broadcaster Jon Gruden. Coach Gruden has been a Sports Matter official ambassador since 2014 and has teamed up with our foundation to raise multiple team donations, ensuring we give every kid a chance to play.

Members of the Salmon River Shamrocks, the girls' lacrosse team featured in *Keepers of the Game*. This all-Mohawk team was from the Akwesasne Mohawk Nation territory, where the game of lacrosse originated.

## CHAPTER 11

# "YOU CAN GO BANKRUPT WHILE TURNING A PROFIT"

Jerry Gallagher was an important source of wisdom and know-how over the first years of our partnership, and I looked forward to our conversations—I almost always ended them smarter than I'd started—and was inclined to heed his advice. But on one subject I thought he was flat-out wrong. I *knew* he was. And that subject was our chief financial officer, Mike Hines.

We'd brought Mike aboard from Staples, the office-supply retailer, while we were in the process of moving to Pittsburgh. He was a Bostonian, a lean six foot six, and not easy to get to know. Once you penetrated his outer reserve, however, he revealed himself as smart, bighearted, thoughtful, intensely loyal, and a blast to be around.

He was a first-rate CFO. Mike had a head for details and the courage to speak his mind. It's all too rare in the business world to find an executive willing to tell his boss he's full of shit, and the fact is, every boss needs such a sounding board. You may not always want it, but you certainly need it, and Mike wasn't shy about playing that role. We complemented each other, too: I was pretty aggressive, he a bit more conservative. He was the perfect counterbalance to me, and I to him.

Gallagher didn't share that view. Early in his tenure, Mike

was a bit unsure of himself at our board meetings. He might have been uneasy about having Dave Fuente sitting across the table—Mike had spent years at Staples, battling Fuente's Office Depot, and I can imagine that it was a little unsettling to suddenly be working alongside a former nemesis. Or he might have been rattled by Gallagher's inquisitional style at our early board meetings. Gallagher would ask Mike questions to which he might not have had immediate answers, then jump on him.

Like I said, Gallagher could be arrogant. It was his style to sniff out what he perceived to be the other guy's weakness and to pick at it, exploit it. Maybe he thought that toughened us up, that such testing strengthened our management team, but the tactic didn't always yield the insight he thought it did. He just couldn't see that we had a great CFO.

Gallagher wanted Mike gone. "You need to fire him," he told me on one occasion. I shut him down. "You see him at board meetings," I said. "I see him in action every day. And he's terrific. I'm not replacing Mike Hines." A year later, I went to see Gallagher at his office in Minneapolis, and again he tried to convince me that I should fire Mike. As our meeting ended, he rode in the elevator with me and crossed the lobby. A cab was waiting just outside to take me to the airport. "I'm telling you," he said, "I want you to fire Mike Hines and get a different CFO."

I looked at him as I climbed in the cab. "Jerry," I said, "I am never going to do that." He dropped the subject after that.

I look back on those exchanges today, and I'm thankful that I didn't listen to Jerry. If I'd done as he wanted, Dick's would be a very different company, if it existed at all. I don't know that we'd have refined our real estate strategy as Mike pushed us to do over the years, or taken the rational and tough-minded approach that we did to where we located our stores. I don't know that we'd have knitted expense control into our culture to the degree we have, which has been key to our profitability. Mike was on top of our numbers, and he had an intense curiosity about every aspect of our business. He wanted to understand *everything* about merchandising, sales, and logistics. He had an intellectually curious mind, and he used it to make us better.

Most important, I don't know that we would have survived the biggest crisis in the company's history. Though it wasn't yet clear when Gallagher started arguing for Mike's replacement, we were in trouble. Dick's was about to hit the wall. And when I reflect on whom I counted on most throughout those days of existential peril, Mike Hines is at the top of the list.


Our move to Pittsburgh and the infusion of new capital marked the start of a period of crazy growth at Dick's. And when I say *crazy*, I mean it: it was crazy to go as fast as we did. In 1994, we had twelve stores. By the end of the year, we had eighteen. Within another few months, we had twenty-two. And over the following year, we opened up eighteen more on that base of twenty-two. We went from being a little family chain to being a serious regional power. As this expansion played out, it seemed at first that all was well. Our sales were terrific. Our margins were solid. Our board was ecstatic. Our new partners had pushed us hard to grow at this clip. We'd delivered.

It wasn't quality growth, however. The view back then among big-box retailers was that you'd move into an area to establish a beachhead—just get stores up and running—and figure out the details later. I thought we could handle it. Opening stores was routine for us now, and I failed to detect any reason to slow down. I was the controlling shareholder, and I went along with the other directors. We thought we had the Midas touch.

But the fact is, we couldn't handle it. We outran our capital structure. Our systems, such as they were, couldn't keep up; we were merchandisers and marketers, not logistics-savvy. This breakneck expansion required having really sophisticated systems in place to move merchandise out of the warehouse and out to the stores, the right stores, at the right time. We had nothing like that; we were still using systems we'd put in place years before.

Our management team was completely overwhelmed. We had too few people trying to do too many jobs, and many details slipped through the cracks. We pulled workdays that were ridiculously long and still couldn't keep up with what was required of us.

Not only did we open too many stores too quickly, we opened bigger stores—we introduced a new Dick's prototype that measured a whopping sixty thousand square feet. The architecture we put into these cathedrals cost more to build—fancy floors, which were just plain stupid, because nobody noticed. Expensive fixtures. Design details that added up fast. The changes probably boosted our overhead with no return on our investment and did nothing to drive additional sales.

We located them in markets where we really didn't know what we were doing; in one year we opened three stores in Cincinnati, three in Philadelphia, and three in Baltimore, all cities in which we had little on-the-ground history or insight. We didn't take time to understand the hunting and fishing business there. What did we know about the catfish culture in Cincinnati, or fishing for rockfish and blue crab in the Chesapeake Bay? Not much. That showed in low sales volumes. At the same time, we made other mistakes. These stores were overinventoried and cost more to run, market, and supply.

Even so, we might have been okay. We could have trimmed our expenses on future openings and wrestled our spending back under control. But with runaway growth, we also lost track of our inventory. We were buying it without proper controls in place, and soon we had pallets stacked on pallets in the warehouse and had a hard time getting it moved out. The stores were already bulging with far too much merchandise. If you'd walked into a Dick's in 1996, I doubt you would have detected any sign that we were in trouble, because the shelves certainly weren't bare. There was an overabundance of stuff to buy. Because our inventory had blown up, we had to cut prices to reduce our surplus of merchandise, which drove down our margin rates. When our margins tanked, our profits plummeted. As my dad used to say, "You can go bankrupt while turning a profit, if you have everything tied up in inventory."

We did. Our available cash dwindled. Store sales couldn't come in big or fast enough to keep up with our needs. Another indication that our operations were out of whack: our shrink numbers rose to 2 percent of sales, double what's usually regarded in the industry as acceptable.

All of these issues were directly tied to our expanding too fast. This wasn't measured growth. In 1996, all of these factors converged simultaneously: We had no money and no prospect of getting more—we were up against our credit limit. We had too much cash tied up in too much inventory and no way to relieve that situation besides slashing costs and taking losses on our merchandise. We were crushed by high operating and capital costs that we'd brought on ourselves. We used primitive systems incapable of helping us run so large a company. And we were spread across too wide an area, without the logistics in place to keep merchandise moving smoothly.

I was already losing sleep when I walked into Mike Hines's office one day, and he looked up from some papers and said, "You realize we're going to be out of money next month?" I said, "Yeah. I realize that." But there seemed little we could do about it. We'd lost control of our ship. Any mistake you can make in retail, we'd pretty much made it. And we'd done it quickly. In 1994, we were healthy. Little more than a year later, we'd lost $13 million, and we didn't have $13 million to lose. This is how bad it was: We set aside a conference room for our incoming bills. They were piled on a table there, all coming due, and we'd go through the daily reports from the stores to see how much they'd done in sales the day before, and decide which of our bills we could write checks for.

We talked with our banks about restructuring our loans, to buy us a little breathing room. The banks refused. They wouldn't lend us another cent. Our venture capital partners refused to put any more money into the company until we restructured our debt—which, of course, required money we didn't have. We were stuck, and a complete collapse was approaching fast.

There was some talk that we should file for Chapter 11. It took me back to my father's stories about Hillcrest. What little he'd said about it turned on one decision he made—he refused to declare bankruptcy. He would not force his creditors to suffer for mistakes he'd made. He sold his house and car so that he could make everyone whole. I'd had that ethic drilled into me from childhood, and I probably felt even more strongly than he had that Chapter 11 was not an option. I was not going to use bankruptcy to escape the debt we'd piled onto the company, even if it made restructuring a lot easier. I could not bring myself to do that.

We talked about selling the company. That conversation didn't last long. Ours was a family business with a long and cherished history. But how to save it?

Now, for the first time, I understood what my father had endured as the Hillcrest store tanked in late 1955 and early 1956. My days were filled with one piece of bad news after another. I remember apologizing to Bill Colombo one day, telling him how sorry I was that I'd gotten him involved in such a mess. You'd have been better off staying at Penney's, I told him. I'd authorized our expansion. I'd pushed to build bigger stores. It was on me.

As bad as the days were, my nights were endless and far worse. I lay awake, sick to my stomach, heart racing at the thought that we might have no way out. Man, had I screwed up.

Then someone suggested we talk to GE Capital.

I knew the name, and what I'd heard led me to believe that GE Capital was a lender of last resort, the one you turned to just before you called Tony Soprano. That's an overstatement, a joke, but the company was known to be tough, very tough, in the terms and conditions it set for its loans. These days, GE Capital is a streamlined outfit that offers financial services to the aviation and energy industries, but in the mid-1990s it had a wide range of customers, from individual credit card holders to commercial real estate buyers to businesses, like ours, that needed capital. In many respects it resembled a gargantuan and multifaceted bank.

We were facing a last-resort scenario here. It appeared that GE Capital might be willing to take on a risky proposition, like us, that the banks wouldn't. So we called them, and they agreed to see us.

Mike Hines and I arrived in New York the evening before the meeting. I didn't sleep much that night. If we didn't make this deal, we were finished—we'd have to file for Chapter 11 and try to reorganize. I would be fired, and Dick's would be owned by someone else. Forty years after my dad had been forced out of business at Hillcrest, here we were, a runaway success in every market we'd entered, and yet in the same spot. Forty years after he'd started rebuilding the company piece by piece, day by day, always scared to death of pushing too far, too fast, I had abandoned his conservative ways and brought it all to the brink of failure. The family business that my dad started. His name on the stores. I'd screwed it all up.

I got up, went for a run to clear my head, grabbed a shower, and called Denise. She told me she hoped things would go well and wished me luck. I got tears in my eyes, talking to her. She tried to sound confident, but clearly, she was as scared as I was. We had five kids to feed, and we both knew that we were at the brink of losing everything. I got choked up to the point where I couldn't speak and had to end the call. I tried to pull myself together, knotted my tie, put on my suit jacket, and started out of the room.

On the way I passed a full-length mirror and caught a glimpse of myself out of the corner of my eye. I stopped and turned around. You know you're in a tough spot when you talk out loud to yourself while looking in a mirror, but that's what I did: I looked myself right in the eyes and said, "You've got to toughen up. Get your shit together, Stack." I stood up straight and buttoned my jacket. "You have to walk in there and talk to these guys like you don't give a shit whether they give you a loan or not. Because you have confidence in this business, and you'll turn this around."

I stepped into the hall feeling better—if not confident, exactly, at least clear in my thinking about what I had to do. A little while later, and a few blocks away, Mike and I took an elevator high into a Manhattan skyscraper, and we walked into a long conference room where ten or so men and women in suits sat around a table. They had me sit at its head, Mike just to my left, then fired a barrage of questions at us, one after another, about how we'd gotten ourselves into such a mess.

Mike answered some, I answered others, and sometimes we'd piggyback on one another. We were a good team. Even so, the tone of the questions was in-your-face, and at one point I found myself thinking, *Man, this isn't going well*. One of the suits asked why we increased our store size to sixty thousand square feet. We answered that sixty thousand had been a mistake, and that our future stores would be smaller. They busted us pretty hard over that, and rightly so.

Another of our interrogators asked whether we had a computerized replenishment system that recognized when a store was about to run out of a particular item and automatically shipped new product. I answered, "No."

"How can you run a business like that?" he asked. The subtext was, "You people are idiots," though in truth, we couldn't replenish a lot of our merchandise that way, even with the greatest system in the world. Automatic replenishment works great at Walmart or grocery stores, where you're selling bottled water and paper towels, but it doesn't count for much when you have to order Nike products six months ahead of time.

They made us feel pretty stupid about our systems, nonetheless. When we'd been answering questions for a while I interrupted to lay out the situation in a more holistic fashion. "Let me tell you something," I said. "We made a series of mistakes. And these are the mistakes we made." I told them what had happened, then moved on to why it had happened: that we'd thought establishing beachheads in new markets was important, but we'd moved into too many, too quickly.

"And this is what we're going to do so that it never happens again," I said. "Our venture group will put additional equity into the business. We're going to be disciplined from a capital allocation standpoint. We'll be disciplined on expenses and growth. We won't allow our growth rate to outstrip our capital."

All told, the exchange went on for about ninety minutes, and I noticed this one guy sitting in the back, taking it all in, saying nothing—about forty years old, dressed impeccably in an expensive dark suit, white shirt, quiet but elegant tie. He was straight out of central casting for a banker.

The meeting ended with no promises made, but as I gathered up my papers this quiet observer came over, slid a chair up beside me, and sat on it backward, arms folded across the top of the chair's back. I'm asked to speak to college business classes on occasion, and what happened next often makes its way into my remarks. The lesson it offers is that if you're in a meeting and there's a guy sitting off in a corner, not saying anything, that's the guy you probably have to convince. He's the decision-maker.

"Tell me the three things I need to do," he said, "so that we can agent this loan."

There were only two. I told him how much money we needed and when we needed it by.

He studied me for what seemed like ten seconds, his head cocked a little to the side, saying nothing. It was a long, strange moment: his eyes and his expression weren't adversarial, not at all—he seemed to be seeking understanding, not delivering a challenge. I think he knew that for all the analytics, this was a gut-instinct call, and this silent appraisal was a form of due diligence. I held his gaze. Finally, he smiled. "We can do that," he said. He shook my hand.

To this day, I don't know who he was.

Mike Hines and I walked out in a bit of a daze. "What just happened?" Mike asked.

I was still trying to process it all, but I told him: "I think we just saved the company."


In truth, we weren't saved just yet, and the cure for what ailed us was, in some respects, mighty bitter medicine. This is a good place to make a point that took me a while to understand and that I now share with young people coming into our business, and with college students when I'm invited to speak to them. It's this: Business success, or failure, doesn't move in a straight line. There are highs and lows, so that although the overall trend of a company's performance might be on the rise, it will incorporate a lot of ups and downs.

My dad ran a business that became a Binghamton institution in the decades after Hillcrest, but even so he lost money some years and faced many weeks when he wasn't sure how he was going to make payroll. So it goes with most every company. Apple consistently ranks among the world's most valuable corporations, but it got there only after a lot of missteps—its failed Lisa computer of 1983, Steve Jobs's departure, the company's near-failure. It returned to profitability with Jobs's return, and the introduction of the iPod, iPhone, and iPad, yet even now, it experiences down quarters.

Even the most successful companies have to fight through tough times. There will be good days and great days. There will be bad days. And some days will be just flat-out awful. Dick's has had its share of all of them. The day we met with GE Capital ranks among our best days, in retrospect. Some of the days that followed, on the other hand, were complete nightmares.

We returned to Pittsburgh with GE Capital having agreed to give us a credit line of $140 million. It was contingent on our venture capital partners increasing their investment. Problem was, those guys wouldn't put in any more money until we'd restructured our debts, which we couldn't do without the loan. So though we now had a commitment from GE Capital that promised to save us, we were still caught in a vise between forces we couldn't control.

For more than a week neither side blinked, and my sleepless nights continued. Ultimately, the venture group didn't want the company to fail—they already had a bunch of their money in it—so they agreed to end the impasse. Following Denis Defforey's lead, they ponied up $35 million.

But that good day brought with it great compromise for me personally. Because with the additional investment came a shift in the board of directors: while I'd had five designees and our outside investors had controlled two seats, now the balance flipped, so that I had two, and they had five.

I still owned a big piece of Dick's, and I remained its CEO.

But I no longer controlled my family's company.


True to its reputation, GE Capital was tough. The loans we got from them had covenants attached, which restricted us to the point where we couldn't do a whole lot without getting their permission first—we couldn't take on any additional debt, for instance. We had to keep our capital expenditures within hard-and-fast limits, and they monitored a host of other metrics of the company's performance, all of which had to fall within certain ranges. By any standard, it was a tough loan. It made the loan structure my dad had set up when we bought him out look like a piece of cake.

The money they made available to us was limited by our inventory—it followed a formula based on the value of our assets. Some of our inventory was set aside, right from the start, as a cushion, and we could borrow against a percentage of the remainder; from what I recall, it played out that we could borrow up to 50 percent of the value of 80 or 85 percent of our inventory. We had to be incredibly judicious about our spending.

Getting their money did not, in and of itself, save the company. It bought us time to make changes that we now recognized were past due. Our first move was to slow our growth. We halted new store openings. For about eighteen months we signed no new leases, and we revisited some of those we'd already signed—went back to our prospective landlords and asked to postpone our opening for a year, or to let us out of the commitment altogether. In general, they were good to us. They had practical reasons for that: they didn't want to build us a store, force us to open it, and then watch us go belly-up and leave them with an empty building.

More fundamentally, we adopted a much more financially disciplined inventory system. We'd always had a model for what and how much we bought, but it had served as a guideline, rather than a set of hard-and-fast rules. No longer. The new system dictated how much of any category of products we could have in our inventory. It identified merchandise that could be marked down and how much. It set goals for receipts and incorporated sales plans for each store, each district, and the company as a whole. In short, we tried to assign measurements to everything we bought, everything we sold, everything we did. If a measure fell outside the range we'd set, we could identify the problem and fix it at once.

The new approach broke down our inventory to a granular level. While we'd had an "open-to-buy," or limit on buying inventory, for categories before, now we focused it far more sharply. It was no longer "golf gear" we kept track of—now it was down to how many golf balls of a particular brand we could buy. Our open-to-buy on athletic footwear became scores of line items, one for each brand and style.

We were able to do this because we had a lot of data that we'd collected over the years but never used to the extent we should have to manage the business. We knew how many golf balls we sold, how many golf tees, how many Nike men's running shoes of a particular style. It was all in our records. We now loaded this data into our new open-to-buy system, and focused on controlling every aspect of our buying and how we distributed inventory among the stores. We developed a merchandising system that kicked out a daily report on sales by store, by category. It tracked our margins down to one-hundredth of a percentage point, and if we were off our margin targets by one-tenth of a point for two days in a row, bells rang and whistles blew, and we jumped in to find the cause.

This isn't sexy stuff, but developing new systems saved us. In a few short months we became maniacally focused on the numbers, and over those same months our situation stabilized. We sold off our excess inventory. We found our balance. The crisis passed. And we resolved that we'd never find ourselves in such a tight spot again. Fear is a terrific motivator. My dad had known that all too well after Hillcrest, and now I understood it, too. We'd peered into the halls of hell, and we were never going back.

Funny thing: GE Capital turned out to be a wonderful partner. If we had an issue or wanted to do something different, they wanted to know about it and to understand our thinking. But I can't recall a single instance when we were mulling some important action and they said no. Their covenants proved far less onerous than they'd seemed; in fact, they were easy to hit. They'd put those in place to keep us from getting ourselves into trouble, and once our new systems were installed and we were back on solid footing, with our inventory under control and our margins back to normal, the covenants were performance bars that we cleared easily.

All told, fixing all that was broken took a little more than a year. By early 1997, we were a far healthier company than we'd been before the scare. Hitting the "pause" button in our growth enabled us to take a more thoughtful approach to further expansion. And with our new systems, we had an almost microscopic view of Dick's operations and a far better sense of what we were doing and why.

We began opening new stores again, at a much slower pace, and these stores marked our return to the fifty-thousand-square-foot model we'd debuted at Vestal and operated successfully in

Pittsburgh. It was a more comfortable and efficient size but still big enough that walking into a Dick's brought a *wow* from shoppers. The first of the new stores were in markets we already had at least one store in. From there we spread our reach into Michigan and down into the Carolinas—our first store in the South. We were apprehensive about it. We'd always been a cold-climate store.

But our first store there, in Raleigh, was a hit beyond our wildest expectations, partly because we visited it regularly after it opened. The heavy outerwear that was our staple in New York and the Great Lakes states was overkill in the Carolinas—*that* we knew before we left Pittsburgh. But what we learned from our store managers down there was more nuanced: we were pulling baseball and softball gear from the stores too early each fall, and waiting too far into the spring to return it. "Guys," one manager told us, "we can sell baseball stuff in January."

All of the new stores were tremendous successes. We were back to making a profit, and in short order we were able to retire a big piece of our debt. Denis Defforey, God bless him, was wonderfully paternal through our return to health. One day we were talking and he asked, "Are you sure you're okay from a capital standpoint?" I told him I thought we were in good shape. "Okay," he said. "Just be sure. You don't want to get into trouble again." When he left, Mike Hines chuckled and shook his head. "Don't you feel like you just had your grandfather ask you, 'Are you sure you have enough spending money?'"

I was confident we had enough. For twenty years now I've been fixated on avoiding debt whenever possible. Twice, Dick's has teetered at the precipice because we were beholden to banks—the first time in 1987, when our Binghamton lender abruptly tossed us overboard through no fault of our own, and again in 1995, when we were reckless and stupid. I do not want to find us in that situation again.

I now understand the scar tissue my dad carried after Hillcrest. You never get over a close call like the one we experienced in the mid-1990s. I will never again be comfortable relying on someone else's capital. I will always be a little paranoid and insist that we finance all we do from our own earnings. It seems to me that it's the only way to control your own destiny. The banks can't take away your business if you don't owe them any money.

So we carry no long-term debt. Self-reliance requires discipline, but we've managed it. I think that's one reason we've survived when so many other retailers have run into trouble, especially our direct competitors in sporting goods. Many have carried a heavy load of debt, pushed on them by their private-equity-firm owners—firms that used these stores, and that debt, to pay themselves. When you're leveraged up like that and have significant interest payments to make, you're not as nimble when things get turbulent.

Wall Street gets on my back sometimes, saying we don't have an "optimal balance sheet," which is its way of saying we have too much cash and don't have what the Street considers the proper amount of debt. Let 'em say what they will. Our balance sheet is optimal for us.

## CHAPTER 12

# "YOU'VE DONE ALL
# YOU CAN DO"

I am grateful, in some respects, that my dad did not know that we'd had such a close brush with death. The news might have brought to life all of his worst fears about the course I'd chosen for the company he started. I can only imagine that he'd have lost a lot of sleep over it, and I can't even imagine what our phone conversations would have been like. Actually, maybe I can imagine. I'm glad they didn't happen.

I'm even more thankful that he did not learn that I'd lost control of the family business. Dick's was nearly fifty years old when that happened. Seeing it in the hands of outsiders would have broken his heart. That I'd lost it would have disgusted and infuriated him. He might not have even bothered to call.

But my gratitude is pure selfishness. The reason he was spared the news, and I was spared his reaction, was far worse than any of that.

As he entered his midsixties, my dad had been smoking non-stop for fifty years or better, and he'd been a drinker for nearly as long. It was probably inevitable that his bad habits would catch up with him. He'd already had a couple brushes with death. I dreaded the day I'd get the call that he was gone.

In the early 1990s, long before we moved to Pittsburgh, there came times when my father would suddenly be gripped by a terrible headache. It came on fast and usually passed in a minute or two, but for the duration he'd feel dizzy and see double, or be so staggered by the pain that he'd stop talking midsentence and have to sit down. We later learned that he was having transient ischemic attacks, or ministrokes. My siblings witnessed them, too. None of us realized how dangerous they were. And he had a lot of them.

I noticed about a year after these attacks started that he was becoming forgetful. He'd tell me something, then repeat the same remark or story a few minutes later. That's when I remember feeling a first real twinge of worry. Even so, he was holding it together physically. He played golf several days a week. On the course he could still hit the ball pretty far and still had a great short game. Considering how long he'd abused himself, he was a medical miracle.

But then, on Easter weekend in 1995, Denise and I were in Florida with the kids. It was a trip we took every year, and my dad and I always played golf at Old Trail, a course affiliated with Jonathan's Landing, near Jupiter, where he lived. We hit some practice balls before teeing off, then climbed into the cart, my dad behind the wheel. He drove us ten or fifteen feet, then stopped and looked at me with an expression of absolute horror. "Eddie," he said, "I don't remember how to get to the first tee."

A wave of alarm bordering on nausea swept over me. He'd played Old Trail hundreds of times. It was clear that my dad had a real problem. We were in trouble. I wondered what our next steps would be, where this was headed. His confusion passed and we actually played the round. I shot about a million that day.

Other episodes followed. While my dad was making his summertime visit to Binghamton the following year, my brother Marty spotted his car pulled onto the shoulder of Route 17, a major highway through town. When Marty stopped, my dad, obviously scared, told him that he couldn't remember how to get home.

The frequency of these lapses increased, and between them my dad would plunge into depression. Dementia is a cruel disease, and in his case it was all the more so because he saw it was happening. Soon enough, he didn't recognize his friends, and eventually, his own family.

At times it seemed impossible to believe that his slide was real. I was sitting with him at his apartment in Binghamton one day while he ate a cream-filled chocolate cupcake. He ate it like a baby, drooling chocolate from the corner of his mouth, making a mess of himself, and I was suddenly sure that he was putting me on, that he was busting us. There was no way this was the Dick Stack I knew—not the man who'd been so formidable for so long. Any second, he'd wipe his mouth, look over at me, and say with a smile, "Had you finky kids going, didn't I?"

But of course, that did not happen, and that scene became just one in a series of heartbreaks that went on for years. My stepmom, Donna, was heroic through all of it. She never left his side. She never complained. As she'd later put it, if love could have saved him, he'd have been saved.

My dad's deterioration stole his ability to golf and fish, his great joys. While that happened, my oldest son, Michael, became obsessed with golf. One evening in March 1998, I suggested we play together the next day, when I knew he was off from school. "You have tomorrow off, and I'll take tomorrow off," I said. "Let's play."

Michael was twelve and never missed a chance to golf. He spent long hours by himself on the course, hitting drives and practicing his chips and putts. He worked hard at the game. But instead of saying what I expected—"Great! I'd love to play"—he replied, "Mom says I need some clothes and she's taking me to the mall tomorrow. So I think I need to go with Mom."

It was completely out of character for him, so odd that I had a strong and immediate sense that the universe was trying to tell me something. "I think I need to go up and see my father," I told Denise. I called USAir and booked a flight to Binghamton for the next morning.

I found him in bed, asleep. He'd been in and out of consciousness for weeks. I sat beside him and took his hand. He didn't stir. I felt sure that I was supposed to be there, that it was important I be there on that day, at that time. "Dad," I said, "you've done all you can do for us. You did all you set out to do. You've raised all of your kids. You've put everyone through college. You built your business, and you were successful. There's nothing more you can do." I had to pause to wipe away some tears. "The business is in great shape. The kids are all fine. I promise you that I'll make sure the business continues on, and I promise I'll take care of everyone." I squeezed his hand a bit tighter and said, "Dad, if you want to go, it's okay. You can go."

He slept on. I sat there for a while, looking at him, my sharp-edged, two-fisted, ball-busting, deeply sentimental, and ultimately good-hearted father. I wiped away more tears, told him I loved him, and flew back to Pittsburgh.

I'm convinced he waited for me and that visit. Kim called at two the following morning to say he'd died.


We held the funeral at St. John the Evangelist, where my dad had been an altar boy, and where, sixty years before, he'd played baseball and acquired a love for sports that he passed on to me. On the drive to the cemetery, the cortege detoured to Court Street and made a slow loop through the parking lot at 345. I sent an email to the 4,300 people who worked for Dick's. "Those of us who knew him and loved him," I wrote, "will miss him very much."

I think my dad's legacy might, to some, be that business he created, a company that, at the time he died, had fifty-one stores in six states, each emblazoned with his name in letters ten feet tall. And of course, the stores are a big piece of his history. But the Binghamton *Press and Sun-Bulletin* ran a story the day after he died that was insightful in how it summed up his life. The first paragraph read: "You can't read the newspaper for more than a week or two without noticing Dick's Clothing and Sporting Goods sponsoring some event to benefit youth sports and community beautification or combat cancer, drugs and drunk driving." The story went on to talk about how he'd grown the business, but I think it's telling that it began not with his company's success, but its involvement in the community. That's how he, and Dick's, were thought of in Binghamton.

By the time he died, I'd abandoned a good many of the examples he set in actually running the company, but the way he made Dick's a springboard for helping the city and people around him stuck with me. I'd grown up with that part of our company culture ingrained in me.

He was making a difference to his community before I knew it was happening, with his contributions to Binghamton's youth baseball programs—work that I directly benefited from and that made my hometown a measurably better place to live. As a teenager I saw him demonstrate that same spirit when he dealt gently and knowingly with that young shoplifter who so desperately wanted to play baseball. I have no idea what became of that kid, but my dad understood the transcendence of sports—that they can channel kids' energies, give them focus and goals, keep them out of trouble, reshape their lives. And he understood that it wasn't enough to wish these benefits on others. He was willing to reach into his own pocket to give that kid a chance at them.

Under my dad's leadership, Dick's contributed to Binghamton charities and causes throughout my years in high school and college, continuing right up to the moment he sold the company to us. I don't think this was altruism, necessarily. He saw that for Dick's to prosper as he hoped, the city around it had to be healthy, that he stood to benefit indirectly by seeking to improve the standards of life in town. More fundamentally, I think he believed that companies have to be more than machines for making money, that in America more than anywhere else, our companies are key building blocks of society—and in return for our patronage, and our service as employees, we should expect our companies to behave as good citizens, to be contributors to the common good.

I disagreed with my dad on many subjects, but I'm 100 percent aligned with him on that. I've tried to follow his example. A few years after I took over the business, I was on the board of the Boys and Girls Club in Binghamton, and I was tapped to help pick the winner of its annual top youth award. We interviewed four finalists, both boys and girls, and I asked the same question of all: "What can be done about the drug and alcohol problem in high schools today?"

Every one answered the same way: Nothing. Can't do anything about it. Kids drink. Kids do drugs. That's the way it is.

I found that really disturbing. As I walked to my car after the Q & A session, I found myself thinking that the kids had been courageous in their answers, though fatalistic. Surely, something could be done about the problem. I didn't agree it was a lost cause—I'd had my own embarrassing experience with beer, but now I mostly avoided drinking. When I thought about why that was, one answer was that my dad's drinking had scared me. But another, and perhaps even more powerful, reason was that I'd been busy. I played baseball and football.

As I drove home my thoughts morphed from *Somebody's got to do something* to *Why isn't anyone doing anything?* By the time I got home, they'd sharpened into: I *should do something*. With that, Dick's helped organize a program called Get Involved. During the back-to-school season, we ran a big campaign encouraging kids to go out for sports teams, join school clubs, try out for the marching band. We didn't push athletics more than the chess club—we knew that not every kid is a wide receiver, or wants to be one.

At the heart of the push was our belief, and my personal experience, that kids need a place to go after school. They need a group, to feel they belong. And in particular, they need a community that provides them with a mentor—whether a teacher, a coach, the director of a play, an editor who volunteers his or her time. They need a reason to not go to the Wigwam.

While we were ramping up that campaign, we kicked off a

fund-raising program in partnership with Students Against Driving Drunk and the Drug Abuse Resistance Education (DARE) program. For every pair of shoes we sold, we'd donate two dollars to a fund to finance antidrinking and antidrug programs. Schools and school districts would apply for help in financing after-hours prom parties and similar events, and SADD and DARE would distribute the cash we'd set aside.

We got a lot of positive feedback from students, teachers, and parents. Too many kids are hurt or killed on prom night, as a result of drinking. A good many pregnancies happen that night, too—it's an event in which kids tend to act with abandon. With our help, schools in the Southern Tier rounded up seniors after the prom and herded them into the gym, for soda and pizza and dancing until daybreak. The kids were probably wired on all the sugar they consumed, but they weren't getting into trouble, and they all made it home alive.

When we opened our stores in Syracuse, we took these programs there. I believe they made a difference. It's hard to know what might have happened had we not helped fund the prom after-parties. But it was a start, a step in our evolution to help the communities and kids we serve. Once you start giving, it grows inside you, becomes more important to you to give. No doubt, my dad figured that out.

So when we heard that some townships in upstate New York were having trouble getting community sports programs together due to a lack of equipment—that they didn't have the balls, goals, and other gear they needed to run practices and games—we decided we'd give them a hand. We put together kits for soccer, baseball, volleyball, and basketball teams. Each consisted of a big gym bag filled with up to a half dozen balls, some cones to mark off a field, a whiteboard and markers, and a couple of whistles. We also threw in sets of pinnies, those bright nylon-mesh vests that distinguish sides in a scrimmage. It was everything you needed to run a practice in one bag.

We started this at about the time we moved to Pittsburgh. We put out word that teams or programs could request a bag, and we'd provide it at no charge. We also created a community marketing effort within Dick's, and our associates would seek out programs that needed these kits. Before long it had spread into Pennsylvania; we were giving out as much as $5 million in gear per year.

I was excited about that program. It worked. I think it's safe to say that we helped a lot of kids. A few years down the road, as the business grew, we'd be thinking much bigger.

## CHAPTER 13

# "THEY'RE NOT GOING TO SAY YES UNTIL YOU SAY NO"

With our growing pains behind us, and new controls and metrics in place, we got back into the rhythm of opening stores. We spread throughout Ohio. We moved into Philadelphia and the Detroit suburbs, into Delaware and Indiana, Illinois and Kentucky. Altogether we opened ten stores in 1997, nine the following year, and thirteen the year after that, for a total of eighty-three by year's end 1999.

By now the design of our stores had been refined to better give the departments distinct identities. Each had signature signage and color schemes. The golf department, which we labeled "The Pro Shop," was wood paneled and clubby. "The Lodge," where we sold fishing tackle and hunting gear, was constructed to look like the inside of a log cabin. The athletic footwear area was big, with almost five hundred styles on display. We used a lot of wood and indirect lighting throughout to make the whole store inviting. Once you walked in, we hoped you'd stay awhile.

You could spend some of that time testing merchandise before you bought it. The new stores incorporated not only driving ranges but running tracks and archery ranges. We would sweat every detail to surprise and delight our customers. We'd constantly visit our competitors' stores, and if we found something we liked, we'd incorporate that, too.

When we opened a new store outside Baltimore in Columbia, Maryland, we included a "Nike Women's Concept Shop" loaded with gear especially for female athletes—long overdue in an industry patronized by as many women as men but never catering to women at an equal level. Today, our sales of women's products often eclipse those of men's, and even so, we constantly battle with our vendors to provide us with more products specifically designed for female athletes.

All of this effort translated into a healthy income that enabled us to accelerate our growth. The year my dad died, we posted $728.3 million in sales—an average of $9 million per store—and netted $11.2 million in earnings. In fifteen years, we'd grown from two stores to a super-regional chain. We had plans to push our footprint out from there, across the Mississippi. Our ambition had grown with the company. We wanted to be not only the best but the biggest sporting goods retailer in the country.

We were nowhere near that yet. The Sports Authority was growing, too, and they'd had quite a head start. They produced more than twice our sales and covered a lot more territory. But this game had just begun.

The key to everything I've talked about—the way the stores looked, the products we sold, the booming sales—was that our leadership team kept visiting our stores. I'd spend two days a week, three weeks a month, out in the field. I'd fly into a city such as Charlotte, where we had several stores, and all the store managers would meet me and our team from Pittsburgh at one store. We'd walk the aisles and talk to them. More important, we'd listen.

I wasn't there to critique their operations. I wanted them to tell me what their customers were saying—about the store, about particular products they liked or didn't like, about what they wanted but we didn't have. I wanted these managers to tell me what we were doing right and, more urgently, what we were screwing up. The longer these visits went on, the more enthusiastic the managers and their staffs were about talking, because it became clear that we sincerely wanted to know what they thought. The insight they offered was the difference for Dick's. It kept us relevant to our customers, and it kept us alert to shifting trends in popular taste. The men and women on the front lines could detect marketplace demand long before we could from our desks in Pittsburgh.

I'll give you an example of how one of these visits changed our business. In 1997, a group of us went to Baltimore to walk through our stores there. Our manager in Columbia was a guy named John Jones. I asked him how things were going, and he told me that kids were coming into the store all the time, asking for this new product, a compression base layer that football players had started wearing under their pads. It's called Under Armour, John said. Can we get some of it and give it a try?

I'd never heard of it. When a store manager tells us we should try something, though, we almost always try it. So we put in an order for Under Armour, which was headquartered in Baltimore. We tested some of their HeatGear and ColdGear. Both fit snugly and wicked moisture; these clothes kept you dry even if you were sweating buckets. And because you stayed dry, Under Armour kept you warmer in cold weather and cooler in hot.

It blew right out of that store. We had trouble keeping the Baltimore stores in stock. So we tried it in a few more stores outside the city. Again, it sold faster than we could order new stock. After eighteen months or so, we put it in all of the stores, and the response was just as robust. We were the first major retailer to carry it, creating what would be a lasting, and important, association between Under Armour and Dick's.

Early on, Under Armour's tops and tights were seen strictly as football gear, and we displayed them in the football section of our stores. But as Christmas approached in 2001, it occurred to me that we should move them to the apparel displays, where we sold Nike, Adidas, The North Face, and other popular brands. Our chief merchant disagreed with me, pointing out that Under Armour saw itself as gear, not apparel. I had a hunch about it, though, and overruled him. We moved it to the power aisle up the middle of the store, and holy smokes, it spread fast from football players to athletes of all types.

From that point on, Under Armour became strategically important to us as a company; if the winter weather was colder than expected and Under Armour sales climbed, we felt it. We were important to them, and they to us. For several years, something like one out of every three dollars they took in came from their sales at Dick's.

The company's founder, a former University of Maryland football player named Kevin Plank, became a great friend of mine. In the years since, the brand has expanded into all types of activewear and has become synonymous with sports. Its logo has become a ubiquitous sight at athletic events all over the world. It's been a real treat to watch that success, and to be part of it. We were two small companies that helped each other grow. It started with that manager, John Jones, who is still with us today as our vice president of store operations.

By this time, most vendors were eager to have their brands at Dick's. Back in the day, that hadn't been the case, as I've mentioned: either they wouldn't open us up, or they wouldn't sell us enough product to distribute to all of our stores, as they were protecting their other accounts. Now, however, we were a pretty big company. We could move the needle for most of the companies we did business with.

Still, a few brands dismissed us, just as Adidas and Puma had done years before. Probably the most notorious example was Callaway. We wanted to be *the* leading golf retailer, and Callaway was *the* premier brand of golf clubs. The company was founded by Ely Callaway, a Georgian who'd already made fortunes in the textile and wine businesses before he bought a small golf company and transformed it into Callaway Golf in the early 1980s. His groundbreaking innovation was the Big Bertha driver, introduced in 1991. At a time when most driver heads were made of persimmon wood, the Big Bertha had an oversized stainless-steel head that could send a ball farther and, some thought, straighter. It seemed everyone wanted a Big Bertha.

Problem was, Callaway didn't want to sell their products through a sporting goods retailer. They sold their clubs through "green-grass" accounts—the pro shops at golf courses and country clubs—or "cement shops" that specialized only in golf. They weren't interested in selling their clubs in a big-box store.

We understood that, but we wanted to separate ourselves from Sports & Rec and The Sports Authority in the minds of the public. We aspired to make Dick's the first destination for all golfers—to become, in essence, cement shops that shared a roof with other sports; to become the best off-course golf retailer in America. We needed Callaway to establish our credibility.

We had several meetings with Callaway, trying to get them to open us up. When it was clear they wouldn't budge, we switched to guerilla tactics. An existing Callaway dealer would sell us its excess inventory at a slight markup, and we bootlegged their clubs. We sold a lot of them. This went on for a couple of years, at least, beginning shortly after we moved to Pittsburgh. We had several conversations with Callaway, in which we continued to press our desire to carry them as an authorized dealer, but they kept giving us the brush-off.

Then one day Bruce Parker, who ran sales for Callaway, called me. We'd met a couple of times, and he hadn't been terribly friendly. On the phone, however, he was warm and enthusiastic. Hey, he said, we'd like to open you up. Why don't you fly out here? We'll have lunch together, and we'll talk about it. I was all ears. Later that week, I jumped on an early-morning flight for San Diego.

We met at one of the restaurants at the Aviara Resort, a five-star Four Seasons hotel, spa, and golf resort in Carlsbad with an Arnold Palmer–designed eighteen-hole course. It was just an amazing place, and it was clear that Parker was in his element there. He came across as king of the mountain. Once seated at a table, he and I exchanged pleasantries for a few minutes before he reiterated that Callaway wanted to open us up. But before we do, he said, I have to ask you a question. Who were you bootlegging the product from?

"Bruce," I said, "I can't tell you that."

"Well, if you don't tell me," he shot back, "we won't open you up."

"Bruce, I'm not going to tell you," I said. "I don't think it's our job to police your brand, and I'm not going to tell you."

I could see he was getting angry. "If you don't tell me," he said again, "we won't open you up." It was pretty clear to me by now that getting the names of the people selling us product was the real reason I was there. I doubted he ever planned to bring us aboard.

I looked him in the eye. "Bruce, my mother taught me two things, growing up. Number one, you go to church on Sunday. And number two, you don't rat on your friends. I'm not going to tell you."

Bruce said it was a shame that we wouldn't be doing business.

I said that I guessed the meeting was over.

I guess it is, he agreed.

I stood, thanked him for his time, and left. I'd been there all of fifteen minutes. Back at the airport, I had to wait until eleven that night to catch a red-eye flight back to Pittsburgh. It gave me time to determine our next move. Once I got home, we organized a Christmas campaign in which we sold Callaway at deep discounts. We advertised these low prices throughout the holidays. It drove Parker and Callaway nuts.

How do I know that? The following month, I was at the annual PGA Merchandise Show—the golf industry's biggest event, attended by fifty thousand pros, manufacturers, and retailers—and I passed the Callaway booth. Bruce Parker was standing inside and started yelling at me, "You can't hurt me! You can't hurt me, you son of a bitch!"

*Well, now*, I thought, *I think I should go over and have a conversation.*

He kept hollering, and in the process ignited my temper. I'm embarrassed to say the exchange grew so heated that it came close to turning physical. I've got some Dick Stack DNA in me, you know.

(Quick aside: My dad was at a golf course once, playing craps in the clubhouse with a bunch of other guys. This one character, a head taller than my dad and about fifty pounds heavier, lost big but refused to pay up. "No problem," my dad said. "But you're not playing anymore." Apparently, this guy had had an issue with my uncle Ed, who at the time was fighting for his life in the VA hospital, and he sneered, "I never met a Stack who was any good." My dad asked him to step outside. As soon as they were through the door, my dad punched him in the face, rode him to the ground, stuck his knee between the guy's shoulders, and mashed his face into a gravel parking lot. So.)

To shorten an already-long story, I got pretty hot. We were never closer than five or six feet from each other, but that's because we were both restrained by colleagues. A bunch of Callaway people clamped onto Parker, and Jay Mininger and another Dick's associate had a hold on me.

After that, I had to resign myself to not doing business with Callaway. A couple of years passed. We'd emerged from our near-death experience and were back to growing fast, and we were selling a brand of putters called Odyssey—we were their biggest customer—when we read in the *Wall Street Journal* that Odyssey had just been bought by Callaway. Well, so much for Odyssey, we said among ourselves. We'd surely have our top putter taken from us, because Bruce Parker and I weren't exchanging Christmas cards.

But Parker surprised me with a call. "I'd like you to come out," he said. "I'd like to clear the air, and we'd like to open you up."

"Bruce, we tried that once before," I said. "And as you'll recall, it didn't go well."

"It's not going to go that way this time," he said. "We've looked at your sales with Odyssey, and you're not only their biggest customer, they say you're their best. They love doing business with you guys. Come on out, and I promise we'll open you."

I said okay, and again flew to San Diego, this time with our golf team, and we made a deal. While I was at their Carlsbad headquarters, I met with Ely Callaway, who by then had a bigger-than-life reputation. He'd been a success at everything he'd ever done, and he'd been doing it since World War II. I was escorted into his office.

We made small talk for a while. Then he looked at me with an impish grin. "We make the most expensive clubs in the world," he said. "Do you know why?"

It was a weird question, and I remember thinking, *Stack, don't say something stupid. You're finally on the verge of getting Callaway to sell to the company. Don't screw it up.* I went with the most innocuous answer I could think of: "No. Why?"

"Because we can!" he said. He cackled.

So began our relationship with Callaway Golf. We're now their biggest account, by a significant margin, and among all the companies that we do business with, Callaway is one of my favorites.


Though we now had quite a few outside investors in the company, my primary contacts with the venture capital group remained Jerry Gallagher and Michael Barach. And it was as our success was becoming apparent that they began to second-guess what we were doing. Now, as I've said before, to succeed for any sustained period in retail you can never allow yourself to relax. You have to constantly question your assumptions, rethink your approaches, reimagine your stores and your product lines. So a certain amount of second-guessing is not only helpful, it's necessary.

This wasn't that kind of second-guessing. Barach was a believer in modeling—using economic models to dictate what the business should be doing. One of the key measures his modeling used was GMROI—gross margin return on investment—in which you divide your gross margin on the sales you make by the cost of your inventory. Stripped to its essentials, it reveals whether you're making money on the stuff you sell.

His figures showed that we sold some products that did very well by this measure, and others that didn't. That wasn't news to me. We knew that we made relatively little money from each firearm we sold, for instance—they cost us a lot to buy, and we couldn't sell them for much of a markup. Next to apparel and footwear, where our margins were better and the inventory turned over faster, guns seemed like a dog.

But to position ourselves as a full-line sporting goods retailer, we needed those categories in our stores. They gave us credibility and authenticity. In short, Dick's had always aimed to go deep in its specialties, and we couldn't well do that if we eliminated too much of the lower-margin products on our shelves. We weren't as valuable to the customer, and we weren't as special in the market, if we carried just the bestselling, lowest-common-denominator goods. We had to have a broad range of merchandise, including some arcane offerings, to win in the marketplace.

Barach's modeling said otherwise. At the time he was crunching his numbers, two big-box footwear retailers had burst onto the market. Just for Feet had started as a small shop outside Birmingham, Alabama, in 1977, but reimagined itself as a superstore ten years later. By the late 1990s, it was operating one hundred forty big, flashy stores throughout the South and Midwest—twenty-thousand-square-foot places that boasted indoor basketball courts, lots of video monitors and rock music, and thousands of shoes. Nike and other vendors had stores-within-stores in these places, and they made such a splash that by 1997, Just for Feet was the country's second-largest retailer of athletic footwear, behind Foot Locker. Sneaker Stadium was a smaller but fast-growing chain of similar stores scattered between Connecticut and the Carolinas. Its giant outlets were little more than clones of Just for Feet, and every bit as intimidating.

Barach watched them grow and became convinced they were going to destroy us. Their GMROI was great—all they sold was shoes and some activewear made by the shoe brands. He tried to convince me we should stop opening sporting goods stores and focus all of our energy on footwear and apparel. "Michael," I told him, "we're not going to do that."

I like to think of myself as a student of retail, and it seemed to me that focusing so much on the GMROI was exactly what had gotten Herman's in trouble. They had been the dominant player until their bean counters insisted that they do away with all their low-GMROI categories, including outdoors and fishing. With that, Herman's became a glorified socks-and-jocks store, undistinguished in a crowded field of apparel and footwear retailers.

I didn't want that to happen to us. One of the enduring challenges of our business model is that there is no typical Dick's customer. The shopper who walks into our store seeking athletic shoes is very different from someone looking to buy a new driver, or a football, or a rifle. In fact, we carry so many different styles of athletic shoe that just that one department serves a wide range of customers—runners, walkers, hikers, basketball players, aerobics practitioners, baseball and football players, boaters. You name it, we probably carry it. So every day we serve scores of different constituencies.

What this means, in practical terms, is that we have to be very good in just about every form of team and individual sport out there, as well as a wide range of pursuits that aren't sports, per se, but fall under the umbrella of outdoor recreation. This has become a lot more complex over the years. It's difficult; it would be a lot easier to just go for the quick buck. But it's what sets us apart, and no one on our team wanted to give that up. We wanted to stay as broad store-wide as we were, and as deep as we could get in each category. Some of what we sold would be high margin, and other stuff low, but we'd be Dick's.

Barach and some of our other outside investors were still pushing for change when Sneaker Stadium cratered, followed not long after by Just for Feet. In 1997, *Fortune* had ranked Just for Feet in sixth place among America's fastest-growing companies; in November 1999, they filed for Chapter 11, done in by too much debt and out-of-control inventory. There but for the grace of God (and GE Capital) went Dick's.

We were still embroiled in the GMROI debate when our venture capital partners tried to take us into the dot-com bubble. It's hard to explain to those who weren't around at the time just how crazily bullish American business was in the late nineties over the notion that the future of commerce lay in the Internet. The time might be coming when many bricks-and-mortar stores can no longer compete with online retailers, but that isn't the case today, and it certainly wasn't in the late 1990s.

Twenty years ago, computers were not the essential household tools that they've since become, and many home systems weren't even connected to the Internet. So right off the bat, the dot-com boom was premature, because the potential audience any dot-com business could reach was just a fraction of the population.

That was just one of the challenges online companies faced. The Web was primitive and clunky, compared to its modern form. We tend to forget how recently our digital age has come to command our lives. Here's a little something to consider: The first iPhone hit the market in—when? 1992? 1995? 1999?

No. The answer is 2007. The iPad didn't come along until 2010. Our lives have been transformed almost overnight. So the dot-com boom was reaching a fever pitch way too early, when computer operating speeds were glacial, online offerings were Stone Age, and the pleasure of online shopping was so-so, at best.

Plus, Internet companies were expensive to get up and running because the one advantage they claimed over physical retail was convenience—the notion that you could find and buy a product without leaving your house—and key to that was speed.

If it took them two weeks to deliver a product you could otherwise get in a drive across town, they weren't competitive. They had to be fast.

That translated into steep warehousing and shipping costs, which they couldn't very well pass on to the customer, or they'd price themselves out of business. So from the start, online businesses faced market, technological, and logistical disadvantages that, it seemed to me, made them unattractive. I didn't see how we at Dick's could make money online—not then or any time soon. (Obviously, that would change in years to come.)

None of this stopped investors from going hog wild for dot-coms. The values placed on some Internet companies were nothing short of Fantasyland. When eToys.com went public in 1999, for instance, its trading price opened at $20 a share; by the end of that first day, its value had almost quadrupled, to $76 a share, and the IPO raised $166 million. In the succeeding months, its stock climbed as high as $86 a share, and eToys had a higher valuation than Toys "R" Us, at the time the toy industry's nine-hundred-pound gorilla.

But eToys, like many Internet retailers, spent mountains of cash on marketing, trying to establish a place in the public mind, and on a pair of giant distribution centers. It failed to deliver many toys on time during the 1999 Christmas season, dealing itself a public-relations blow from which it never recovered. Losing millions of dollars a quarter and finding itself almost a quarter-billion dollars in debt, the company saw its stock price free-fall to nine cents a share. It was gone shortly thereafter.

When the dot-com boom was at its height, however, some of our venture capital partners had caught the fever. Michael Barach pushed hard to get us into online sales—in fact, he argued we should stop opening stores and shift our focus to the Web. Lebow started K2, a company that sought to bankroll retailers hoping to get into e-commerce.

On the Dick's board, Dave Fuente and I were deeply suspicious of the craze and thought it would be stupid to jump in. But we were in the minority. So under pressure from our gung-ho venture capital partners, we spun off a separate company, DSports.com, that Bill Colombo ran for a while, under the heavy hand of Steve Lebow and Henry Nasella, a former president of Staples who was also involved in K2. We weren't thrilled with the DSports name, by the way, but Dicks.com was already taken—it was a gay pornographic site. That made us all totally crazy. We repeatedly tried to buy it, but it was years before we succeeded.

We and K2 each invested $10 million in our online program and launched it on Super Bowl Sunday in January 1999. It was a modern site for the time, with search buttons by category, brand, and price, and we soon had 34,000 items for sale there. Before long we were offering Nike, Adidas, The North Face, and other brands, with coupon offers that knocked our already-low prices down further, at significant cost to our margins. We spent a ton of money advertising on ESPN and Fox Sports.

My aim in the experiment wasn't to make money—I didn't think we could do that. Rather, I just hoped to limit how much it cost us. I remember sitting with Lebow and Nasella one day, and Nasella saying to me, "You clearly don't want to win in this, because you're not willing to lose more money." He was right about that. The eToys story, and dozens of other examples of high fliers gone bust, were cautionary tales that I thought we'd be fools to ignore.

My lack of enthusiasm for turning Dick's into an Internet-only business caused some heartburn among our investors. It came to a head when, right about then, I decided to take my first vacation in years. Denise and I flew off to Cabo San Lucas, Mexico. We were having a great time when I got a call from my assistant back in Pittsburgh. She thought that there might be a coup under way. We cut the vacation short, and once home I called Barach. His message to me was unequivocal: "You shouldn't be CEO."

We agreed that he'd fly in from Boston to see me. His flight was due to land at six thirty p.m., but I didn't want to waste time waiting for him when I could be working, so I told him to call me when he got to the hotel; we could get together at the Embassy Suites, which shared a parking lot with our offices, to talk. He called at seven fifteen p.m., livid: Where are you? You're supposed to meet me!

Michael, I'm at the office, like I said I'd be, I replied. You were supposed to call me when you were settled in. He started hollering that it was like Truman and MacArthur, insubordination and whatnot. I remember wondering what the hell he was talking about. In the days that followed, he tried to have me removed as CEO, but Denis Defforey, Fuente, and the rest of the board—even Gallagher, also a K2 investor, and as pro-Internet as he was—wouldn't go along with him.

Our investors' fire for the dot-com boom was unaffected, however. Gallagher, Barach, and others were desperate to get into it. One way to do that was to take Dick's public, which would enable them to pull out all or part of the investments they had in us and put them to work in online companies. I wasn't interested in going public. I'd have been content to stay a private company forever. But one upside to becoming a publicly traded company was that we'd be done with our venture capital partners. I wasn't as eager to see them go as they were to leave, but they'd been wearing out their welcome, what with all the fuss they'd made over GMROI and the Internet.

We drafted an S-1, which is a form you prepare in anticipation of offering shares to the public. It gives the Securities and Exchange Commission, as well as potential investors, a detailed look at a company's balance sheet, its historical sales and earnings, and its assets. It also lists the possible risks of buying in and lays out the company's plan for what it'll do with the money it raises from the public.

We learned very quickly that our timing was bad. For the past couple of years our profits had been good—very good. But we'd been driving sales with discounts and promotions that we didn't think were sustainable in the long run—we were churning a lot of merchandise into and out of our stores, but our margins had fallen in the process. We'd addressed this by cutting back on the promotional nature of the business. Our sales had flattened, but our margins had increased, which was a healthier place to be. We were actually making more money.

Although our earnings were up, sales were an important measure for Wall Street. In particular, it's comp sales that the Street looks at closely when assessing a retailer—that is, sales at stores that have been open for more than a year. Inflated sales driven by new stores are removed from consideration, and you get a more accurate picture of how business is going. It signals whether you're gaining or losing market share in the places you do business.

When we met with our investment bankers, they wanted to know how our comps were going to be for the coming year, by quarter. We told them they'd be flat to plus 1 percent, though we anticipated that number might be higher. "You can't go public," they replied. "The Street wants to see strong comp gains." We didn't make the grade, in particular because Wall Street wasn't much interested in bricks-and-mortar retailers—like our own venture capital partners, the financial community was crazy for dot-com investment.

At the next board meeting I broke the bad news: "Our bankers have told us we can't take the company public."

Jerry Gallagher was sitting across the table. He was a smart guy. He knew we couldn't take the company public. But he sneered at me. "I think you're not going public because you don't want to go public. I think you could, if you wanted to."

"Jerry, actually, that's not the case," I said. "We were ready to go."

Our agreement with the venture groups included something called a mandatory redemption provision. It says, in effect, that a shareholder can declare, "I own this much stock. I'm hereby cashing it in. I want you to buy me out." It's included in such documents as a mechanism for investors to pull their stake. Thing is, the arrangement doesn't work if the party obligated to buy the stake doesn't have money.

Even so, Gallagher announced he was invoking the mandatory redemption provision. Because he knew we didn't have enough money to buy out our venture partners, he said, "I'll move the mandatory redemption provision out a couple of years. But I'm going to make it hurt." Meaning, in lieu of payment, he wanted a bigger share of the company—and he'd take it from my family's piece.

I looked across the table at him and thought: *It's time for you to go. You're no longer acting like a partner.* It was a ballsy thought, admittedly, because I did not control the company. But to my mind, he'd gone from venture capitalist to vulture capitalist. He knew we couldn't go public. He knew we couldn't meet the conditions of the mandatory redemption provision. It was a setup to give him and the group a bigger piece of the pie.

And true to his word, he made it hurt. Our venture partners took another 3 percent of the company.

I didn't dwell on the situation for long. The solution to this dilemma, it seemed to me, was to buy out the venture capital folks by any means necessary, even if it meant taking on debt. I knew we couldn't, as a company, afford to buy all of their stakes—that would have cost $100 million, and the idea of borrowing that much struck me as far too risky. But I was confident that we could live with a $60 million loan, and if we were to buy 60 percent of their shares back, we could reduce their voice in the company's affairs by the same percentage. I could regain control of the company, and eventually get them out all the way.

Which is what took me back to our friends at GE Capital, who, I want to stress, had proved to be real friends since our near-death experience a few years before. I explained that I wanted to buy out a majority of the venture capital investment in the company, and they were wonderful in putting together a deal that enabled that to happen.

When I broached the idea with Gallagher and the others, they were thrilled. They so desperately wanted to take chips off the table. There were a lot of players involved: after the initial buy-ins, several other investors had put money into Dick's. They appointed Gallagher to negotiate the deal on behalf of the group.

We talked. He squeezed me quite a bit on share price and conditions, but we finally got to the point where both of us were able to say, "We're good." Ah, but then Barach called to say, "You know, I think the deal's fine, except for this part and this part." He squeezed a little more, and I adjusted until I thought we'd finalized the thing. And then another player called, trying to squeeze more dollars out of us.

This went on until Mike Hines walked into my office. Remember, you always need someone on your team who's unafraid to tell you that you're screwing up. "You know what?" he said. "You need to realize that they're not going to say yes until you say no." Which was great advice. Gallagher was so wrong about Mike. Because the next day, when another in our roster of venture capitalists called to get his piece, I told him: "We're done. You either want the deal, or you don't."

Lo and behold, they said yes.

So we had a deal. It was done. Or so it seemed. We distributed paperwork laying out how much we'd pay per share, how many shares we were buying back, all the details. A few days later, a Friday afternoon, I was playing golf with some vendors when my assistant called. "You need to get back here right now," she said. "We have a problem." I asked what was going on. "We got a fax," she said.

"Okay. Read it to me."

"I don't want to do that," she said. Her voice quavered.

"Please, just tell me what it says."

It was a letter from Leonard Green & Partners, a large private-equity investment firm out of Los Angeles that owned pieces of

Rite-Aid drugstores and Petco, among other retail outfits. The letter offered to buy the shares of our stockholders at a higher price than we were offering—and to buy all of them, not just 60 percent. We evidently had a mole. To this day, I cannot say for sure who it was, but someone who was privy to the paperwork that was passing back and forth between board members leaked it, and Leonard Green had recognized that we were in play—and ripe for a hostile takeover.

I wasn't the only person at Dick's to get this letter. Leonard Green sent it to everyone on the board. I knew we didn't have the money to match their offer, and I knew that Gallagher and Barach were prepared to sell; this represented a huge windfall for guys who'd been looking to put their money elsewhere anyway. It seemed that I was outmatched. If Leonard Green's takeover succeeded, I'd be fired immediately. I stood to make some money—the new owners would buy my shares, along with everyone else's—but neither I nor any other Stack would be part of the family business. It was a deadly situation.

My one ray of hope was that the three biggest shareholders were me, Denis Defforey, and Paul Allen's Vulcan Northwest. I knew that Denis enjoyed being part of Dick's for the same reason he'd invested in other companies—to lend a hand to entrepreneurs in building their businesses. He enjoyed seeing good ideas brought to fruition, and if he made money in the process, great; he was always willing to play the long game with his investments. I called Steve Lebow, who was still Denis's investment banker, and Steve agreed that Denis might not be interested in the Leonard Green offer. He said he'd set up a call.

A few days later, Denis called me from Paris. He'd received a copy of the letter, and Steve had already briefed him that other investors wanted to sell. He asked one question: "Ed, do you want to sell your company?"

"Denis, I don't want to sell it for this price," I told him. "I don't want to sell it for twice this price."

Without a pause, he said, "Then neither do I."

Not long after, Paul Allen's group announced through Lebow that it wasn't selling. And with that, we blocked the takeover. We rejected Leonard Green's offer and proceeded with our buy-back of the venture group's shares. With that out of the way, we reconstituted the board of directors to reflect the venture capital group's reduced investment in Dick's. Of the seven board members, I'd name four, they'd name two, and we'd have one that we all agreed on.

Even if that last board member sided with the venture capital group, I'd have a majority of the votes. I'd regained control of Dick's.

## CHAPTER 14

# "YOUR INVESTMENT BANKER IS NOT YOUR FRIEND"

'd come to like Dave Fuente a lot during his time on the Dick's board. He'd had a storied career—he was a college marketing professor and was a division president at Sherwin-Williams before he joined Office Depot as chairman and CEO in 1987. It had ten stores at the time. He took the company public and grew it into the biggest office-supply chain in the country, with hundreds of stores and billions in sales. Dave was really smart, confident, and was a lot of fun to be around. He'd always gone out of his way to help me. He was a great mentor and friend.

I wanted him to be one of my four board designees and told him so. "I'd really be happy to be one of your designees," he said. "But that's not how you want to play this."

"Really?" I said. "Why?"

"You want me to be the guy you all agree on," he said. "We both know that they'll definitely agree to have me be that guy." That hadn't even occurred to me, but he was right. The venture capital folks respected Dave, with good reason. And sure enough, Dave became that guy, which effectively gave me another board member I could always trust to do the right thing for the company, long-term.

And so I regained my place at the head of the family business, and we got to work. Dick's opened twenty-two new stores in

2000, and another twenty in 2001. We pushed west into Wisconsin, Iowa, and Missouri, and south into South Carolina, Georgia, and Alabama. As we had from the beginning of our expansion, we favored medium-sized cities over big ones, which gave us hundreds of thousands of potential customers to ourselves—instead of fighting our way into Atlanta, for instance, we set up shop without serious competition in Macon. But on occasion we'd blitz a metro area, as we did in Kansas City: in the fall of 2000, we opened five stores there on the same Sunday. That gave us instant scale in KC, and our team made that market into a great success.

By now we had a pretty sophisticated system for deciding where to put our new stores. We looked at the age, income, and size of an area's population, as well as the number of kids playing team sports there. We'd study the performance of an existing store with similar characteristics. Before we committed to a location, we projected annual sales for the store, knew the capital we'd have to put into it, and had built a profit-and-loss statement for its first three years of operation.

Our model was that we had to earn a 40 percent cash-on-cash return by the third year, which means that the store would have to generate an income equal to 40 percent of all the cash we'd invested in the deal. Let's say to open a store we spent a net $1 million on inventory and $200,000 on fixtures, plus $100,000 on pre-opening costs, giving us $1.3 million invested. By year three, that store had to net 40 percent of that, or $520,000 per year.

We quickly found that to be too easy a target, so we bumped it up to a 50 percent cash-on-cash return—or, using the same example, $650,000 of net earnings by year three. And as we broadened our footprint and introduced ourselves to new markets throughout the eastern United States, we found that even that target was a low bar to clear. Our typical store brought in $8 million to $10 million a year, and netted 12 to 15 percent of that before taxes, so it often turned a profit the first year out of the box.

We were now far too big and widespread to continue supplying the stores from a single warehouse, so we opened a second distribution center in Pittsburgh. It covered 383,000 square feet, which seemed almost absurdly big to us—between it and Conklin, we figured we could service twice as many stores as we had.

Even with that outlay, we were rapidly paying down the $60 million loan from GE Capital and used our excess cash to open new stores. It seemed we could keep doing it until we ran out of places to put them. Our model seemed a machine for profitable growth. We'd be able to stay a private company, minding our own business, for as long as we wanted.

One Tuesday morning in September 2001, I got up well before dawn and flew to Saginaw, Michigan, accompanied by Dan Ostrowski, our director of stores. We expected to be in Michigan for a day and a half; we were scheduled to visit our location in Saginaw, then go on to Detroit to see some other stores. It was the sort of trip I made almost every week.

We got to the Saginaw store at about eight thirty, which tells you how early we'd left Pittsburgh. As soon as we walked in, someone told us that a plane had flown into the World Trade Center. We assumed, like so many people, that it was a private plane—that some poor guy had suffered a heart attack at the controls while over the city and crashed into one of the towers. We were walking the store with the local managers when we heard a second plane had hit. Our walk-around stopped; we all gathered at the store's TV. The news reports carried word that a third had hit the Pentagon, and another had gone down in Shanksville, Pennsylvania—not far from home. When the first tower fell we were stunned. People in the store were crying. I got a call from Lynn Uram, our senior vice president for human resources, who told me that the home office was in a high state of anguish. She wanted to close up and send everyone home. "Absolutely," I said.

When we saw the second tower collapse, the three of us decided we needed to be with our families, so we drove back to the airport. The pilot reported that all flights, including private planes, were grounded. We could either hunker down in Saginaw or rent a car. So we hit the road, listening to the radio as we crossed Michigan. The country was reeling. The world felt crazy, dangerous, out of sorts, and we worried there were more attacks to come. I needed to hear Denise's voice, so I called her at home and asked, "How are you doing?"

"Elaine and I are going to the store," she replied in a panicked but defiant tone, "and we're going to buy a shotgun and bullets and then we're going to pick up the kids at school and bring them home."

This was a shock. I hadn't expected Denise, of all people, to take up arms. I was sitting beside Dan Ostrowski. He and his wife, Elaine, lived catty-corner to us, and I couldn't picture Elaine with a gun, either. "You're not going to buy a gun," I told Denise.

"Yes, we are," she said. "We're going to the Cranberry store to get a shotgun and some bullets, and then we're going to the school to pick up our kids."

"Denise, please don't do that," I said. "First of all, bullets don't go in a shotgun. Shotgun shells go in a shotgun. Bullets go in a rifle. You don't know how to load a gun, let alone shoot one. You're going to hurt yourself or one of the kids." I pointed out that the North Hills of Pittsburgh weren't a likely target for the next terrorist attack. Even so, when we hung up, Denise was still insisting that she was headed to the nearest Dick's to buy a gun.

I turned to Dan: "This is a problem." If Denise and Elaine were reacting to the attacks like this, there were going to be other people showing up at our gun counters, and some would be even less qualified to buy a gun than those two. With no idea what they were doing, they'd hurt themselves, hurt their kids, hurt a stranger. Maybe worse, I worried that in this crazed atmosphere we might sell guns to people who would march down the street and use them to shoot their neighbors of Arab descent, just because they vaguely resembled the terrorists. I called the office from the car. "I want you to take every single gun off the shelves and every box of ammunition off the shelves," I said. "In all the stores. Until further notice, we're not selling any guns."

We kept the guns and ammo out of sight for four or five days, until everyone calmed down a little. It seemed the right thing to do; we didn't announce it, we just did it. But people noticed, just the same. We were getting to be a pretty big company by now, and we got a slew of nasty calls and letters. One guy reached me on the phone. "You son of a bitch," he roared, "if I want to buy a gun, you're going to sell me a goddamn gun!" He sounded completely unhinged. "I'm sorry," I told him. "We're not going to sell you a gun. And the more you yell, the more I'm convinced we should never sell you a gun."

He was an extreme case, but I was surprised by the general intensity of the public reaction. It was a primer on just how emotional we Americans can be when it comes to our guns. I'd get a clearer picture in the years to come.

The September 11 attacks were a wake-up call in another way, in that they got me thinking a lot about the company and its responsibilities. As soon as the second plane hit the World Trade Center, the worldwide economy went into shock. The New York Stock Exchange shut down and remained closed for the rest of the week, but stock prices in Europe and South America plunged, and when the American market reopened, the Dow Jones Industrial Average dived more than six hundred points, at the time the biggest one-day drop in its history.

Over the following month the market recovered and achieved a tentative stability, but a mild recession that had started earlier in 2001 deepened, and I worried about the long-term effects of the tragedy. If the country experienced a serious economic downturn, we could be in trouble. We were healthy: We were in the process of posting a billion dollars in sales for the year, the first time we'd achieved that milestone. We had, or were building, 132 stores in twenty-four states. Our profits were healthy. Still, we had considerable debt to retire. I wasn't confident that our balance sheet could survive three or four rough years.

I'd have preferred to stay private, financing our own growth and remaining below the radar, and I still feel that way to this day. But we employed thousands of people. They depended on us for their livelihoods. They had families, mortgages, car payments. The world suddenly seemed a scary, unpredictable place, and we didn't know whether another September 11 was on the horizon or if the attacks might spark a war that would throw a wrench into the economy. If the company's health were compromised simply because my personal preference was to remain private, I'd be doing a disservice to a lot of people.

Besides, I knew the venture group wanted to pull its remaining stake out of Dick's—it remained eager to put its money to use elsewhere—and I wanted to help it do that. Going public would be the easiest way to achieve multiple goals at once.

So in the spring after the attacks, we planned another run at an IPO. Dave Fuente had taken Office Depot public back in 1988, and in several conversations he tried to prepare me for what lay ahead. Mike Hines and I would be embarking on a "road show" to introduce the company to potential investors, he explained. We'd go from city to city, meeting with the people who ran mutual funds, big pension funds, investment houses, and we'd have to keep at it for weeks. "You're going to hate it," he promised. "It's an absolutely grueling process. By the time you finish you'll be exhausted and sick, and you and Mike will be ready to kill each other."

I told Mike what Dave had said, and we resolved that our experience would be different. This was probably the only time in our lives that we'd do this, and we'd make sure that we not only did it right but had a good time. We were ready to file our S-1 with the SEC in early July, but we held off doing so until July 17. It was my dad's birthday. Call me superstitious, but I thought he might be able to help.

• • •

We hit the road for nearly three weeks that fall, and as Dave had warned, it was exhausting. We were on the run from dawn to close to midnight every day, flying from one place to the next, making a pitch to every group we met. Each put us through the wringer, trying to determine whether we were winners or losers. At day's end we'd be utterly spent.

But for all that, we had a great time, too, in part because we met some real characters along the way. I can't remember the group they represented, but in Kansas City a couple of guys played good cop, bad cop with us. The good cop would quiz me about our strategy, our business philosophy, our expectations. The bad cop just fixed on me with an icy stare. It was so overt that it was all I could do to keep from laughing. At one point I looked over at Mike and nearly lost it, because he was staring back at the guy with the same expression; if he could have taken him outside to kick his ass, I think he would have. As we walked out of their office, we had a good laugh about those assholes.

But the trip brought bad news with the good, and in ways that Dave hadn't predicted. In October 2002, the interest in any IPO was lukewarm at best, and the market for retail was downright cold. No one had tried to take a major retailer public in months, and few of the people we talked to seemed excited by our story.

Moreover, our stock price would be based on comparables, just as real estate agents set house values. The market would look at the already-existing stocks of companies in the same business, and in most cases price the newcomer about 10 percent lower. If we were as good as we believed ourselves to be, we'd see our price rise after our debut, but our initial price would largely be a product of how well, or poorly, others were doing. And the obvious comparable for us, The Sports Authority, wasn't doing well. Its stock was drifting downward, and taking us with it.

Before we embarked on this road show, our investment banker

had told us we could expect to price at $18 to $20 a share. As our comparables continued to flounder, he revised that number to $16 to $18. And we were riding with him in Los Angeles, more than two weeks into this backbreaking tour, when he informed us that we no longer had a shot at even that range. "Sports Authority is taking a real hit," he said. "We're probably going to be in the thirteen-to-fifteen-dollar range."

We were pulling up outside an LA office building, where we were about to undergo another hour or two of close examination, and his announcement pissed me off. I glanced over to Mike. We'd been working together for seven years and had become good at wordlessly reading each other. I could see that he was disappointed, but his expression told me he was thinking the same thing I was: the ground had shifted under our feet. Everything we'd been told, all that had made this IPO seem a smart financial move, had changed. "We're done," I told the banker. "We're getting our brains beat out from a stock-price standpoint. We're not going to do this right now."

He took that in for a moment. "We can call off the IPO, no problem," he said. "But we have this next meeting in fifteen minutes, and it'd be poor manners to cancel it." It was a good point, because sooner or later we might be back at this. We agreed to do the meeting and gave our presentation to yet another group of skeptical investors.

When it ended, we stepped back out into a cloudless Southern California afternoon. Mike had already called his wife to say we were headed home. Our banker seemed resigned to the idea that the IPO was off. But something gnawed at me. In place of the relief I should have felt at a decision made for a good reason, I felt only uncertainty. We were about to climb back into our SUV and set off for the airport when I told them that I needed to take a walk.

I set off through town, trying to examine the situation from every angle. The new price range was lousy, no question—we'd raise a lot less money than we'd expected. And there was always a worst-case possibility to consider: that after opening at $13 a share, our stock could slump below the opening price—a kiss of death for a new offering, one from which few recovered. Then there was my long-standing preference to stay private. On the other hand, we might never get this chance again. We might never have another shot at strengthening our balance sheet against unforeseen trouble. The environment was becoming ever more hostile to retail IPOs. The window might be closing for a very long time.

And a thought came to me, in my father's voice—a memory decades old, from an exchange otherwise forgotten—delivered in his signature tough-guy style: "If you start something, you finish it. End of conversation." I might have just as easily conjured another voice, my gramp's: "If you tee off on number one, you putt out on eighteen."

I was four blocks into my walk. We could minimize the effects of the lower stock price by limiting the size of the offering—we'd put less of the company's stock up for sale, so that no matter how it fared, it would affect us only so much. And if the stock took off, we could do a secondary offering and get the higher price we deserved.

My anxiety lifted. Resolute calm replaced it. We'd make it work. I returned to the parking lot, where Mike and the banker were waiting beside our SUV. "We're going to finish what we started," I told them. "Let's go to the next meeting."


Many IPOs see a company's management team take chips off the table: the influx of outside money enables them to cash out part of their stake in their company and thus put a few dollars in their pockets. Some other managers sit tight, hang on to their shares, and if things go well, wind up owning a piece of a more valuable company down the road.

I thought I could stress to Wall Street just how committed I was to Dick's and our IPO by doing neither of these things. Instead, I'd buy *into* the IPO—I'd use our public offering to buy more stock in a company I already controlled. Doing that is pretty much unheard-of. When I unveiled this idea at our next meeting in LA, the guy we were pitching leaned forward in his chair, amazed. Others we talked with at later meetings were shocked, too. By the time we wrapped up our road show, I could tell our audiences that I wasn't alone: Mike Hines and Bill Colombo were buying in, too. I'm convinced that caught the attention of investors who might have otherwise given us a pass.

As our preparations fell into place, Mike Hines and I jumped on a plane for Geneva. Denis Defforey, who'd saved us from a hostile takeover and at every turn proved himself a caring and generous shareholder, as well as a terrific human being, was so ill he'd given up his board seat and was no longer up to traveling to Pittsburgh. We wanted to thank him for all he'd done, though, so we went to him.

We met him at his flat, and he looked terrific—really, if I hadn't known he was ailing, I would have never guessed it. We sat and talked. I thanked him for his friendship and told him how much he'd meant to the company. "If it hadn't been for you," I said, "none of this would have happened." I explained that we were taking the company public and mentioned what had happened with the stock price on our road show.

He shook his head. When he had put together Carrefour's IPO years before, he "didn't get the thing public at the price [they] wanted," he said. "But if you have a low price, it's easier to go up, and everyone will always be happy about that. So don't worry about the price." We went to lunch at a nearby restaurant. Denis still owned a pile of Dick's stock. He looked over at his nephew, who was also his financial adviser. "As long as I'm alive," he told him, "I never want you to sell a single share of our Dick's Sporting Goods investment."

That meant a lot to me. And it's my understanding that he was good for it. Denis's paternal feelings for the companies he invested in really showed in his relationship with Dick's. We were one of the lucky companies he nurtured. He was a class act.

Back in New York, we met with an investor from a hedge fund who announced he wanted to buy 25 percent of the IPO. We'd never have allowed someone to buy that big a cut of the company, but it was a great endorsement. A few days later, on the evening before we were to go public, we were in the office of our financial adviser, Ken Berliner. Our main investment bankers were Goldman Sachs, Merrill Lynch, Thomas Weisel Partners, and William Blair & Company. We'd already worked with them to reduce the size of the offering. Now they were reading the mood on Wall Street and advising us on the price we should set for our stock. It was the moment of truth.

Months before, when we'd talked about the road show, Dave Fuente had shared another piece of hard-earned wisdom with me. "You have to understand that your investment banker is not your friend," he'd said. "He's doing this one deal with you. He'll be trying to sell Dick's to the likes of Fidelity and Janus and other funds. That's going to be the extent of your interaction. But afterward, he's going to keep working with Fidelity and Janus on other deals. So, remember: your investment banker is not your friend."

His words had come to mind briefly back in Los Angeles, when our banker told us that we were likely to sell for $13 to $15 a share. Now, in Ken Berliner's office, the investment bankers reported what they were hearing. "Look, this is a tough deal to get done," they told us. "We think the right price is twelve dollars a share." This, after I'd nearly killed the deal at $13.

"We may be able to get twelve fifty," they said, "but we wouldn't recommend that. We don't think it'll trade well in the after-market. And at thirteen dollars, there's no deal. You can't get the deal done."

Mike, Bill, and I huddled. We called Fuente. We weren't selling that much, which took some of the sting out of the news. And our venture capital partners would be leaving us, at long last, which argued for proceeding. We had to make a decision then and there, and the four of us agreed that we'd do the IPO at $12 a share. I had previously committed to buying eighty thousand shares.

Our families were waiting at a restaurant across town, and we climbed into a car with our Merrill Lynch bankers and set off to join them at a dinner celebrating the day's work. On the way over, I got a call. It was a woman from the Merrill Lynch trading desk. "We understand you have interest in buying eighty thousand shares of Dick's Sporting Goods stock," she said. "I am happy to tell you that you are going to be allowed to participate in the IPO."

She had no idea she was speaking to the Dick's CEO. "But," she said, "the deal is so oversubscribed that we have to cut you back. We can't sell you eighty thousand shares. We need to cut you back by ten percent. You have been allocated seventy-two thousand shares at twelve dollars each." I repeated out loud, for the benefit of those in the car, "I can't buy the amount I want. You're going to cut me back by ten percent?" One of the bankers from Merrill Lynch was sitting next to me. He and our other investment bankers had lowballed us. They'd set an unnecessarily low price for our stock at the last minute.

"Would you still like to participate?" the caller asked.

"Yes," I said. "I will."

As soon as the call ended I turned to the banker. "You've *got* to be kidding me," I said. "You stood up there and told us the deal had to be done at twelve dollars, that we couldn't do a deal at thirteen dollars—and now I get a call from your trading desk saying you have to cut me back because it's so oversubscribed?" I was not happy. Not because I'd been cut back—I already owned plenty of Dick's stock—but because people who'd long been involved with the company had cashed out some of their investment, and their payout had been whacked by fifty cents a share, a buck a share, $1.50, whatever it should have been. For no reason I could think of. "Dave Fuente told me that your investment banker is not your friend," I told the banker. "Now I know exactly what he meant."

The banker didn't have a response. The rest of the ride was very quiet. At dinner, I sat next to Ken Berliner and my family. I didn't have much to say to the investment bankers.

• • •

Morning brought a surreal trip to the New York Stock Exchange to ring the opening bell. I'd spent eighteen years running the company, and most days it didn't seem much different from when we had two stores. Of course, I understood that, in an objective sense, the company bore very little resemblance to the Dick's of 1984, but its place in my head and heart hadn't shifted much as it grew. It had always been, for me, a mission—no less when we were at 345 Court Street than when we'd opened our hundredth store.

It was something like the experience I'd had as a parent: my kids grew up, but they stayed my kids. When I stopped to think about it, I recognized that they'd changed over the years, but in my heart each was a bundle of all the stages they'd passed through—an infant in my arms, a toddler, a fifth grader, a teenager—and that bundle was indivisible, bound by the constancy of my love for them.

That morning on Wall Street, I realized that Dick's was about to undergo a big change. But it was almost an out-of-body experience, to be up on that podium with our entire management team and to push the button that rang the bell that opened the session. Afterward we took a tour of the exchange, had breakfast, then flew home. And, of course, we checked our stock price through the afternoon.

Our shares opened at $12.25 and closed at $13.15, or nearly 10 percent over our offering price. By late November, the stock was trading for more than $20 a share.

Did things change much after we became a public company? Only in the sense that now, everything we did was open to public scrutiny. Everyone knew who we were. That contrasted sharply with an experience I'd had ten years before our IPO, when we won an award at the National Sporting Goods Association. When the emcee announced it, he said, "This goes to Dick's Sporting Goods. Ed Stack, please come up." Two guys were sitting at the next table, and one said, "Who are *they*? Never heard of them." I thought that was wonderful because we strove to fly below the radar. We believed it was key to our survival. Now our financial statements were everyone's business. Our good days and bad were newsworthy, when before, both had passed unnoticed. That took some getting used to.

But otherwise, life at Dick's changed very little. We were, and are, a controlled company. We have two classes of stock. Our Series B shares, held by me and my family and not traded, get ten votes for every share. The Series A shares, traded on the market, get one vote per share. We control well over 60 percent of the votes, and thus the company. We built that structure into the IPO, because it enables us to do what's right for the business over the long term, rather than worry about how things are going from one quarter to the next.

Don't get me wrong: We care about quarterly results. We want to deliver the best possible return on investment for our shareholders. But we're not going to mortgage our future for the sake of one quarter. If we hadn't received the ten-to-one vote differential, we wouldn't have gone public because I know we wouldn't have been allowed, over time, to keep our focus on the horizon.

Another change that came in 2002 was easy to make. In 1999, Bill Colombo had come back to Dick's after leading our Internet company, and I'd talked with him several times about stepping into our presidency. He was unparalleled in his ability to execute our strategy and a creative genius in running stores. I thought he'd be great in the job. Bill wasn't so sure he was up for it.

Late in 1999, Bill had gone to the executive MBA program at Harvard Business School. He found it really useful and would later say it changed him as a businessman. When he returned the following year, he and I had gone out to dinner, and I'd asked him: "So, what do you want to do next?" Bill had answered, "I want to be president of the company."

I was thrilled to hear him say that. In 2002, we made it happen. Bill became Dick's president and took a seat on the board.

• • •

We got back to work, resolved that we'd never fail to meet the Street's expectations for our performance. I was especially fixated on making our numbers the first several quarters after going public. So many sporting goods companies before us had cratered at that juncture. The world didn't need another.

It so happened, however, that the fall after our IPO was a warm one, and third-quarter sales at so many of our stores depended on cold weather. Business wasn't great. Little more than two weeks before the end of the quarter our controller walked into my office to announce, "I don't think we're going to make our numbers."

I was beside myself. We were about to be exposed to the world as total idiots. Then, the last week before quarter's end, it got really cold across the country, and we sold a ton of Under Armour and outerwear. I mean, piles of it. And we made our numbers. That was too close for comfort, and we've taken great pains to ensure we've calculated all the variables that can affect earnings. In sixty-plus quarters, we've fallen short of our guidance only a few times.

At the risk of beating a dead horse, an important ingredient of that success has been getting our leadership team into the field. Our stores are spread over the entire country these days, from Portland, Oregon, to Portland, Maine, and if it weren't for the fact that the leadership makes the time and effort to visit our store managers and listen to what they have to say, we'd have far less insight into what our customers need and want.

I alluded before to the other big ingredient, too: we've been willing to constantly redesign our stores. We'll build a prototype, and as soon as it's up and running, we get to work on a new one. In fact, we're often working on a *new* new prototype before the new one is complete. We're always trying to come up with new ways to present the merchandise and inspire our customers. To live by the words of our mission statement: "To be the number one sports and fitness specialty retailer for all athletes and outdoor enthusiasts, through the relentless improvement of everything we do."

It's not easy. We'll never be content to kick back and relax. In an environment in which so many big retailers have failed to change with the times and technology, we have come to see it as necessary. Complacency kills.

CHAPTER 15

# "PEOPLE SHOULD KNOW WHEN THEY'RE CONQUERED"

I've mentioned that I've long been a student of retail. Beginning with books about captains of the industry that I read after college, I've sought to understand why some companies have failed and others have grown into giants. One of the themes that emerges time and again is that once successful, too many outfits fail to take their smaller competition seriously, right up to the moment that the little guy grows big enough to do them serious harm.

Decades ago, when Adidas was the world's premier athletic footwear company and the category's biggest player, it seemed to dismiss the emergence of the running craze, which enabled Nike to single-handedly create the running shoe market. Had Adidas taken the upstart seriously and recognized that it had a good idea, the Germans would likely have stunted Nike's growth while it was still finding its legs.

Nike grew into a behemoth but overlooked the huge untapped market for women-specific athletic footwear—in particular the sneakers you'd use for aerobics. That left room for Reebok, which had been around since 1958 but remained all but unknown, to introduce the Reebok Freestyle, which it seemed that every woman in America bought. In a few years, Reebok became the official footwear supplier to the NFL and the NBA and saw its sales soar. A little later, Adidas, Nike, and Reebok overlooked the

211

opportunity created by compression clothing, which opened the door for Under Armour.

You have to pay attention. You can't take anything for granted, and that goes for not only competitors but shifts in public tastes or habits. F. W. Woolworth grew into one of the world's biggest retailers by snagging prime downtown real estate in city after city. It operated 2,850 stores at its peak after World War II; its lunch counters were among the biggest suppliers of prepared food anywhere. But Woolworth failed to anticipate the public's exodus to the suburbs, and by the time it saw what was happening, its downtown real estate was a millstone. It closed its last five-and-dimes in 1997.

Yet Woolworth is also a success story, because in 1974 its Kinney Shoes division opened a new specialty store called Foot Locker. Kinney shut down not long after Woolworth's department stores, but Foot Locker prospered in the sneaker explosion of the 1980s and beyond. Today it's the country's biggest athletic shoe retailer, and a major Dick's competitor. At least some people at Woolworth were paying attention.

As a company, we've tried to stay alert to what's happening in the market and in the country at large. We've kept an ear to the ground regarding trends. And no matter how big we've grown, we've tried to keep tabs on smaller competitors, to give them our attention and respect. I remember reading that Sam Walton would walk into a Kmart or other Walmart competitor and take stock of what its people were doing right, rather than dismiss them for what they did wrong.

It's easier said than done, but that's an important piece of guidance. You have to view your competition as inspirations for improvement, because they often have something to teach you. Blow them off at your peril. That lesson is part of our own history, because if Jack Smith at Sports Authority hadn't waved off our importance to Jerry Gallagher, we might not be around today.

All of this is prelude to a visit I made to a massive sporting goods store in Columbus, Ohio, in the mid-1990s. It was called

Galyan's, and it was a sexy, two-story palace of a place—seventy-five thousand square feet, with a forty-two-foot climbing wall, a towering glass façade, an open atrium occupied by a lavish steel tree, putting greens, an archery range. Outside was another forty thousand square feet of play and product-test space: basketball courts, a pond for test-paddling kayaks, hiking trails, and a mock campground for tent set-ups.

This was theater as much as it was retail, but it was damn good at both. You could spend all day at this store. It was fun. It was hands-on. And the merchandise it sold went even broader and deeper than ours: while we catered to the beginner, the intermediate athlete, and the enthusiast, Galyan's offered the more arcane and expensive gear that appealed to the super-enthusiast. I was impressed, and more than a little worried by what I saw. These guys were really, really good—so much so that for the first time in my career I found myself thinking that I'd met a competitor who might be better than we were. No might about it. They were better. I was particularly taken by the way the store's design split the merchandise between two levels. It gave us a lot of ideas.

Galyan's was still a little company at that point, but it was poised to grow fast. It dated back to a grocery store opened in 1946 by Albert and Naomi Galyan in Plainfield, Indiana, just west of Indianapolis. The store sold hunting and fishing gear on the side and evolved until, by Albert's death in 1975, it was devoted solely to sporting goods. His son Pat took over management of the store, bought out his mom three years later, and started expanding a few years after that. By the early 1990s, the chain had four stores in central Indiana, all fairly standard big-box stores of under forty thousand square feet. With that Columbus store, though, it introduced a new Galyan's prototype and started calling itself "the World's Coolest Sports Store."

I kept my eye on the company as Pat Galyan retrofitted his first four stores to emulate his flagship, then opened a sixth. I grew more uneasy when, in 1995, the small chain was bought by the Limited—very good store operators and meaningfully bigger than us. The new owners announced plans to build up to fifty new Galyan's megastores by 2000. Meanwhile, a group of us visited the Galyan's stores in the Minneapolis area and came away further unsettled. The selection they offered, especially on outdoor gear, hunting, and fishing tackle, was amazing. I couldn't say whether they were making money, but their stores looked great, were well stocked, and had a lot of people working the floor. It was clear that if they perfected their model, they'd be lethal to anyone in their path, us included.

Our first response was to build a two-level store of our own at a mall in Hartford, Connecticut, in an effort to better understand them. We hired a design firm to work with me, Bill Colombo, and our head of stores, Joe Schmidt, and together we came up with quite a few interesting elements for the place, including a simulated hockey rink in the part of the store where we sold hockey gear. But the whole turned out to be less than the sum of its parts. We overengineered the store, making the simple complex at every turn, and the resulting eighty-thousand-square-foot beast cost a bundle to build and never quite worked. It was a rarity among Dick's locations: it never made much money.

While we tried to get a handle on what had gone wrong, Galyan's upped the stakes. It moved into Chicago, established a firm hold on Atlanta, and announced plans to open in Pittsburgh. We managed to intercept their lease at a suburban Pittsburgh shopping center, putting a Dick's there instead. But where we went head-to-head, we didn't fare well. They took a bite out of us.

The easiest solution was to buy them before they got too big, so we approached the company. I sat down with their CEO, had a conversation. He more or less told me, as politely as he could, to pound salt.

About a year later, they gave us an opening. We noticed they were outrunning their capacity to manage the business, just as we'd done a few years before. They were opening too many stores, too quickly, over too big an area—from their Indianapolis base they were trying to ride herd on gargantuan stores from Las

Vegas to Chicago to Boston to Atlanta—and they hadn't built the systems they needed to manage such growth. They didn't seem to have a cohesive real estate strategy, either. It's always tempting to move too soon into big, high-profile markets, and we figured that was what they were doing. So they stumbled. They didn't open even half the stores they'd talked about—by the end of 1999, the chain boasted twenty locations. At that point, the Limited sold a piece of its stake to a private investment firm called Freeman Spogli & Co.

The ink on that deal had barely dried when we caught wind that they were making a second run at Pittsburgh. They aimed to put a store in the planned Mall at Robinson, almost within sight of our offices near the airport. We defended our turf. I drove two hours to meet with the developers, who were based in Cleveland. We had dinner, and as it was clear that getting the deal done meant beating Galyan's at its own game, we promised that we'd build a two-level store in their mall that would equal or better the other guys. I hit it off with the old-school retail owner of the development firm, and they agreed to include us.

The project packed a lot of risk. We'd already tried the two-story format and hadn't done it well. If we bungled the job here, it would cost us a lot of money, and it would make us a laughing-stock in our own backyard. But we had to do it. We had to perfect this two-story format if we were to head off the threat that Galyan's represented. We couldn't be competitive with our standard, one-level stores, good as they were. Besides, this was home. This was where we'd make our stand.

So we redesigned our two-level prototype from top to bottom, avoiding all the design and inventory mistakes we'd made in Hartford. The Robinson store was a beautiful place, and when it opened in February 2001, it was a sensation: it did nearly $20 million in sales its first year, far outpacing anything we'd done before. We were so confident that we had the model down that we opened another two-story store in Richmond, Virginia. It scored big, too. Within a couple of years, we'd grown so com-

fortable with these bigger, more complex stores that we decided to go on the offensive. We'd take the fight to Galyan's.

It was in the midst of all this drama that my marriage spun into pieces. Its end had been coming for years. I'd been focused on the business. Denise and I were each other's best friend, but we grew more distant, and though we struggled to get our marriage back on track, we couldn't. This is one of the biggest regrets of my life. Denise is a wonderful, warm woman and has been an exceptional mother to our five children. We broke each other's hearts.

I was fortunate to get another chance at love. Donna Burnett had worked at Dick's for years and was having problems in her own marriage. We both sensed a spark between us but steered clear of each other for a long time. Until we didn't.

I moved out of the house in 2003. Denise and I divorced three years later.

At Dick's we studied our adversary, seeking to understand it. In 2001, at about the time we opened the Robinson store, Galyan's had issued an IPO. In the wake of its stock sale, Freeman Spogli owned about 30 percent of the company, the Limited about 22 percent, and the public the rest. Galyan's public offering opened their books to us, providing a wealth of details about their sales and earnings.

When we analyzed the numbers, it became clear that they made a lot of their money in central Indiana and Columbus, where they were most firmly established. We did market research on their customers in those places and found that while they loved the selection of merchandise Galyan's offered, they were frustrated by having no alternative to the chain and suspected that it was gouging them on prices. There was room for another player. What we had to do was obvious: go into Indianapolis, where they were strongest, and pulverize them.

So we put up three stores right on top of theirs—two double-decker, eighty-thousand-square-foot boxes and a single-story fifty-thousand-square-footer—and we poured our resources into getting them ready. In the spring of 2004, eight weeks before we opened, we ran ads in the paper, on billboards, on the radio and TV, even on the sides of buses, that consisted simply of the word *Wait*. It was a refinement of our entry into Syracuse seventeen years before, and it sparked a tremendous response—all around Indianapolis, people were wondering and talking about these ads.

The next round of spots featured kids and adults playing baseball, basketball, soccer, golf and other sports saying, "I'm going to wait," or "Of course, I'm going to wait," or "Why wouldn't I wait?" One radio talk show invited listeners to call in with guesses on what it was all about. The show's hosts concluded that they were ads from a Christian group out to convince kids to abstain from sex.

Finally, we unleashed ads explaining it all—that Indy was about to get stores with Under Armour, great selection, low prices. We promised to be the better choice for the city's sporting needs. We opened all three stores on the same day in April, and by close of business took in a million dollars. That bears repeating: we had never done a million dollars in sales from three stores *in one day*. And we were just getting started. We did ad blitzes thanking the city for the biggest grand opening in our history and promising great events to come. We dialed up the pressure and never let up. When the quarter ended, Galyan's hadn't done so well. We made another overture to buy the company and were again rebuffed. This time, we didn't take no for an answer.

We could have waged a war of attrition with them, and I'm confident that we would have prevailed. But buying them made a lot more sense. First, it got them out of the way. Plus, it got us into markets where we didn't overlap—expensive markets such as Atlanta, Boston, Chicago, Dallas, Denver, Las Vegas, Salt Lake City, and Washington, DC. Had we tried to shove our way into those places on our own, we'd have been the third sporting goods

217

retailer on the scene and faced a tough, costly fight to establish any respectable market share.

So we gave them what's called a "bear hug"—basically, a letter to a target company's board, putting it on notice that a takeover attempt is under way, and to which it must respond. We sent word to Galyan's directors asking to buy the company. We offered a premium price per share, high enough that the board had to take it seriously. The company responded by arranging to meet us surreptitiously at an out-of-the-way hotel in Boston's Back Bay neighborhood. They sent a delegation, and I went with Mike Hines and a couple of others on our management team. The guy who was representing Freeman Spogli & Co. wasn't a fan of our offer. He was upset that we'd given them the bear hug and seemed committed to resisting it in any way he could. Freeman Spogli did not want to sell.

The Limited wanted to hear us out, however, and we figured that if our price was right, we'd entice a sufficient number of public shareholders to vote with the Limited to sell. We went back and forth on social issues, such as where the company would be headquartered (Pittsburgh, naturally), and a litany of terms and conditions. Following the first meeting, I didn't participate in the face-to-face discussions—the guy from Freeman Spogli was so mad at me that we didn't think it helpful to have me in the room. Over the next several weeks, our general counsel, Bill Newlin, led the negotiation for Dick's. Ultimately, the only thing to wrestle over was price, and in the wee hours, Bill called me. "Just got done negotiating," he said. "They want another quarter." As in, an additional twenty-five cents per share.

"Okay," I said, "what do you think we should do?"

"Screw 'em," Bill said. "I wouldn't give them another quarter." He sounded annoyed, which was unusual. Bill was typically the picture of calm. I understood his position. We were already paying a lot for the company—more than it was worth, objectively speaking. Still, it was worth a lot to us to make this deal.

"Bill, another quarter amounts to four and a half million dollars," I said. "In the grand scheme of things, it doesn't make that much of a difference, and we want these stores in these markets."

"So you're telling me you want me to give them another quarter?"

"Yes, Bill," I said. "I'd like to give them another quarter."

"Fine!" he said. He hung up. Ten minutes later, he called back. He sounded back to his usual calm self. "Yeah, everything's good," he reported. "They took the quarter."


We paid $362 million for Galyan's. The day after the deal was announced, Bill Newlin and I flew to Indianapolis to meet Galyan's management team. And let me tell you, the reception we got was icy cold. We weren't made to feel welcome.

We talked to them about how similar our businesses were—that they'd both been founded as tiny, family-owned stores and had expanded only after years of small-town operation. The Galyan's people didn't want to hear it. They were gut-shot that their bosses and shareholders had sold them out to the enemy. We never got a good grip on the company culture, but I think it was built around the idea that they were better than everyone else—which, actually, might have been true—and now they couldn't fathom how the lesser mortals at Dick's had won the fight.

It was clear that it wasn't going to be an easy assimilation, so Bill Colombo moved to Indianapolis to guide their integration into our systems, then shut down their offices and move the operation to Pittsburgh. He had his hands full. We had inventory coming in for the holidays. Galyan's had inventory coming in. Some of our merchants decided we should have similar merchandise in both, so they bought more inventory for Galyan's. An overabundance resulted. We didn't control our inventory well, which resurrected unwelcome memories from the mid-1990s when we'd nearly tanked.

This time, however, we had a different balance sheet. We could weather the mistake. We marked down a bunch of stuff to move it out of the stores. We met our quarterly numbers, but the integration's costs prompted us to lower our future guidance for the balance of the year. Our stock got hammered for a bit.

Bill found it a daunting task to work with Galyan's people. He and I are big movie buffs, and we both like *Gladiator*, which opens with Russell Crowe's character, the Roman general Maximus, overlooking a field at which a great battle is about to start. His vast army holds the high ground. A ragtag army of barbarians waits below. Maximus sends an emissary to seek peace from the other side, and the barbarian leader emerges from his army holding the envoy's severed head. At which Maximus's second-in-command says to him: "People should know when they're conquered."

That fall, Bill was talking with the Galyan's folks about marketing, and they weren't making it easy for him. He called me up and didn't say hello. Instead, he began the conversation with: "I hate it when people don't know they're conquered."

"What's wrong?" I asked.

"We're telling them how we're going to market with this tab for a couple of Sundays, to drive some traffic, and they tell me, 'Well, that's not what we do. That's not consistent with our brand.'"

I had to laugh at that. Their brand was history. "Well," I said, "I'm sure you'll figure it out."

"I will," he growled. *Click.*

And he did. For all the heartburn it caused us, the Galyan's acquisition accomplished two important things for Dick's. First, it got us into those key, highly competitive markets where Galyan's had already built stores and established a beachhead. Today, the markets we picked up in the deal are some of our most profitable. Our two top-performing stores are in former Galyan's locations.

And second, the transaction made us America's biggest sporting goods chain, edging past the Sports Authority. A showdown loomed.

• • •

I love a street fight. As I've pointed out, half of my DNA comes from Dick Stack, and while our fighting styles might differ—Bruce Parker is the only guy I've come close to brawling with in my adult life—I do enjoy going at it with a competitor, the bigger the better.

Not long after we hit the billion-dollar mark, we had an off-site leadership meeting, and ahead of it I had everyone read *Good to Great*. It's a terrific book by Jim Collins, who led a research team in studying the habits of companies that had "made the leap" to superior, long-term growth. The eleven he focused on included retailers such as Walgreens and Circuit City, and it famously included the idea that all of these great businesses had a "hedgehog," a big, hairy, audacious goal that inspired passion in everyone who worked there—something that set them apart, that they did better than anyone else.

We had to identify our hedgehog. Collins encouraged his readers by asking, "What gets you excited? What do you, and we, do better than anyone else?" So I asked everyone in the room, "What gets you excited about our business? What are we really good at?" We went around the room. "Customer service," one said. Another said he was "jazzed about the products we sell." Someone else said, "Our marketing." Eventually it was my turn. "You know what, guys?" I said, with just the hint of a smile. "I'm going to go to the bathroom and throw up, after what I've heard. I'll be back in a couple of minutes." I got up and walked out of the room. I'm sure they were all wondering what was going to happen when I came back.

Which was this: "Really?" I asked them. "Is that what we're passionate about—customer service? Important, yes, but is that what gets us up every morning? Is it really the content we sell?" No, I told them. "What gets us up every morning? What gets us really jazzed? We love to be in a street fight. We *love* a street fight. We loved fighting Galyan's. We love fighting Sports Authority. We love to be in a street fight, and we're good at it."

221

All around the room, heads nodded and people yelled, "Yeah!" Because it's true: as a company, we love the game. We love the competition. Retailing is a sport, as surely as the football, baseball, and basketball we help our customers play. We're in it for that struggle under the boards, for that lunge past a swarm of tacklers that ekes out a first down, for that deciding "this is it" play to get the win.

Soon enough, we had ourselves a street fight, because Sports Authority came after us. They made noise that they were going to enter the Ohio Valley, which we absolutely owned. They were going to come into our stronghold and compete head-to-head, and beat the hell out of us.

Sports Authority was a roll-up of four different sporting goods retailers that had been around for a long time. In 1928, a paperboy started Gart Bros. Sporting Goods in Denver, and did it selling fishing rods that he borrowed $50 to stock—a story a lot like Dick's beginnings. Gart Bros. opened its first superstore in 1971 and swallowed up some smaller chains to become a regional power in the mountain states. At the same time, Sportmart, out of Chicago, grew to sixty-odd stores in nine Midwestern states and California. Gart and Sportmart merged in 1998, and in 2001 the combined company merged with Houston-based Oshman's, which had fifty-eight stores.

Meanwhile, The Sports Authority was created by a group of venture capitalists in Fort Lauderdale in 1987. It was owned by Kmart for a while, then spun off, and grew to two hundred five stores in thirty-three states. We'd been eyeing them as a threat for a long time, since years before Janet Hickey sang their praises during our walk-around in Buffalo. It was The Sports Authority that Jack Smith headed when Jerry Gallagher asked him about us and he blew us off as insignificant.

In 2003, Gart and TSA merged to form Sports Authority, minus the *the*, creating by far the biggest sporting goods retailer in the United States. So skip ahead seven or eight years, and we'd just had our best quarter ever. We'd absolutely blown away Wall Street's expectations, and our comp sales were among the top in retail. We were just about to have our fourth-quarter earnings call when Sports Authority started this talk of moving onto our turf, and despite our amazing quarter our stock price got crushed.

I don't often get upset about our stock price because I figure that if the Street gets it wrong one quarter it'll correct its mistake the next time. But I was steamed in this case because our stock price had been taken down by a subpar retailer that I knew couldn't do what it said it would do. Sports Authority was poorly run. Its merchandising philosophy wasn't coherent, perhaps because it had never quite managed to fully systematize and consolidate all of its component parts.

Because it was warehouse format, brands such as Nike didn't give them their best lines, and some vendors didn't sell to them at all. Even within the warehouse-format world, they'd never impressed me. Sports Authority paid almost zero attention to customer service, and it tended to carry entry-level, lower-end brands. We carried products for the beginner, the intermediate athlete, and the enthusiast; Sports Authority carried stuff for the beginner up to maybe the middle-intermediate. So if you were a real athlete, you'd find little of interest there. You'd come to us, instead. We had them dead to rights on customer service. We had a much better selection of product. Our stores were bright, clean, and well organized, while theirs consistently struck me as dingy. So when I heard their talk about taking us on, my first thought was, *Bring it*. We were in the mood for a fight.

I shared my feelings at a quarterly leadership meeting the afternoon the stock fell. We gather about 150 of our top management people for these meetings so that they can ask about what's going on and we can explain what we're thinking. I got pretty revved up talking about Sports Authority, as well as some other retailers that had badmouthed us. "The only thing we can do is to kill 'em all," I said. "Our objective is to kill them all. We're going to do it legally"—heated though I was, I thought it important to add that—"but we're going to go out there, into a street fight, and we're going to kill them all."

We didn't wait for Sports Authority to come to us. In market after market, we'd open a store right on top of theirs. In part, that was unavoidable, because they were already established in the markets we wanted. In general, they did a poor job of selecting real estate. While Dick's aimed for locations in the middle of power centers, surrounded by the kind of stores that drive traffic—Walmart, Target, Costco, Best Buy, and so on—many Sports Authority locations were slightly off the mark, I suspect to get lower rent. The old adage "location, location, location" is on the money when picking store locations. We'd aim for the best spot we could find, and if that was right across the street from Sports Authority, that's where we'd go.

But we *wanted* to be close, too. It meant a shopper would encounter both of us simultaneously and have to choose. We weren't bashful about forcing the choice. We beat the other guy on excitement, expertise, selection, and service, and at least tied them on price. So we'd open across the street, leveling the playing field from a real estate standpoint, and let the best store win. Which we knew would be us.

The first couple of markets we tried this, we beat them bloody. Feedback from the marketplace was that as soon as we opened nearby, a Sports Authority store would lose 20 percent of its sales. When, on the other hand, they showed up in a city after we did, we experienced little or no downturn in our business. They had virtually no impact.

That signaled that our real estate strategy was more than just ballsy, it was good. And as time went on, we noticed an interesting shift taking place among commercial real estate developers. These folks have preferences when they're planning the mix of retail in a shopping center. They'll choose a Target over a Kmart. They'll shoot for Best Buy over other electronics stores, and Bed, Bath & Beyond over other home goods stores. And with time, as word spread that we were doing really well, they'd call us first when seeking a sporting goods retailer tenant. As we received those calls in one market after another, Sports Authority was squeezed out of the prime real estate.

We were winning the street fight. And this was on *their* turf, or in cities new to both of us. As for the Ohio Valley, they never tried to open there. Not a single store.

## CHAPTER 16

# "THOSE YANKEES. I WAS SO DISGUSTED LAST NIGHT WITH THOSE BOYS."

Years ago, I asked our head of human resources to conduct what you might call a DNA analysis of the company's best employees. Instead of asking for hair or blood samples, we asked several dozen of Dick's most successful people, at every level of the organizational chart, to participate in an array of personality tests administered by an industrial psychologist. What we learned was that these were among the most competitive people you could ever hope to meet, but they weren't competitive with each other—their drive to succeed was *outwardly* directed, at people and entities outside Dick's. They weren't out to keep others from advancing within the company. They weren't bent on getting ahead of the guy at the next desk. They were committed to succeeding *with* their coworkers.

That was gratifying to learn, though not a surprise. We've always been wary of showboaters with too much self-regard, the type who catch a twelve-yard pass and act as if they've single-handedly won the Super Bowl. That type of character reminds me of an acquaintance of mine who lived in New York City and every day drove FDR Drive, up Manhattan's East River waterfront, to get to work. While he was at the wheel, he had two objectives. The first was to get ahead of the car in front of him. The second was to block the car behind him from passing.

A lot of companies have cultures that reward that style of naked ambition. They think a guy who's willing to submarine his coworkers to get ahead is *hungry*. At Dick's, we've never had that culture, and if someone like that slips through our hiring process and becomes part of the team, it isn't long before he reveals himself and the team cuts him. We try to reward people who understand that they have a job to do, and do it well, but who recognize that their job is part of a greater whole. People who see that success relies on the same three ingredients in both business and athletic contests: discipline, execution, endurance.

You can't get ahead at Dick's without discipline. Our expectations are high. You have to use your time well. Hitting your numbers requires focus. You have to execute, too—to finish what you start. You have to think clearly. And neither matters if you aren't able to keep doing it, day after day, year after year, improving all the while. As our mission statement says, *through the relentless improvement of everything we do.*

We try to build endurance into our team by insisting that our people maintain a work-life balance. We don't have meetings at the office at five p.m. and never schedule them on weekends. We try to provide our teammates plenty of time with their families. We figure that's important to keeping them.

And we're eager to keep those who staff our stores because they're the most important players on the team. Our organizational charts are in the shape of an inverted triangle. I'm at the bottom, the least important player, because I'm the farthest from day-to-day contact with our customers. The closer you get to the customers, the higher up the triangle your position. Our store associates are at the top. This customer-focused, teamwork-based culture has been at the heart of the company's growth and success.

At the risk of sounding boastful, let me walk you through the numbers our team has delivered for Dick's in the first few years of the millennium, because they underline just how quickly we went from regional to national. At the end of 2001, the year we broke over a billion dollars in sales for the first time—$1.07 billion, to be exact—we made $23.2 million in net income. We had 125 stores, all but a handful east of the Mississippi. Two years later, our sales had increased by 40 percent, to $1.47 billion; our net income had more than doubled, to $52.4 million; and our store count had climbed by 38, to 163.

It had taken us 53 years to reach the billion-dollar mark. We achieved $2 billion just three years after the first. In 2004, we posted $2.1 billion in sales and, helped along by our acquisition of Galyan's, operated 234 stores in 33 states. That was 71 more stores than we'd had the year before. We now had a two-store toehold in Texas; a strong presence in Minnesota, Missouri, Kansas, and Colorado; and far-west outposts in Utah and Nevada. We expanded our distribution center outside Pittsburgh and started revamping the Galyan's warehouse outside Indianapolis to try to keep up.

Just two years later, in 2006, we reached $3.1 billion. We achieved a 6 percent comp store sales increase that year, too, and ended the year with 294 stores. So, to recap: we hit a billion dollars in sales in 2001, two billion in 2004, and three billion just two years after that.

With the exception of the Galyan's takeover, which got us forty-eight of their stores, this expansion was primarily organic—we built our own stores from scratch in new markets, or in markets where our sales and research told us we needed a bigger presence. We preferred that do-it-yourself growth over swallowing up competitors; between inventory issues and cultural differences, Galyan's had left us with a pretty long-lasting case of indigestion.

But in 2006, golf was nearing a peak in popularity around the country, and we had an opportunity to buy Golf Galaxy, a chain based in Eden Prairie, Minnesota, outside of the Twin Cities. The company had been founded by two guys who'd worked for Best Buy early in its history and rose through its leadership while it grew into the country's premier big-box electronics retailer. Both avid golfers, they decided to apply what they'd learned to a golf-only superstore concept and opened their first Golf Galaxy in 1997.

Unlike Galyan's, this was a friendly takeover. They agreed to be bought for $226 million, which amounted to a 20 percent premium on their stock price. We got sixty-five stores, each as much as twenty thousand square feet, in twenty-four states, and instant status as the number one golf retailer in the United States. With a well-funded parent company, Golf Galaxy was insulated against the ups and downs of the golf category.

We inked the deal in February 2007 and built on the purchase by opening sixteen new Golf Galaxy stores; even so, we paid off the entire cost of the buyout by year's end. They were beautiful places, with indoor driving bays, full-sized putting greens, and state-of-the-art golf course simulators and swing analyzers.

Then, late in 2007, we bought a privately held, fifteen-store chain of Southern California sporting goods stores. Chick's, founded in 1949, was one of the biggest regional chains in the country, with big-box stores that were about the size of our one-story locations. We assumed the company's $31 million in debts and paid its owner, Jim Chick, $40 million in cash, for a deal totaling $71 million. In retrospect, that was a bargain, because it gave us an immediate strong presence in Los Angeles. Dick's was coast-to-coast.

But in hindsight, we should have waited on the Golf Galaxy deal. Unknown to us, the housing market was about to collapse, and when that came to pass in 2008, it dragged the entire US economy into the abyss. Job losses numbered in the millions. Discretionary spending dried up—and you'd have a tough time finding purchases more discretionary than golf clubs.

We struggled through those lean times. Company-wide, our comp sales were down by 4.8 percent. Our cash flow fell from $263 million to $160 million. Still, we were much better situated to ride out the crisis than most retailers. For one thing, we had zero debt; our close call back in the mid-nineties had taught us hard lessons. For another, we knew that liquidity was more important than earnings in such a crisis. We trimmed inventory by nearly 13 percent, kept our short-term borrowing low and our expenses down, and against all odds, broke four billion dollars in sales for the year.

Among our not-so-secret weapons throughout this almost unimaginable growth was Bill Colombo. My old college buddy was terrific at execution, at putting our plans into motion and seeing them through to completion. I oversaw our merchandising strategy, what we actually chose to put in our stores—I'd always taken a strong personal hand in that—and our skills dovetailed so well that, with a financially disciplined approach and an expanding and competitive team, we were able to keep up with the company's growth. At the pace at which we were expanding, and with the territories we had left to penetrate, we projected that we'd someday have eight hundred or even nine hundred locations.

But Bill's brother fell ill with leukemia while in his fifties and was given a 30 percent chance of recovery. That got Bill thinking. Life is short. He thought he might wake up one day and find himself facing similar odds. He told me he wanted to retire, and in February 2008, he stepped down as president.

His successor, Joe Schmidt, had been with the company for eighteen years, most recently serving as our chief operating officer. He was smart, capable, and visionary, and had been actively involved in building the culture that had brought us success. I was pleased to have him, and he served in the role for five years, from 2009 to 2014.

Bill didn't leave outright, however. Dick's had outgrown a succession of leased headquarters in Pittsburgh's western suburbs, and we now sought to custom-build a Store Support Center, as we called it, that would accommodate our leadership team, the thousands-strong force that oversaw the details of our operation, and our budding e-commerce efforts. I asked Bill to head up the project. We wanted a true home for the company, a place that our teammates were eager to be.

And holy smokes, did we ever get it: a campus of five connected buildings totaling 670,000 square feet, with soaring lobbies and atriums, a full-sized store mockup, and an auditorium seating about five hundred. Our team has, within steps of their desks, a full-service food court and a sit-down restaurant, indoor basketball and racquetball courts, an indoor running track, and a state-of-the-art health club. Outside are tennis courts, a soccer pitch, softball and baseball diamonds, and a hiking trail. The whole campus is certified green.

Five stories tall, topped with a sloping "victory wing" that juts from the roof over the main entrance, the Store Support Center occupies a wooded site in Coraopolis, beside Pittsburgh International Airport. A long drive winds through forest before the complex erupts into view, and let me tell you, that first view of the place never fails to excite me. We took up residence in 2010.

Still, Bill wasn't finished. We had need of a marketing head late that year, and I asked him to fill in through Christmas. He was two years past ready to retire, but he agreed to do it while we searched for a new marketing boss. We found one in Lauren Hobart.

Lauren grew up in the New York suburbs, graduated from the University of Pennsylvania in 1990, and spent five years in commercial banking before returning to school for her MBA at Stanford. From there she joined Pepsi, where she worked in the company's finance group for four years, then switched to marketing. Then, after ten years in marketing roles at Pepsi, she decided it was time to leave.

As luck would have it, I'd met a former boss and mentor of hers who caught wind that we were looking for a chief marketing officer. So Lauren came to us and impressed us at once with her smarts, energy, and creativity. She joined Dick's in February 2011, and was destined to rise to the company's presidency a few years later.

Bill finally retired on his anniversary date with Dick's, after twenty-three years with the company. Even then, we didn't let him shake loose completely: he remained vice chairman of our board of directors. He remains on the board today.

• • •

Whenever we had the chance, Donna and I got away to Florida. I'd inherited my dad's love for the place and bought a house on the Atlantic coast, not far from where he'd spent so much time. My stepmom, Donna, lived nearby, and my siblings spent a lot of time in Florida, too.

My mom did the same—winters in Tequesta, summers in Bing-hamton—and I saw quite a bit of her in Florida over the years. For most of them, she remained the same demanding, me-first personality I'd known in childhood. But in 2005 she fell ill and learned that she had cancer. It started in her gallbladder and spread to her lungs, then to her brain.

This terrible news came with a bleak prognosis, but it sparked a wondrous transformation. After a lifetime of being needy and undemonstrative, my mom became warm and loving. Whereas before she'd been self-absorbed, now she became giving and com-passionate; her mind-set shifted to "How can I help? What can I do?" And in place of the bitterness that had long consumed her, she was accepting, even happy. It's one of those terrible ironies that an effective death sentence brought her the most satisfying years of her life and the happiest time we kids spent with her, but so it was: she struggled against her cancer with dignity, humility, and concern for all around her. She became a lovely human being. In the end, she got it right.

At some point she was given the choice of brain surgery and the possibility of a longer life—but with pretty good odds of dying on the table—or, alternatively, living out her few remain-ing days in relative comfort. She chose the surgery, and though the doctors bought her time, she never really recovered from the procedure. She was lucid but so compromised physically that she never left her bed. She might have become even more loving after that.

One thing that never changed: like everyone who'd spent years at 16 Ardsley Road, she was a Yankees fan. I remember walking into her room in the fall of 2009, during the major-league play-offs, and asking, "Mom, how are you doing?"

"Those Yankees," she said, sighing. "I was so disgusted last night with those boys."

The Yankees ended up winning the World Series that November. My mom died two months later, on January 15, 2010.

By then my family had been in Pittsburgh for sixteen years. My son Michael was out of college, Brian was soon to graduate, and Katie was halfway through her studies. Denise and the two younger kids lived in the house we'd built upon moving from Binghamton. I lived a few miles away.

For years, I was unsure I'd ever get married again; I was consumed by guilt and regret over the failure of my marriage to Denise. But Donna and I proved a really good couple. She went to bed happy every night and woke up the same way. She was big-hearted, funny, and patient with me—that last part a key ingredient to our success, given the time that Dick's required. She was a wonderful mother to her young son, Ryan, and unfailingly kind to my kids. Plus, she was fun, energetic, and as crazy for golf and skiing as I was—a tomboy, the prettiest tomboy I could imagine. My guilt never left me entirely, but I fell in love with Donna, and she helped me get past it.

When we started to get really serious about where our relationship was headed, we decided she shouldn't work at Dick's anymore. She moved to Nike, where she was a strategic account rep. The job was important to her. She'd worked since she was sixteen, had always made her own way through life, had always built her own financial security. That wasn't going to change—not after we became engaged or, she thought, once we were married.

Except that six weeks before our wedding—which took place in August 2013—Nike let her go. She called on Dick's buyers as part of her job, and evidently the company didn't want her doing that as my wife. Donna was devastated. I was pissed. She had no shortage of job offers and wrestled with whether to take one; she was sensitive to people's thinking, *Oh, she married Ed Stack so she doesn't have to work anymore.*

I left the decision entirely up to her, listening as she ticked through the pros and cons, until after weeks of anguish she asked me for advice. "If it was me," I told her, "I'd consider not going back to work. If you really miss it, you can always go back, but Ryan's eleven. When he goes off to college, you're never going to think, *Gee, I spent too much time with my son.*" Also, I pointed out, she loved spending time with her mom, who lived a few minutes from the house.

A few days later she announced that she wouldn't accept any of the jobs she'd been offered. She's instead thrown herself into all sorts of things—she's joined the boards of several private foundations—to the point where her calendar is probably fuller today than it ever was when she was selling for Nike. She says to me now, "I'm way too busy to work."

Ryan lives with us half the time. I've watched him grow into a young man who makes both Donna and me proud, and a talented student and athlete. I've come to love him like one of my own.


While my personal life was changing, Dick's continued to grow. We had 444 stores in 45 states by the end of 2010, added another 36 in 2011—at the same time topping $5 billion in sales—and the following year, with the financial crisis now firmly behind us, had 518 stores and were closing fast on $6 billion. While we flourished—our growth now so carefully and thoroughly researched and practiced that it approached the reliability of an algorithm—our competition faltered.

And by that I mean Sports Authority, because by now it stood alone among our challengers on the national scene. In 2005, our old nemesis was neck-and-neck with us in sales. The following year they were bought by Leonard Green, the same private-equity outfit that had attempted to snatch us up. Their new owners flattered us: they introduced a new look to Sports Authority stores, with well-defined departments arranged like boutiques under one roof. Even so, by 2010 their sales hadn't budged, while ours had nearly doubled. As we opened new distribution centers in Atlanta and Phoenix, and solidified our hold on the West Coast and some of the country's biggest metropolitan areas, they oversaw a flat-lining store count and mounting debt. In 2015, according to news reports, they owed their creditors a billion dollars.

We received hints that they'd welcome a merger. We couldn't imagine how that would work. We already owned the markets where we overlapped, and in those where they were better established, we'd have had to spend a ton of money to reconstruct their stores to resemble ours. We had several conversations, but they went nowhere. It was clear to us that we could simply wait them out. We were in forty-six states and had only two major markets left to capture: South Florida, where we were making inroads against Sports Authority's greatest concentration, and the five boroughs of New York City, where we were unwilling to spend the ridiculous sums necessary to buy or lease real estate. For the time being, we left that to Modell's.

Our attention was shifting to a new adversary, anyway. A dozen years after our venture capital partners tried to push us into becoming an online-only business, Amazon had emerged as a growing threat. Until now we'd been able to out-position our competition with smart real estate decisions. That wasn't as effective when the competition was a click away. While I hope there'll always be demand for a bricks-and-mortar, sensory, in-person shopping experience—for the entertainment aspect of shopping—we and every other retailer had to develop new strategies and tactics to keep up with a changing, tech-savvy consumer. Shoppers' time is the linchpin of success or failure: they want what they want how they want it, and they want it *now*. We have to be able to answer those demands.

Michele Willoughby had led our e-commerce effort for years, and she had done a wonderful job positioning Dick's to compete online. Under her guidance, we turned a small, insignificant aspect of the business that was losing money into a profitable engine that posted more than a billion dollars in sales. When Michele retired in 2016, we put our e-commerce business in the hands of Lauren Hobart.

It was largely her task to transform Dick's from a physical retailer to an "omni-channel" player. While the Internet is often blamed for the demise of retail, the fact is that our stores and our online presence complemented each other—they could, working together, make Dick's the go-to sporting goods provider regardless of where our customers were and when they wanted to shop. We could actually build customer loyalty by fully integrating our online and physical "channels" into a seamless whole.

If we executed correctly, we knew our websites should benefit from our great network of stores, and they from a robust online portal. In fact, our stores gave us a decided advantage over the competition. A customer could order an item online and choose to pick it up at the store, or order it online at the store and have it shipped to his or her home. A shopper could return or exchange an online purchase at the store, which is far less of a hassle than shipping packages back and forth. Most important, that shopper could review our offerings online, then come to the store to experience them firsthand—because, convenient though the Internet might be, there's no substitute for trying on a jacket, feeling the quality of a piece of gear, stepping on a treadmill, or lacing up a pair of running shoes.

By 2013, increasing synergies between our channels enabled another advance: a customer could shop online, and our integrated systems relayed the order to the store nearest them, which arranged for delivery—faster for them, cheaper shipping for us, and it enabled us to use store inventory to fulfill online orders.

Our theories about symbiotic benefits seemed to be affirmed by something we noticed along the way. Eight in ten of our online orders shipped to customers who lived within an easy drive of a Dick's store. When we opened a new Dick's store, our online orders in that area typically doubled. Growth in one channel did, indeed, appear to drive growth in the other.

It didn't take long to capture a meaningful share of online business. From 2009 to 2012, the online sporting goods market experienced a compounded annual growth rate of 19 percent; during the same period, Dick's e-commerce sales grew by 41 percent. They took off from there. In 2013, our online sales jumped by 65 percent. They accounted for 10 percent of our total sales in 2015. A year later, they surpassed a billion dollars for the first time.

Meanwhile, the sporting goods landscape was becoming littered with empty big boxes. Austin-based Golfsmith, long a strong competitor with more than one hundred locations, was dragged into bankruptcy by building too many of its stores too big and went belly-up in 2016. Gander Mountain declared bankruptcy in 2017, and under new ownership (and a new name—Gander Outdoors) reopened less than half of its chain.

And Sports Authority, which had been wallowing in debt and mediocrity for years, missed a $20 million interest payment early in 2016 and declared bankruptcy shortly after. At first it announced it would close only 140 of its 460 stores, but the chain couldn't reach a deal with its creditors, and in May it announced its liquidation.

In the space of little more than a year, twenty-two million square feet of sporting goods space emptied—sales floors that had been devoted to doing battle with Dick's. "The disruption . . . positions us well to optimize our core business," I wrote in an annual report. All that market share was up for grabs, and the new real estate environment "allow[ed] us to be patient for the best locations at the best terms."

We bought Golfsmith's assets and inventory at auction and opened Golf Galaxy stores in some of their better locations. We snatched up some of Sports Authority's prime spots. Of the forty-three stores we opened in 2017, nineteen were built in the shells of former Sports Authority locations. The retail apocalypse, as the press was calling it, was good to us.

I'm going to stop this litany of success here because I'm getting ahead of myself. I instead want to talk about a tragic event in the nation's history that opened a defining chapter in the Dick's story.

It started on a Friday in December 2012, when a young man walked into Sandy Hook Elementary School in Newtown, Connecticut.

CHAPTER 17

# "IF WE WERE TASKED
# WITH SOLVING A PROBLEM,
# WE'D SOLVE THE PROBLEM"

Newtown, Connecticut, was a quiet place. Through most of 2012, it retained a small-town charm that seemed to contradict its location just an hour's drive from New York City. In the previous ten years, it had recorded just one homicide.

That changed on the morning of December 14, when a troubled twenty-year-old misfit shot and killed his mother in her bed, then drove across town to Sandy Hook Elementary. Once inside the school, he gunned down twenty little kids, all six or seven years old, along with six staff members. At the time, it was the second-worst mass shooting in American history.

We didn't know the details until hours after the shooting stopped. I had a TV on in my office as they emerged, horror by horror, in a slow drip that afternoon. The victims were *little* kids, completely defenseless. The gunman had cornered most of them in their classrooms and shot them point-blank. It was an act so unthinkable that my coworkers at Dick's, hundreds of miles away from the carnage, cried and hugged each other in the halls. I was having trouble wrapping my mind around what had happened, and in the solitude of my office, the revulsion and grief I felt at the act itself was sharpened by an all-too-familiar anxiety. The school was not far from a couple of our stores. I waited for the networks to mention the gunman's name.

Elsewhere in the Store Support Center, our people were preparing to launch a frenzied search of our records for that name, an effort that had become a terrible routine in the wake of any high-profile shooting. Dick's, like every licensed firearms dealer, kept a record of every gun transaction—in a six-page Form 4473, which is paperwork required by the federal government, and in our own logbooks listing the details of every sale. Completing the 4473s required us to verify the purchaser's identity; enter his or her name in NICS, the National Instant Criminal Background Check System (and record the number the NICS spit out when it okayed the purchase); and have the buyer fill out an affidavit swearing that he or she was eligible under federal law to buy a gun. It was an exacting process.

Naturally, we hoped we wouldn't find a match. It wasn't so much that we worried we'd made a mistake that put a gun into the wrong hands: we were downright obsessive in our attention to every letter of the law, every box on the forms. We knew those 4473s had to be perfect, every time. But we were a big company. We sold a lot of guns. And although we consistently did everything we could to ensure that every sale hewed to the law, there was this nagging fact: the perpetrators in the vast majority of mass shootings had come by their weapons legally. We could do everything right and still wind up selling a rifle, shotgun, or handgun to someone who'd later use it in terrible ways.

So it had become our habit, in the first hours after a mass shooting, to conduct a search through the files, to pin down whether we'd been dragged into a story that we wanted no part of. And if we had, to decide how we would respond to it.

So far, we'd never had to.

One detail emerged early: the shooter had used an "assault-style" rifle, meaning some variant of the AR-15, a civilian cousin of the US military's M16 rifle. Compact, light, and accurate, the AR-15 fires a 5.56-millimeter round—essentially an elongated and more powerful version of a .223-caliber bullet. It rips to pieces whatever it hits.

Within the gun industry, these weapons are called "modern sporting rifles," a term coined by a trade group three years before Sandy Hook in an unsuccessful attempt to get people to stop using the "assault-style" label. Fueling my unease that afternoon was the fact that we stocked MSRs at Dick's. We hadn't been carrying them for long, but we'd added them to the inventory over the previous year or so because they were popular—they're among the biggest sellers at gun retailers around the country— not because we saw any particular merit to them. We were simply answering a demand. As we waited for a name, I wondered about the wisdom of that decision.

When it came, we found that the gunman hadn't purchased his assault-style rifle at Dick's. But not long after, somebody called the media and reported that they thought they saw the shooter in one of our stores a couple of days before the massacre. The police asked to review our security camera footage, and we cooperated fully.

Even though they knew this guy hadn't bought from us, some media outlets demanded to see the video, too. They got really aggressive with us, even airing stories saying that this nut had been seen in a Dick's store. We weren't about to share the tape with them. I'm not sure we could have, even if we'd wanted to— we were cooperating in a mass-murder investigation, for God's sake. But some TV people didn't give a shit about confirming their information and went with stories we were sure were bogus. Then CNN and some of the other big outfits started calling, wanting to know what was going on.

Our management team huddled on the phone, late into the night, trying to figure out what to do. We emerged from that long conversation with two decisions. One, the media could pound salt. We weren't going to be handing over our tapes. We'd stress to anyone who asked that we hadn't sold this nut a gun and leave it at that.

The second decision inspired a lot more debate. We went back and forth over whether MSRs had ever been a comfortable fit at Dick's. They weren't traditional hunting rifles, which served our primary clientele. In demand or not, they were out of step with our mission as a company—it was a stretch to consider them at all "sporting." As long as we sold them, we'd be giving them an implicit Dick's seal of approval. And as we were among the biggest gun retailers in America, that made us part of the problem they caused. The fact that we hadn't sold a rifle to the shooter was beside the point.

Every so often comes a moment when you have to stop thinking of your company solely as an engine for making money and broaden your view to consider its role in American life. It seems to me that all of us, not just doctors, should strive to hold true to the Hippocratic oath: first, do no harm. I don't see why that shouldn't go for companies, too. Earning a return for the shareholder is important—without that, a business can't do much else, good or otherwise—but a company's income should be a reward for not only worthy products and good business strategy but responsible behavior. Put simply, to be a good company, you have to do good.

That may seem a surprising platitude from a guy who just a little ways back was talking about how much he loves a street fight, but there's a difference between a metaphorical pep talk and real life.

Anyway: we hashed out what to do about the weapons in that marathon late-night conference call. Four of us went around and around for close to three hours about it—besides me, David Mosse, our general counsel, was in on the call, along with Joe Schmidt, our president, and Lauren Hobart, who was running our marketing. We struggled to find the overlap between what was in the best interest of the company and what was the right thing to do.

The decision came down to this: On the one hand, we made some money from selling assault-style rifles, and we followed the

letter and spirit of the law in doing so. We were within our rights to keep doing business as usual. On the other hand, twenty-seven people, including twenty little children, had been murdered with a weapon uniquely suited to mass killing. It wasn't the first time an AR-15 had been used that way, and it seemed a safe bet it wouldn't be the last.

By the end of the call, it looked like a no-brainer.

We had to stop selling the damn things.


Our decision to suspend the sale of assault-style weapons wasn't the first time Dick's had been moved by a sense of civic duty to do such a thing. I'd yanked all firearms and ammo after September 11, you'll recall, but there was an even earlier precedent: thirteen years before that, we'd done something similar after a burglary at our first Rochester store. The thieves stole ten handguns and eleven shotguns and rifles.

At the time—October 1988—we had just a few stores and hadn't yet developed the sophisticated security systems we have in place today. The crooks weren't subtle. They used a sledgehammer to smash the front door, cleaned out the gun display cases, and dashed back out. We talked about how to respond. One idea was to build a cage around that whole part of the store so we could lock it down at night. We talked about taking the guns out of the cases at closing time and discussed where we could keep them safe. But we worried that if we did either, thieves bent on getting guns might show up while we were open, and somebody would get hurt.

We were wrestling with this question, two or three days after the break-in, when the police called and said they'd found some of the guns. They were in a house in a rough part of Rochester, in which they'd also found a bunch of teenage gangbangers. The city's SWAT team had launched a massive raid on the house after word on the street said the kids had stolen the guns with every intention of using them, and soon, against rival gangs, the police themselves, or both. We were staggered. I talked it over with Bill Colombo, who was our head of stores at the time, and we decided we were done with handguns. If we couldn't safeguard the inventory, we figured that other tragedies were just a matter of time. We sent some guns back, sold out our inventory of some others, and got out of the handgun business.

It wasn't a permanent decision. Years later, when we expanded into Texas, we found ourselves up against Academy Sports + Outdoors, a chain about one-third our size that was based in the Houston area. It didn't take long to see that without handguns, we wouldn't fare well against Academy, so after some long and really spirited conversation, we returned handguns to a few stores in Texas. That morphed into a few more stores. Today, I'm guessing we sell them in about 25 percent of our locations.

But back to the initial decision: When we pulled the handguns, we didn't announce it—we just transitioned out of selling them. Nobody seemed to notice. Then again, we were a smallish regional company. Nobody paid much attention to anything we did.

So those were a couple of touchstones in the evolution of our corporate conscience about guns, and our responsibilities as a firearms dealer, before the Sandy Hook massacre. As in those cases, we decided after Sandy Hook to merely pull assault-style rifles from the shelves without announcing what we were doing. We had no desire to get into a Second Amendment debate; our aim was simply to satisfy ourselves that we'd taken action to limit the availability of weapons that seemed attractive to mass shooters.

Which they certainly are. I'm writing this from the perspective of several years later, and the pattern that has emerged is undeniable: AR-15s and other military-style rifles are like catnip to the deranged. Don't get me wrong—they're popular with a wide range of buyers, the vast majority of whom are law-abiding citizens who never use them improperly. That said, a *proper* use for them is elusive. In combat, they are terribly effective, but that's all they have going for them. The military variant of the AR-15 has just one purpose: to kill people.

And it might be that, right there—along with their scary appearance, and the badass, deadly aura they give anyone who totes one—that makes them so irresistible to people who get it into their troubled heads to slaughter a lot of innocents. Tick through the mass shootings of recent years, and you'll find assault-style weapons figuring prominently in a great many, and at the center of the worst.

So: I was not heartbroken to pull them. We put out the word to the stores, and late in the evening, down came the assault-style rifles. Ah, but this was not 1988 or 2001. Almost immediately, the word of what we were doing spread on social media. Some customers may have been in the stores and may not have liked what they were seeing. Without a doubt, some of our own associates were displeased with the policy. Either way, we came under attack on social media. We were caving to the left. We were antigun. We were denying people their Second Amendment rights. We were against the Constitution and hated America and its traditions. It blew up fast and furious, with a *lot* of people really upset with us, and within a day or two we were sitting on a full-blown public relations crisis.

We'd expected some flak; the reaction to our 9/11 decision told us we'd get it. But we weren't prepared for the ferocity of these broadsides and the huge numbers of people joining the fray. It was a wake-up call regarding just how passionate some people are about any perceived threat (*perceived* being the operative word here) to the Second Amendment. We'd challenged their core beliefs.

Meanwhile, a customer and his young son, five or six years old, came into one of our stores near Sandy Hook Elementary, and as they passed the gun displays the little boy became highly distressed and screamed for his dad to get him away from there. When I heard that, I decided we had to go further in the stores around Newtown. This was Christmastime, when we have a lot of kids in the stores, and I didn't want any to be confronted with a reminder of the trauma they'd just survived. I ordered those stores to take all the guns off the shelves until further notice—handguns, hunting rifles, the works. We shut down the gun departments there.

The public frenzy over our wider assault-gun decision continued. Thousands of our customers let us know, often in really colorful language, that they'd never step into our stores again. We decided that we had to issue a statement. It was short and to-the-point. "We are extremely saddened by the unspeakable tragedy that occurred last week in Newtown, Connecticut, and our hearts go out to the victims and their families and to the entire community," it read. "Out of respect for the victims and their families, during this time of national mourning we have removed all guns from sale and from display in our stores nearest to Newtown and suspended the sale of modern sporting rifles in all of our stores chainwide."

It didn't cool any tempers, but at least it explained why we'd made the move. The thousands of people who promised to boycott us were true to their word. We lost their business, and it hurt. Dick's went through a difficult time in the weeks and months after. We were overinventoried, not only in guns but in other departments where customers who felt strongly about their guns had shopped in the past. It took a long time to recover.

But we weren't about to change our minds. We took those rifles out of the stores because we felt it was the right thing to do—for us, and ultimately, for everyone. We didn't want to sell them anymore, and we weren't going to sell them. And as far as I was concerned, if some people didn't like the way we ran Dick's, they could take their business elsewhere.

Now, before you go off on a rant about how I'm a scourge to gun owners everywhere, let me point out that I'm one, myself. I support the Second Amendment. I have guns and respect them. I grew up around them. Ours was not a household where pistols were considered the devil's right hand; they, along with rifles and shotguns, have helped put food on the table since long before I worked at Dick's. As far back as I can remember, they've been part of my daily life. When I went to work at 345 Court Street, the hunting department was a busy place, especially in the fall, and in the course of a day's work I'd often handle rifles, shotguns, and handguns, discuss them with customers, demonstrate their use. I unpacked them, assembled them, and put them on display. They hold no mystery for me. I see them for what they are: tools. And I understand that like any tools, they're as good or bad as the person wielding them.

It's just that with assault-style rifles, we've presented the public with an all-too-effective tool and no appropriate job to do with it. On this issue, mine is not a voice in the wilderness. On September 13, 1994, the US Senate passed a ban of these weapons, which was signed into law by President Bill Clinton on the same day. The vote came after former presidents Gerald Ford, Jimmy Carter, and Ronald Reagan wrote to Congress in support of a ban, citing a 1993 Gallup poll that showed that 77 percent of Americans favored abolishing the manufacture, sale, and possession of semiautomatic, assault-style rifles.

The ban, a subsection of the Violent Crime Control and Law Enforcement Act of 1994, expired after ten years. Since then, no attempt to renew the ban has gained traction. And each year since, agreement of any kind on firearms control has slipped further out of reach.

What happened after Sandy Hook illustrates my point. Five days after the shootings, President Barack Obama appointed Vice President Joe Biden to head up a task force charged with developing concrete proposals for stemming gun violence. Biden had a month to complete the job—a reflection of Obama's grim understanding that the nation's grief over Sandy Hook might not last. The task force immediately set about meeting with stakeholders in the gun control debate—the White House would later say

Biden and his team heard from 229 different people or organizations in the course of their fact-finding. Among those vested interests were the big retailers who sold firearms.

So it was that we were invited to be part of a delegation of retailers meeting with Attorney General Eric Holder in January 2013. We sent Dave Mosse, our general counsel, and another Dick's lawyer, Beth Baran. Both had been building a government affairs specialty within our legal team and understood our need, as a corporate citizen, to not only hear out the government's concerns but serve as a source of information; we had, after all, been among America's biggest gun retailers for years and had practical experience to share.

So David and Beth went to Washington. Before the meeting with Holder, they joined some gun sellers at a nearby law office and were surprised to find that most had sent not senior executives, as we had, but midlevel compliance officers, which suggests to me that they had no intention of getting involved in a substantive back-and-forth about guns or any other subject.

And indeed, the talk among the other retailers at that pre-meeting get-together was centered on just one thing: so-called Fix NICS legislation, which would improve state mental health databases and get that data into the NICS system. They didn't talk about a ban on any type of weapon or gun accessory. The attitude in the room seemed to be: Let's not let anyone use this tragedy to leverage us into a reduction of rights.

We didn't have that mind-set, and I don't think Walmart, which also was represented by senior executives that day in Washington, did, either. But it didn't really matter, because once the retailers got to the meeting with Holder, it became clear that he didn't have the time or inclination to dive deep on the subject. The gathering lasted maybe twenty minutes, during which there was no real attempt at conversation; later, David told me that it seemed a "check-the-box" exercise, enabling the Biden task force to say it had sat down with all who had a piece of the issue.

Meanwhile, two or three weeks after Sandy Hook, I was down

in Florida, on the golf course with John Boehner, then the Speaker of the House, and a couple of other guys. The country was still grieving and angry about the shooting. The airwaves were full of demands for commonsense gun reform. The Biden task force was still at work.

As we were getting ready to play, I looked at the Speaker and said, "John, what's going to happen with gun reform?" He was a Republican, but so was I at the time, and I expected him to say that something had to be done, even if that something was pretty narrow. I wouldn't have been shocked if he'd said that Congress might discuss resurrecting the assault weapons ban, or employing a universal background check, or—at the least—raising the minimum age for their purchase. I was good with all of those possibilities.

Instead, he looked at me with a quizzical expression on his face, then shook his head. "Nothing," he said.

That shocked me. "Really?" I asked him. "Nothing?"

"Nothing," he said. "Both sides can't come together."

He didn't explain, but I interpreted the remark to mean that Republicans and Democrats had become so entrenched in their positions, and the gulf between them had grown so wide, that both had come to view compromise as capitulation. To budge was to lose. And in fact, when the Biden task force finished its work, its recommendations were either hollow or unattainable. The one legislative recommendation from the task force that gained any traction—a modest measure on expanded background checks—died in the Senate that spring. Virtually *nothing* was done—not even the "Fix NICS" reforms the gun retailers favored.

Perhaps it's not worth it to either side to give up a talking point it can use against the other. Whether it's guns, health care, race relations, education inequality, or the minimum wage, the two sides hold fast to their positions because it establishes their brand. It sets them apart from the other guys.

Let me tell you a quick story from my own life. A few months before Sandy Hook and that golf game with John Boehner, I was having dinner in Florida with Donna, my sister Kim, Larry Schorr and his wife, and Glenn Small and his girlfriend; Glenn, you'll remember, was the Binghamton banker who saved us during the S & L crisis. I'd long been a registered Republican, though I considered myself a centrist—a conservative on foreign policy and the economy, and fairly liberal on social matters. Kim was and is a liberal Democrat. Larry is a staunch liberal, too.

President Obama was campaigning for reelection against Mitt Romney at the time, and we started talking about the race and politics in general, and in no time the exchange grew heated. And I mean *fierce*. And all of a sudden it struck me as funny, and I started laughing. The others looked at me like I was crazy. Still laughing, I said, "Even *we* can't agree on anything."

I turned to Kim and told her: "You know I love you from the bottom of my heart." To Larry I said, "You and I have been the best of friends for more than twenty-five years. You're the lead director on our board. We've been through so much together.

"And here we are. The three of us can't compromise on *anything*. No wonder the guys in Washington can't."

Here's where the comparison ended, because Larry now offered what I thought was a really profound observation. "You're right," he said. "We have very different views on many different subjects. *But if we were tasked with solving a problem, we'd solve the problem.*"

Bam. There it is. If you have a job, you figure out how to get it done and you do it. Period. In the wake of Sandy Hook, Congress had yet to adopt that attitude. And the country, though wracked with grief and anger about the shooting, didn't hold Congress's feet to the fire. In fact, Sandy Hook had a strange and troubling effect on gun sales: they spiked after the massacre. In the midst of all the talk about gun reform, Americans went to gun dealers by the millions and bought guns and ammunition. Women bought handguns in numbers we'd never seen.

Human nature, I suppose: whenever there's talk about gun control, the public stockpiles weapons. We saw the same thing during Bill Clinton's presidency, when it became clear that his administration was serious about curtailing assault-style rifles. We saw it again when Obama was elected. The fear that guns might be limited boosts sales.

A British journalist named Dan Hodges summarized the political situation in brutal but accurate fashion in a June 2015 Twitter comment. "In retrospect Sandy Hook marked the end of the US gun control debate," he wrote. "Once America decided killing children was bearable, it was over."

Our struggle to balance the twin goals of doing right for the company and doing good for society didn't end with Sandy Hook. It would take many forms in the years to come, some having no connection to guns. I'm immensely proud of the soul-searching we've done and the fruits it has yielded.

But perhaps the most tortured debate within the company centered, after Sandy Hook, on what we should do with a new store we had in the works called Field & Stream. We'd long been working on the concept for a spinoff hunting, fishing, and camping store, a direct competitor to Cabela's and Bass Pro Shops—a thematically focused superstore that brought us full-circle back to the company's beginnings on Court Street. We'd locate these stores in markets where outdoors activities were especially important to the population, and stock a far wider and deeper array of gear to satisfy every level of practitioner, from novice to expert.

We had a store already under construction when the shooting took place and had signed leases for several others. We'd worked long and hard to buy the Field & Stream name. We carried a broad line of outdoors clothes bearing the Field & Stream label. Those clothes had been sold by the Gordon and Ferguson Merchandising Company, which dated back to 1871—so we included that year on the logo we designed for the place, which was dominated by a drawing of a bald eagle in flight. We were excited about the concept and planned to open thirty to thirty-five stores by 2017. We thought we'd found a new growth vehicle.

But Sandy Hook presented us with a dilemma: it was one thing to pull MSRs from all the Dick's stores, but could we open an authentic firearms and fishing chain that didn't stock them? Our merchandising team said we couldn't. The stores would never gain acceptance with the hunting fraternity with that huge hole in their inventory. We wouldn't stand a chance against Cabela's, or Academy, or any other hunting retailers. Besides, if we kept MSRs out of Field & Stream, we could count on being boycotted by the National Rifle Association, which translated into millions of customers.

The other side of the question was just as thorny. Could we put MSRs in a subsidiary of Dick's after we'd pulled them from the parent chain? True, we at Dick's had always said that we'd *suspended* sales of the rifles, rather than declared that they were gone for good, but that was hair-splitting; inside the company, we were committed to never returning them to the Dick's stores. As far as I was concerned, there was no going back.

So the debate evolved into this: Could we sell MSRs at Field & Stream while staying true to our philosophy at Dick's? Could we argue, on the one hand, that these rifles had no business in civilian hands while putting them into those hands at this differently branded line of stores? Could these different positions coexist within the same company?

I was among several members of the leadership team who thought this contradiction did not work. I entered the debate convinced that we shouldn't have assault-style rifles in our stores, no matter what name was over the door. We'd taken a position that our customers would expect to extend across all of our brands.

But in days and days of meetings, the merchandising teams and the team of store managers who'd be running our Field & Stream locations argued that we *could* make a distinction between the two chains—that although it would be no secret that Field & Stream was part of Dick's, we could frame the new venture as aimed at an altogether different customer. We'd position Dick's as family oriented. Field & Stream would be an adult-centric, authentic hunting and outdoors store. There'd be some overlap in customers, but not much.

That's where the argument stood when we called for an informal vote. The leadership team was split. I broke the tie. I went with our merchants and agreed to sell the rifles at Field & Stream. It was a tough place for me to get to. I wasn't comfortable with stocking MSRs there or anywhere else. But if we were to proceed with the new chain, we had to have them, and it was too late to scrap the chain.

Five years later, we'd learn that a lot of people, the press included, never made a distinction between Dick's and Field & Stream. The media would report that Dick's suspended MSR sales in 2012 and lifted the suspension when we opened the first of the new stores outside Pittsburgh in August 2013. That wasn't exactly right: Dick's never lifted the suspension. But I can understand that version of events. It required some mental gymnastics to see it any other way.

That first Field & Stream grand opening was quite an occasion, by the way. Willie Robertson of TV's *Duck Dynasty* spoke at a wedding held in the store, for which both bride and groom wore camouflage. Retired pro wrestler Shawn Michaels, who was hosting an adventure show on the Outdoor Channel, signed autographs.

The store performed spectacularly well in its first months, and its popularity only increased.

## CHAPTER 18

# "WHY ARE WE NOT TALKING ABOUT THIS IN THE PRESIDENTIAL DEBATES?"

I can name every coach I ever had.

From age nine on, I was shaped, encouraged, motivated, and inspired by my coaches. They left imprints that remain part of who I am. What they taught me, what I learned from my teammates, and what I had pounded into me on the field were some of the most important lessons I would ever learn. I've said it before, but it bears repeating: sports made me, and probably saved me. They kept me away from the Wigwam. They kept me focused on a goal. They taught me that hard work is its own reward. And they made clear that the universe doesn't revolve around me.

My dad had already made these discoveries years before I came along, and his entire working life, and mine, was shaped by them. And years into running Dick's, I saw my own kids receive the gifts that sports confer. It took me back to my own teenage heartbreaks and triumphs to see how excited they got about their games, how much their teammates meant to them, how eager they were to sweat and sacrifice for the game.

I remember being in the car with my daughter Katie one day during the summer before she started high school. It's a big move, going from middle to high school, and like most parents I worried about how she'd make the transition—especially because she'd tried out for varsity soccer and made the squad as an incoming freshman. She'd just gone through Hell Week, and we were in the car, making small talk about nothing in particular. We stopped for a red light. She fell quiet, looked off into space. A long moment passed. Then she turned to me and said, out of the blue, "Dad, my soccer team—we are so *tight*." In that moment, any concerns I had about how she'd manage in her freshman year vanished. She had a sense of belonging. She had a place, a group, a purpose. I knew she'd be fine.

My son Brian played high school soccer, too. A lot of the guys on the team had been playing together since the fourth grade. They'd grown into big, strong, fast kids, and they were tough. They had to be. Anybody who thinks that soccer isn't a contact sport hasn't been to a high school or college game. I'd never seen any of these kids cry. I'd seen them get concussions, blow out their ACLs, and break bones, but through it all they'd never shed a single tear.

Brian's school had never made the playoffs, but in their senior year they got there. They were playing near our house at Quaker Valley High. The score's tied, one to one, with under a minute left. Suddenly, there's a player on the opposing team running down the right sideline. Everyone's yelling, "Runner! Runner!" Brian's teammates are streaking after him, trying to cut him off. Brian sees a kid coming down the middle of the field who's going to get the cross pass, so he charges that way with a teammate, looking to get to him before the ball does, and as all converge, the guy on the sideline makes an absolutely perfect cross. All three kids in the middle go up for the ball, and somehow this one kid on the other team gets to it. With eleven seconds left on the clock, he heads it in, and the game's over.

You could have heard a pin drop on our side of the field. We couldn't believe what had happened and how suddenly it happened. After the kids got a speech from their coach and gathered their gear, I walked over. All of them had their hoods up, and every one had tears streaming down his face. They were hugging each other, crying, as I reached my son. "Brian," I said, "are you crying because you lost or because it's over?"

Suddenly, this big, tough kid of mine was five years old again. Gushing tears, he said, "Dad, it's over. It's *over*." The loss was tough, but far harder was the knowledge that they'd just played their last game together. The team was a huge piece of each of them. They'd never replicate what they'd had with each other. And they were all changed for the better by the experience.

Joe Schmidt, who was our president and a very good friend of mine, had a similar story about his son Colin, who played hockey—triple-A high school hockey, big-time stuff. When Colin was a sophomore, his team won the state title. The following year, they were trying to do it again, made it to the playoffs, and got beat in the state final. When Colin was a senior, his team made it to the playoffs again but lost in the first round. It was a shock and a real disappointment.

So Joe was waiting outside the locker room after the game for Colin to come out. Players trickled out, one after another, but no Colin. He waited and waited. A few more players. He waited. The last of the team came out—the last except for Colin. After waiting a little longer with no sign of his son, he walked in. He found Colin sitting in front of his locker, crying. He looked up as Joe approached and said, "It's over."

We understand the importance of these experiences at Dick's. They fuel us, because we believe we're doing more than just selling athletic gear: we're fostering activity that brings positive change to athletes' lives, whatever their age. Once Lauren Hobart was running our marketing, we shifted our message to reflect that belief.

Part of what drove the change were some troubling statistics that Lauren found in a youth sports participation study she was reviewing. The conclusion: participation was declining. Our initial reaction was that kids were spending too much time on their phones and playing video games, but we ultimately discovered an even more frustrating cause. All around the country, public school systems were running into budget crunches, and districts were cutting billions of dollars from their athletic programs. In the 1999–2000 school year, 11.3 percent of public high schools in the United States did not offer interscholastic sports. By ten years later, 22 percent of public high schools—more than one in five—no longer fielded sports teams. In 2013–14, the number had crept even higher, to 22.7 percent. If the trend persists, in a handful of years a quarter of our kids in public schools will not have the opportunity to play interscholastic sports.

That got my attention, as did some other worrisome trends. Some 40 percent of those school districts that still offer sports programs require fees from the players and their families. These "pay to play" requirements preclude many poor students from participating. In fact, a study that we at the Dick's Sporting Goods Foundation commissioned, and that was released in 2019, showed there is a 25 percent gap in sports participation between children of higher- and lower-income families—84 percent of kids from families making $75,000 or more per year participate, versus just 59 percent of young people whose families earn less than $30,000. When asked why their kids didn't participate, more than four in ten of the parents in those low-income households cited expense.

Some cash-strapped school districts are closing schools and combining their student bodies with those of remaining campuses. The result: fewer schools, with fewer teams, and fewer opportunities for student athletes. This consolidation puts more kids at risk.

There is more at stake than the sports programs themselves. Studies have shown that physically active kids are less likely to engage in risky behaviors—alcohol, drugs, and violence—and that their test scores are significantly higher. Student athletes have far better attendance records and fewer detentions, suspensions, and expulsions. They also graduate at a considerably higher rate and are four times more likely to attend college.

In many school systems that have suspended play, other extra-curricular activities—band, orchestra, the student newspaper and yearbook, clubs of all sorts—have also been eliminated. All of this adds up to a crisis. Take a moment and think about what your own middle school or high school experience would have been like without sports and other after-school programs. Kids need a place to go to be with their friends, where they feel they're part of something—where they're supervised, challenged, and mentored. Millions of kids today don't have those places, those influences, that camaraderie.

Coaches have an especially strong influence, because they make the decisions so important to their student athletes—who plays on Friday night. They're in a position to say, "You get your butt home and do your homework," or "You better be in class on time," and make it stick. I can tell you that from my own experience.

When we first learned of the situation, few people seemed to realize this was happening. There wasn't any great pub-lic hand-wringing about it. When the media did pay attention, it was with the apparent assumption that classroom spending trumped athletics in importance. The thinking seemed to be: if tight budgets demand cuts, sports should go first.

On one level, we could understand that. But we could also see that the sports programs facing the most immediate threats were in schools and school districts that served low-income, minor-ity communities: our research shows that high-poverty schools are two and a half times more likely to not offer interscholastic sports. And it rubbed all of us wrong that it was this very fact that had enabled the severe cuts to happen without a huge national fuss being made. I mean, if sports programs had been suspended in *my* kids' schools, it would have been splashed all over the papers. But that wasn't happening. It seemed to me that because the most affected kids were African American, or Hispanic, or Native American, society was saying, "Who cares?"

Well, I can tell you that we did. Our foundational principle—that sports build not only muscle but character, and offer lessons that students carry with them through their lives—might be more relevant in disadvantaged neighborhoods than anywhere else. Schools and students denied resources and opportunities in the classroom know well the power of sports to transform lives.

So, together with our foundation, we launched a campaign to build awareness of the problem around the country. We called it the Sports Matter initiative and were fortunate to recruit Jon Gruden, then a pro football analyst and former NFL coach, and actor Michael B. Jordan to be its spokesmen. We thought it was important to help these kids, especially those in the inner city who needed sports the most. Dick's and the foundation initially committed $25 million to the cause.

As I've mentioned, we'd thrown ourselves behind youth programs before this: Our Community Youth Sports Equipment Kit program had helped a million kids get on the field each year. In 2007, we'd become a partner in Thanks and Giving, a fundraising effort for St. Jude Children's Research Hospital.

In 2011, we'd established the Dick's Sporting Goods Foundation to coordinate all of our philanthropy. It wasn't always easy to get money to kids in need. Some of the laws that regulated our giving were incredibly restrictive, and at times seemed downright silly. In the wake of Hurricane Alex, for example, we wanted to help rebuild the youth sports programs that had been devastated, and we proposed that the Sports Matter initiative buy product from Dick's at cost to donate to them. Our lawyers stopped us. Can't do that, they said, because that's self-dealing: we'd make no money on the deal, but we couldn't, as a company, sell to a foundation over which we had control.

At first glance, and maybe in most cases, that makes sense. But here we were taking a baseball that we could get for a fraction of its retail cost and selling it to the foundation for exactly what it cost us. The foundation's money went much further. It could buy more balls. Dick's merely served as a conduit for the product. I remember saying to our general counsel, "So you're telling me that we could go to Sports Authority, our competitor, and pay much more money for the same stuff, and we'd be fine donating it?"

"That's what you have to do," he answered. "We can't buy it from ourselves."

What we elected to do in that case was leave the foundation's money untouched and just donate product straight from Dick's.

Sports Matter required a more ambitious style of giving. In 2014, the foundation launched its own crowdfunding site to give away millions of dollars to the most at-risk youth sports programs we could find. The following year, we found a more sustainable means of helping public school sports programs in a remarkable crowd-funding organization called DonorsChoose.org. It was started by a high school social studies teacher in the Bronx, Charles Best, who found he was spending a lot of his own money on supplies that his students needed but couldn't afford. It occurred to Best that people might be willing to help, if they knew exactly how their money was being spent. So in 2000, with the help of his students, he built a website that connected needy classrooms and would-be philanthropists.

It's beautifully simple. A teacher in need goes to the Donors Choose.org website and lists a specific need for his or her class, including a line-item budget. People who want to give go to the site and find a need they'd like to help meet. They can donate as little as a dollar. When the budget for the need has been met, DonorsChoose.org buys the requested supplies and ships them directly to the teacher. And when those supplies are put to use, the donor gets a letter from the teacher (and students, in the case of bigger donations) and a report on exactly how the money helped.

At first, the program served only those in the New York metropolitan area. But in June 2003, Oprah Winfrey shone a spotlight on DonorsChoose.org, sparking $250,000 in almost overnight donations and so much sustained traffic that, by 2007, the program was available to every public school teacher in the United States.

It didn't take a lot of smarts to see that partnering with Donors Choose.org would get our money to where it was needed most, because the people closest to the needs would be making the requests. We set up our partnership so that we'd match donations to any sports-related request—a project would need to achieve only half its crowdsourced funding before we'd step in with the other half.

Between 2015 and 2018, the partnership pumped more than $10.5 million into needy programs across the country, directly helping more than 650,000 students. On Giving Tuesday in late November 2018, we committed another $5 million to the effort, to be parceled out over three years. We'll keep doing it for years to come.

Apart from our partnership with DonorsChoose.org, our foundation created an in-house community grant program aimed at helping high-poverty schools, leagues, and sports programs. We put up a million dollars in cash for a wide range of uses, from buying equipment to field repairs to subsidizing player participation fees.

In 2016 alone, Dick's and the foundation together gave more than $30 million to teams, leagues, community groups, and schools to buy gear. Our customers pitched in, too. In every store, at every register, during every transaction at certain times of the year, they could choose to make a donation to the Sports Matter program. During the 2018 holidays, we also held in-store events starring pro athletes and benefiting more than three hundred underserved kids. Chiefs quarterback Patrick Mahomes II, Eagles linebacker Nigel Bradham, and Phoenix Suns star Devin Booker were among the pros who took kids shopping at Dick's, giving them a once-in-a-lifetime experience along with the gift of sports.

• • •

Sports Matter occupied a lot of our attention. We made it central to our Web presence and to signage around the registers in our stores. But the most successful and surprising of our strategies might have been the stories about real athletes that we put before the public in the form of movies. If you'd told me a few years ago that Dick's or its foundation would be in the movie business, I'd have called you crazy, but in truth, it just makes sense as part of who we are. When we say that sports change people's lives for the better, it isn't pro athletes we're talking about. It's amateurs, often kids struggling against all sorts of odds to play, let alone play well. Amateur sports abound with great, dramatic, true stories, and we realized that by telling them well, we could push the message that sports matter far more effectively than if we bought a dozen Super Bowl commercials. We could *show* that they matter, rather than just insist that they do. We could invite people into the lives of student athletes and, by sharing their pain, uncertainty, commitment, victories, and defeats, as well as the challenges they face off the field, bring home the message that sports are essential to building a vital society and not mere luxuries when it comes to public funding.

We had no idea how to do this, so we got help. Tribeca Digital Studios, based in New York, pairs with companies or brands to produce content-driven documentaries, legitimate nonfiction film narratives that help their clients make a point. Some are ninety seconds long. Some are full-length movies.

We teamed with TDS to find and film stories that made our point. The first was a series of short documentaries that followed high school football players preparing for their upcoming season at a weeklong sleepaway summer training camp. The first *Hell Week* doc took a week of shooting, and we realized, in the process of putting it together, that we liked stories that took a while to tell.

Philadelphia gave us an opportunity to go even deeper. In 2012, the city's school district grappled with a shortfall of more than $300 million by instituting its infamous "doomsday budget," shuttering twenty-four schools, laying off thousands of teachers, and canceling many extracurricular programs, including athletics. Among the schools shut down was Germantown High School, violence plagued and for generations the bitter rival of similarly troubled Martin Luther King High. The stage was set for a great drama. First, the district decreed that Germantown's students would be attending MLK. That was bound to be stormy. Second, MLK planned to field a football team combining players from both schools, despite (a) the long history of enmity between the two, (b) having no money for the program and no paid coaches on staff, and (c) MLK's abysmal gridiron record—the school had won just one game in two years.

It was risky. To begin with, we didn't know how the experiment would turn out—this wasn't a story we could script ahead of time. The school's attempt to unite the two teams into one might fall apart for any number of reasons. The environment was gritty, the players unpredictable. "I educate the kids no one else wants," as MLK's principal put it. Half or more of the school's students failed to graduate. Odds were, it *would* fall apart.

But the MLK story epitomized the crises going on all across the country. We decided we'd take it on, and however it came out, it came out. This was real life in an American inner city. Tribeca's group was equally excited to tell this story. They introduced us to a wonderful filmmaker named Judd Ehrlich. Once he came aboard, our main job was to stay out of Judd's way, as he and his crew practically moved in with members of the team and its volunteer coach, a laid-off Germantown math teacher named Ed Dunn.

The result was *We Could Be King*, a feature-length documentary about the MLK football team's 2014 season. If you haven't seen it, you should—I won't spoil it by telling you how it turns out, except to say that it's an amazing story, inspirational beyond our hopes, and a great testament to the redemptive power of sports. It's got a lot of heroes, but none as impressive as Coach Dunn. This guy was so good to these kids, so supportive, and so important to them. As you watch the film, one truth comes to the fore: without football, a lot of these kids aren't going to school. There's a scene at a school board meeting where a former student says as much, and for me it's the most profound statement in the movie. Football is the best thing these kids have, their slim tether to self-respect and a future. If they're not practicing, working hard, what are they doing? It's tough to get to a good place with the answer. And if you broaden their situation to include kids at the hundreds or thousands of American schools like Martin Luther King High, the importance of sports—and the key role they play in the country's health five, ten, fifteen years down the road—really hits you.

*We Could Be King* premiered at the Tribeca Film Festival. Four hundred people were in the theater, including the MLK football team, their parents, the principal, Coach Dunn. None of them had seen it. Everyone was blown away. The event's emcee was Mike Golic, the host of ESPN's *Mike in the Morning* and a former Notre Dame and Philadelphia Eagles standout, and when the closing credits finished rolling, he stood up. "You know, I had a pretty good football career," he said. "But I had one more thing that I wish I could have done in my career. I wish I could have played for you, Coach Dunn." The place went nuts.

After that, the movie was shown on ESPN. The *New York Times* decided it had "a memorable season's worth of moving stories to tell on and off the field, as rich as any in *Friday Night Lights.*" That article, and a rush of other press, established a linkage between the movie's message and Dick's. "Forget sports equipment and sneakers," the *New York Post* wrote. "Dick's Sporting Goods is focusing on the human drama of athletic competition through movies these days. Via its foundation, which focuses on youth sports, the retailer is generating a lot of buzz."

*We Could Be King* won the 2015 Emmy for Outstanding Sports Documentary, which generated still more media attention, cementing our connection to the film. The overall Sports Matter program also won a Grand Clio—the Oscars of the advertising world—for integrated marketing. Which brings up an interesting question: does this kind of purpose-driven investment in storytelling really work? In terms of making the case that sports matter, there's no doubt about it. *We Could Be King* argued the point in ways we, at Dick's and our foundation, couldn't. But here's a benefit that might not be so obvious—being associated with a story that people can get behind, their good feelings about the story rub off on us. We did well by doing good.

There's a lesson in that for American business.

Lauren Hobart, who did a lot to deserve the Emmy statuette she received, got to know the coach and many of his players over the course of filming. She came to really like one kid, a gifted cornerback who, halfway through the season, missed several games because he was jailed in a case of being in the wrong place at the wrong time. "You know what?" she told him. "You get out of high school and you go to college, and then come see me, and I'll give you a job." We'll have to see what happens, but it could be that the movie will bring us further benefits.

Our experience with *We Could Be King* made us eager to try another story. Again with Judd Ehrlich at the helm, we focused on a group of Native American girls at upstate New York's Salmon River High School who were trying to organize an interscholastic lacrosse team, despite fierce resistance from their Mohawk elders, who felt the game was a sacred gift to men, and men alone.

As producers, our foundation team recognized that women's lacrosse wouldn't gain the immediate traction with audiences that football enjoys. But we felt it important to make the point that the transcendent value of sports isn't restricted to the big four games. You don't need to pack a stadium to enjoy the benefits of sports.

So, knowing that the whole film could implode, Judd again glued himself to the students, their parents, their coaches. Some of these kids faced life-and-death challenges off the field. Partway through the season, one girl tried to commit suicide by drinking chlorine bleach. Over time, her lacrosse teammates brought her back to life. The team's unity of purpose, its camaraderie, restored her. Other kids struggling with self-esteem issues, parenting troubles, and academic woes blossomed over the course of the season. Again, I won't say too much about what actually happens in the film, but I was amazed at how intimate it was. You can't help thinking, as you watch it, *How on earth did they do this?* Judd's cameras witnessed really private moments that are startling in places and rich throughout. The result, *Keepers of the Game*, is a terrific movie.

Our foundation premiered it at Tribeca in 2016. Lauren came up with the idea of assembling a panel to talk about the importance of sports right after the screening. We thought we'd invite 250 people to dinner, to hear this panel of athletes and others involved in sports, and to be honest we worried a little, as we sent out the invitations, about whether we'd get enough panelists. You know what? We got so many positive responses that we put together two panels. John Skipper, the president of ESPN, appeared, and Kevin Plank, founder of Under Armour, and Mark King, president of Adidas North America. Tim Finchem, commissioner of the PGA Tour. Rob Manfred, commissioner of Major League Baseball. Tom Brady, Serena Williams, Missy Franklin, and Jessica Mendoza.

Hannah Storm, the ESPN anchor, moderated the discussion, and the stories these athletes told about how important sports had been to them, and how vital they were in general, were just fantastic. Serena Williams was a wonderful spokesperson for the cause. Brady was great. "This is so important," Tim Finchem said. "Why are we not talking about this in the presidential debates?" The event, like the film, attracted another round of wonderful media attention and hammered home the message that sports really do matter in our kids' lives.

I'm tremendously proud of *Keepers of the Game*. I'm so pleased that we were able to tell this story. I hope a lot of people see it. I defy anyone who does to be unmoved and to not understand the stakes involved.

I've always felt, as I suspect my father did, that our country's most precious natural resource is our children. They're our future, and right now we're not investing enough time or money in them. We don't prioritize their educational, emotional, and social development.

That's especially evident at under-budgeted schools serving underserved populations. I believe income inequality is one of the metastasizing cancers in our society, and that its root cause is educational inequality. We need to come together as a nation and make a real priority of providing a quality education for every one of our children, no matter their means. With its wealth and know-how, America should have the best primary education system on the planet. We fall far short of that.

To nurture, protect, develop, encourage, and empower our most precious natural resource, we must educate our children. Our health as a country and the place we occupy in the world is dependent on it.

# CHAPTER 19

# "READ ME THE NASTY ONES"

In February 2018, when I caught the first word of another mass shooting, this one at a school one county away from our Florida house, I was heartsick. Five years had passed since Newtown, and similar shootings had happened with growing regularity since. Yet as a society, we were no closer to solving the issue of gun violence in America. In fact, we were probably further from meaningful dialogue than we'd ever been.

The response to these terrible events had become numbingly predictable. In Washington, both political parties went right to their respective playbooks, and the media did the same. Networks and newspapers would crank out stories that bolstered whichever side they'd hitched their wagons to. And so there was never any serious effort to sit down and discuss the problem, let alone seek a solution. Everyone would talk past each other until another controversy came along, after which the matter would be dropped. John Boehner had been right.

Now, inevitably, it had happened again. I turned on the TV in my office and watched the coverage from Parkland, Florida. Saw aerial footage of kids filing out of Marjory Stoneman Douglas High School, escorted by police. Listened as reporters repeated a few scant details of what had happened inside the building. Felt my heart sink as it became clear that many students, and perhaps a few teachers, were dead. Waited, along with many at Dick's, for a mention of the shooter's name.

It was Valentine's Day.

As that afternoon unfolded, more details of the tragedy emerged. Seventeen students and teachers were dead. An equal number had been wounded. It appeared the shooter was a former student at the school, who was arrested as he walked home through a nearby neighborhood. I don't recall whether we had the gunman's name by the time Donna and I took off for Florida, but we were both preoccupied on the flight; our conversation centered on the day's news. I remember feeling deeply saddened and thinking that something had to be done to stop the madness. *Something* had to be done.

And a thought came to me that wasn't entirely welcome. Maybe we were part of the problem. Maybe the fact that we did everything by the book didn't matter. Maybe that was merely an excuse, a justification. We went through corporate torture every time one of these incidents happened, worried sick that we'd sold the means to cause harm. Why keep doing this?

We hadn't been long on the ground when I sent an email to Lauren Hobart, who by now was our president, and Lee Belitsky, our CFO. "Lauren/Lee," it read, "I would like us to develop a plan to exit the gun business."

Looking back on it, amid my frustration and horror at the day's events, I felt compelled to do *something*—to make some gesture that not only ensured we wouldn't be part of the story when these events happened, but that also threw light on the alarming regularity of the tragedies and maybe, just maybe, provoked a wider response.

That seemed even more necessary when, shortly after I sent that email, our corporate manager of investigations ran the Parkland shooter's name through our files and came up with a hit. "The shooter has been identified as Nikolas Jacob Cruz, 19," he wrote in an email to the Dick's leadership team, "and he is linked to the purchase of one Maverick 12 gauge shotgun.

"The gun was sold at a Dick's Sporting Goods, store 684, Boynton Beach, FL on 12/9/17," the message continued. "He also purchased 12 gauge ammunition on 11/21/17 and 11/25/17 from the same store." My God. There it was. A mass shooter had armed himself at a Dick's store. "At this time," the email concluded, "it cannot be definitively determined if the gun purchased from the company was used in this incident."

Donna and I drove to a restaurant a few minutes from the house and about an hour's drive from Parkland. What followed was not a romantic Valentine's Day dinner. From where we sat, we could see TVs over at the bar, tuned to continuing news coverage of the murders. Students who'd survived the mayhem were interviewed on-screen, along with a procession of rattled parents. We couldn't hear what they were saying, but we didn't need to. The story was all too familiar.

Donna and I talked about those parents—how we couldn't imagine seeing our own kids off to school, to a supposed safe haven, a place we trusted to look after them, then getting a frantic afternoon call from a friend or another parent, asking: "Have you seen the news?" The terror that would bring—or, many times worse, the blood-freezing experience of having the police show up at our door, speaking the unspeakable—would be a parent's worst nightmare.

That the Parkland massacre fell on a day traditionally devoted to love made the brutality of the act all the harder to get our heads around. How many Valentine's Day mornings had we sent our kids out of the house with a kiss, expecting that the hours ahead would be filled with the promise of puppy love? Donna had tears in her eyes. "If that ever happened to us, I don't know how I could go on," she told me.

It was hard not to personalize the deaths. My own kids weren't long out of school. This could have been them. I got pretty emotional, sitting there. I felt so strongly for the parents. Couldn't fathom what they were feeling and didn't want to try too hard to

273

do it—it seemed so big a hurt that it scared me. I felt even more resolved that we had to do something.

We weren't much in the mood to linger long after dinner. Back at the house, we turned on the TV and watched more of the coverage. We couldn't stay away from it. And by now, more details were trickling out. The shooter had arrived by Uber shortly before classes were dismissed, had pulled a fire alarm, and had stood in the hall as the kids left their classrooms, slaughtering anyone who came within range. And he hadn't used a shotgun—meaning he hadn't used the weapon he'd purchased at Dick's. He'd used an AR-15. News reports indicated he'd fired one hundred fifty rounds in six and a half minutes.

While we sat in front of the TV, the Dick's team was busy back in Pittsburgh, preparing to answer any questions that might arise from our having sold this lunatic a firearm. Those questions would almost surely come, regardless of whether he carried that particular firearm into the school. Shortly before eleven p.m., Lauren sent me a draft of a statement we might release "if we should get embroiled in a discussion" about this suspect. She and the staff were continuing to work on it, she said, but in the meantime she wanted my feedback.

The statement said that we were saddened beyond words by the loss of life. It noted that the shooter "did not purchase the firearm involved in Wednesday's horrific tragedy from our store." If the word was out that this guy had shopped at Dick's, we'd acknowledge selling him a shotgun but stress that he "purchased the gun in compliance with all state and federal laws and background checks." It concluded by underlining our commitment to the safety of our customers, our employees, and the communities we served.

"Sounds good," I wrote back. "This is such a tragedy! I feel like we are watching Sandy Hook all over again!"

I knew, even as I typed, that we'd have to do more. Limiting our response to denying that we'd had a role in this particular tragedy wasn't near enough. We were a major gun retailer. We had to be part of a solution. Besides, if this guy bought a shotgun from us, he could have bought any firearm. It was an accident of geography that we hadn't sold him the AR-15. We didn't have any Field & Stream stores in Florida, but we had five of them within a ten- or eleven-hour drive of Parkland—one in South Carolina, one in Georgia, and three in Alabama—and thirty more across the country. Soon enough would come other mass murders, and the next time we might find ourselves the ones who'd put the weapons in the shooter's hands.

Through the next day, and for two days after that, Donna and I seemed to spend more time in front of the TV than at any other point in our marriage. We were riveted by the most remarkable part of the Parkland story, which came after the smoke had cleared: the surviving students of Marjory Stoneman Douglas stepped forward and declared that no other teenager should ever endure the heartache and fear they knew—that every American kid had a right to safe schools, a right to live without menace from guns. The country's "grown-ups" had failed them. They couldn't fail others. The violence had to stop here.

And this was clearly not going to be a short-lived campaign. These kids were serious about keeping the issue of guns and school safety in the country's face. "Never Again" was their battle cry. They were incredibly well-spoken in front of the cameras. I marveled at their courage. And the parents of slain students expressed their anger and sense of loss with a steady-nerved eloquence that I knew I couldn't have mustered. Donna and I found ourselves shaking our heads in wonder and feeling, at some level, a certain degree of guilt—one we shared with America's other political and corporate leaders. All of us, an entire generation, had shirked our responsibilities. We were failing the nation's children. *We had to do something.*

Fueling my sense of urgency was a bit of unwelcome news from Vermont. Just a day after the Parkland shooting, a troubled eighteen-year-old was arrested after making detailed plans to shoot up his former high school in rural Fair Haven. An alarmed friend turned him in, precluding an attack, but a check of our files revealed that we'd sold him a twelve-gauge shotgun that he evidently intended to use.

I'm not much of a crier. I'm a pretty stoic guy. But over those days in Florida I cried more than I'd cried since my mother died. So that weekend, I wrote a first draft of a position paper for Dick's. It opened by saying how much respect we had for the young people behind the "Never Again" drive, and that our thoughts and prayers were with "so many of you that have lost loved ones, friends and mentors." But thoughts and prayers weren't enough, I wrote. "We need to take action to address this problem."

I then offered a list of recommendations. Some were vague— the first item on the list was "revision of gun laws"—but others were aimed at specific targets: A "ban on assault-style weapons." A change in laws nationwide "to include 21 as the required age for buying guns." A ban on the bump stock. A nationwide waiting period for gun sales, during which a buyer's social media posts, as well as his or her criminal record, would be checked.

"We respect the Constitution and the Second Amendment, and we are not asking for a ban on guns," I wrote. "We sold Cruz a shotgun. While it was not the gun used in the Parkland shooting, it could have been. We followed all the rules and still sold a gun to this kid."

Further along, I switched from "we" to "I." "I encourage our lawmakers to come together to find a solution to this problem," I wrote. "That's your job! The country needs for you to put partisan politics aside and thoroughly discuss and pass a practical solution. We do not want to hear partisan discourse, and we implore each side to work toward a comprehensive solution. This is too important."

I was in emotional turmoil when I wrote one of the final points I made in the document: "Until we are confident there are checks and balances that ensure we are not going to sell a gun to someone who plans to walk out of our store and kill, we are suspending the sale of guns."

• • •

Monday morning, back in Pittsburgh, we convened a meeting of the leadership team. We start each week with a meeting as a matter of course, but this one was hours earlier than usual, and everyone knew that the Parkland shooting had affected me in a big way. I opened by saying we had to take some dramatic action. I said, "We have to take a stand here. We don't want to be part of this. And we can actually do something about it—a small thing, maybe, but it's a start. And we should." I had the draft with me and started to read it—and halfway through, I got so choked up that I couldn't speak. Our chief of staff, Ami Galani, took the paper from my hand and read the rest of it.

All ten people in the room favored most of the points I'd made in my draft. Just one caused concern—suspending the sale of guns. Some people asked: Are we sure we really want to do that? The problem, they pointed out, wasn't all guns—it was specific weapons. And what kind of impact would such a move have on the bottom line? I didn't care about that second point and said so. It seemed the right thing to do, and that was more important to me than earnings. I asked them: "Do we have to wait for this to happen to one of our kids?" Well, okay, Lee Belitsky said, but I'm just going to run some numbers so we have them. We're a public company, and we're going to have to guide the Street about what we're doing, and the first thing everyone will want to know is how it will affect revenue and earnings.

The conversation turned to discussing in greater detail just how extensive this suspension of sales should be. And really, that conversation continued for the next six days, because as a group we found it a tough question to fully answer. Here was the issue: the margin rate on guns was not great, but hunters bought not only guns, they also bought hunting coats, boots, socks, and a host of other products that are very profitable. All told, our hunting and outdoor business approached $1 billion in sales per year.

Beyond that, hunting had been a mainstay of Dick's business

since the company's earliest days. It remained an important category for a lot of our customers. If we stopped selling guns altogether, we'd be punishing those customers, some of whom had been with us for sixty years—men and women who knew to treat firearms with respect and who used them for legitimate sport. Did it make sense to needlessly alienate loyal Dick's customers who bought shotguns and deer rifles, and were law-abiding and do-right citizens?

The draft I read at that February 19 meeting was just that, and over the following week it went through a lot of changes as we tried to come up with a stance that made a strong statement but wasn't pointlessly broad. Even as we talked, the "Never Again" movement was gaining traction, and we started getting calls from customers and the public at large, asking whether we planned to take any action on guns.

Eventually, we reached a consensus that we might have more impact if we narrowed our focus down to the actual source of trouble—the guns favored by mass shooters. Which is to say, AR-15s and similar rifles, along with the accessories that went with them. We had never put assault-style rifles back on the shelves at Dick's after Sandy Hook, but as I've mentioned, we did sell them in our thirty-five Field & Stream stores.

You might think that we wouldn't have much at stake by pulling just the assault-style rifles: how much money could we lose by cutting one type of product at just 5 percent of our stores? Ah, but that's not how this works. Guns are such a polarizing issue that we stood to lose a *lot* of customers. There were millions of people out there who might not have owned or wanted an AR-15, but who would be plenty pissed that we'd removed them from our stores, and I mean angry enough that we'd never see them again.

We'd learned that after Sandy Hook. We'd won accolades from a lot of people after we pulled those rifles from Dick's, but we got an equal or greater response from people who vowed they'd never give us another penny. A couple of years later, the folks who'd supported our decision didn't even remember we'd made it. But you can bet that the people we'd pissed off remembered, and they'd been true to their word. They never came back.

So there was a lot more to lose than just the income from a few rifles at a few stores. The people we'd anger didn't just buy firearms from us. They bought baseball gloves, running shoes, and sportswear for themselves and their families. We estimated that the damage would amount to well over a quarter-billion dollars. The numbers crunching that Lee undertook after we met that Monday soon arrived at that figure: two hundred and fifty million dollars in sales, at a *minimum*. We got our finance group working on it and ultimately concluded that we could survive the blow. We'd have to work hard at it, but we thought we could offset the loss by boosting sales in other categories.

Even if we fell short, I was okay with it. The choice seemed plain. If those kids from Parkland could muster up the courage to take their fight to the country, we had to be brave enough to make this move. Still, it would hurt. And we'd take flak for some of the other pieces of our emerging position. We proposed to pull large-capacity magazines along with the rifles and reaffirm our commitment to never carry bump stocks. We would no longer sell any firearm to anyone under twenty-one years of age, though many state laws allowed teenagers to buy and possess rifles and shotguns.

As Friday approached, we made arrangements to consult with the board of directors. We have an active board. It meets quarterly, plus once for a strategic meeting each year. Its Audit Committee meets an additional time each quarter to review our performance and our strategy for releasing and framing our quarterly results. So it's very hands-on, very involved. Naturally, the members would want to chew on what we were proposing to do.

As we often do when we have an urgent matter to discuss with the board, we set up a telephonic board meeting. Actually, we set up two—one to unveil our plans, and a second after the members had had time to digest it, to get their official approval. Before the first call, I spoke with Bill Colombo about what we had in mind. With all we'd been through together, I owed it to him. And, of course, I valued his input—though I was pretty sure he wouldn't like the plan. Bill had long been a vocal defender of Second Amendment rights. He had a permit to carry a concealed handgun. He was an active target shooter.

Sure enough, he pushed back. Yes, he said, the country had a real problem on its hands, but it wasn't with guns—it was with the people who used them. The shooter at Parkland had used an AR-15, but if he hadn't had that, he would have used another weapon, perhaps the shotgun he'd bought from us. And if he couldn't get to that, he might have used something else. The problem was the nut job, not the implement he chose.

I understood his argument, though the *New York Times* had not long before published a report that made a convincing case that our "astronomical number of guns" does, in fact, contribute to the higher incidence of mass shootings in the United States, compared to other countries.* The article relied on a 2015 study that found a strong correlation between a country's rate of gun ownership and the likelihood of mass shootings there. I believed we owed it to ourselves, as well as our fellow Americans, to take a principled stand. Somebody had to be the first to *do* something, instead of talk about it.

Bill ultimately supported our decision, despite his reservations. The board as a whole supported us as well, though not without questions about the effects of our plan on sales and earnings. The board shares our fiduciary duty to our shareholders, and they wanted reassurance that we'd thought this through. Satisfied that we had, they gave us the green light.

I suppose that the fact that I sat down and wrote up that draft manifesto in Florida suggests that I always intended to take a

---

*Max Fisher and Josh Keller, "What Explains U.S. Mass Shootings? International Comparisons Suggest an Answer," November 7, 2017.

public stand about guns in the wake of the Parkland shootings. But I don't know that I did: when I read—or tried to read—the draft to the leadership team, I viewed it as an internal document, a position paper that we could use to guide our corporate behavior, but not something that we'd necessarily be sharing with the outside world. My default style in such circumstances is to simply take action without announcing it, as we had after Sandy Hook.

But members of the leadership team were quick to remind me that that approach had blown up in our faces in 2012. Because we never spelled out what we were doing when the assault-style rifles vanished from our shelves, we opened the door to others with their own agendas to interpret our actions to the public. We lost control of our own narrative.

None of us wanted to see that happen again. So by the time we consulted with the board, we were mulling how we might make it absolutely clear what we were doing and why. We needed to reach three different constituencies with the message: our customers, first and foremost; our stockholders; and not least, our teammates, the forty thousand people who worked for the company.

It seemed to me that we ought to simply release the edited statement, which announced the changes we were putting into effect at our stores, and also urge Congress to get off its collective duff and get its act together on some meaningful reform. Put that out, pull the guns from the stores, and be done with it.

Our leadership team, along with our outside public relations consultants, argued that if we wanted to have the greatest possible impact with our announcement—if we wanted to truly influence public opinion—we might want to go bigger than a press release. This is a big deal, they said. This deserves something more.

We weren't sure what that might look like and were still trying to sort that out when, on the second weekend after the shooting, Lauren alerted me that she'd heard from a well-connected friend in Washington. "He is observing the dialogue down in DC actively," she wrote, "and believes there is mounting frustration with the lack of [political response to Parkland]. He feels that the tide might turn toward calling for boycotts on gun retailers such as Walmart and possibly us. . . ." That put a fire under me. I wrote back that I wanted "to make a statement before we are forced to make the statement we are planning to make anyway. I don't want it to look like we caved." Which meant moving quickly.

We'd planned to hold an off-site strategy meeting beginning the next day. We should have canceled the thing and dived straight into figuring out how to get our message on guns out immediately. But we didn't—we all convened in Sea Island, Georgia, the next morning, and only once we were there decided we should get back to Pittsburgh and hammer out a strategy, that it couldn't wait. We spent maybe two hours on the ground at Sea Island.

Back home, the team talked with our public relations advisers and proposed that we announce our decision on national TV— that we book an interview with one of the morning news shows as soon as possible so that I could explain what we were doing and how important we felt it was. I wasn't enthusiastic about the suggestion. I'd been on TV a few times but was hardly a recognizable face, which suited me fine. There's little real advantage to being a celebrity CEO. I enjoyed simply running the company.

But the issue was extremely important to me, and to Dick's. If we, as a major firearms dealer, recognized that the country's gun laws had too many inconsistencies and not enough spine, we should stand up and say so. Maybe some good would come of it. And besides, I couldn't stop thinking about those kids and parents in Parkland.

Which worried me, because every time I did think of them, I got emotional. I was scared to death that I'd lose it on the air. Even so, I agreed to do two shows—ABC's *Good Morning America* and the morning show on CNN. So it was that at 7:08 a.m. on Wednesday, February 28—two weeks after the shooting—I sat with George Stephanopoulos on the *Good Morning America* set.

By sheer coincidence, that was also the morning that classes resumed at Marjory Stoneman Douglas, and the airwaves were packed with stories about the kids and how they were faring.

While we were waiting to be ushered into the studio, I'd avoided the reports. And once seated across from Stephanopoulos, I kept one hand under the desk and pinched the hell out of a finger, hard enough to cause a fair amount of pain, just so that I'd stay focused and keep from tearing up.

I told him how saddened we'd been by the attack, that we'd felt compelled to take action in response. We discussed the fact that the shooter had bought a shotgun from us. That had been part of our impetus for taking the assault-style rifles off the shelves, I explained: "The systems that are in place across the board just aren't effective enough to keep us from selling someone like that a gun."

Stephanopoulos: "Any regrets at all about not taking a move like this sooner? After Newtown, after Sandy Hook, you announced a temporary suspension of assault weapons sales but then came back to selling."

Me: "We did. We said we were going to temporarily take them out of the Dick's stores, the Dick's Sporting Goods stores. We never put them back in the Dick's stores. They've not been in the Dick's Sporting Goods stores. And then, in 2013, we developed a chain, Field & Stream, which was a full-on hunting and outdoors store. And we put them in those stores.

"But based on what's happened, and looking at those kids, and those parents, it moved us all unimaginably." I was fighting, here, to keep my voice from cracking. "And to think about the loss and the grief that those kids and those parents had, we said we need to do something, and we're taking these guns out of *all* of our stores, permanently."

Stephanopoulos: "So yeah, no chance you're going to reverse this?"

Me: "Never."

Stephanopoulos: "Are you ready for the backlash?"

"We are," I told him. Over the previous few days we'd refined our estimates of what this move would cost us: at least $300 million in sales, possibly more. We estimated our business would be flat, or worse, for the year—in a company that rarely failed to see growth. I didn't share all that, instead saying: "We know that this isn't going to make everyone happy."

Stephanopoulos changed tacks. "You want Congress to act as well."

"We do," I said. "We hope that they'll act and pull something together. We don't want to see the partisan politics, where one side espouses their position, the other side espouses their position, and they actually never do anything."

At the end, Stephanopoulos nodded. "It's a big move," he said. I walked out of the studio, relieved that it was over. Only really, the day's excitement was just beginning. While I was on the air, my executive assistant, Vanessa Ellis, had mass-emailed a letter I'd written to every Dick's employee. "Dear Associate," it read. "Today, our Company is taking a stand in support of the kids in Parkland and all children across our Country who are unifying to have their voices heard following the tragic, unimaginable loss from gun violence." From there, it laid out exactly what we were going to do in our stores and what we hoped Congress would do.

At the same time that letter went out, we posted an announcement of our actions on the Dick's website. Within minutes, the *New York Times* published a story about my ABC appearance. Members of the leadership team held a conference call with store managers.

All of this happened fast, but not as fast as the public response. It was the number one trending story on Twitter. We had more than an hour before I was due to appear on CNN, so when we reached its studio I had a Coke and Lauren started to read some of the reactions to me from Twitter and elsewhere. She started with the nice comments. Thousands were writing to thank us. Some said they'd never shopped at a Dick's store before but would now. There were so many warm, emotional comments from parents thanking us for making the world safer for their kids that I got choked up, listening—I told her to instead read me the nasty ones, so that I could get ahold of my emotions.

And oh, there were so many to choose from. Most of the worst on Twitter have been removed, but here's a sampling of comments made on newspaper websites just after they picked up the story:

*"I hope this goddamn place folds and goes under! They have always been politically correct. . . . Any hunters, target shooters or sportsman should cease doing business with this rathole, Dick's. F\*\*k 'em!"*

*"This is FACISM. . . . You stupid puppets who can't think for yourself will be the downfall of America as we know it. You gulp down propaganda like it was the word of god. You stupid sheep don't know how YOU are being used."*

*"What the dickheads at dick's don't understand is, any weapon can be used in an assault. Assault is an action, not an object."*

*"I will never buy anything from a Dicks. I can not stand businesses that can not mind their own business."*

*"I will never buy from you again. . . . After serving nearly 30 years in the military, I don't know how you can justify not selling a gun to a military member who may be under 21."*

*"As expected, the gun-hating maggots ooze forth from the cesspools of their ignorant fascist lives."*

*"In other news, Dick's Sporting Goods announced a change in the company name to Pussy's Sporting Goods which more accurately reflects the recent change in policy."*

Believe me, there were worse. Much worse. Many hung some choice labels on me, personally. Some were even more poorly spelled and punctuated. But hearing this blowback had an invigorating effect on me. It got my adrenaline pumping. It pissed me off. And anger is a clean burn. When I went onto the CNN set for my sit-down with Chris Cuomo, I was no longer in danger of breaking up on camera. I was ready for a street fight.

When I finished that interview, an avalanche of interview requests was rolling in—we got more than four hundred of them. I wasn't interested. We'd said as much as we needed to, and to continue going on TV to repeat the message would have made us look like publicity hounds. I said no to all of the requests but one: Lauren and our communications director, Jennifer Moreau, convinced me that I should do one evening news spot. We taped an interview with NBC that aired that night.

By the time we left New York, all hell was breaking loose. The response of some people was so unhinged that Lauren and I both had security details for the next couple of weeks—we were tailed by serious-looking guys wherever we went, and they stood sentry outside our houses. Donna got a bit exasperated by it all. "Can you do me a favor?" she asked me. "The next time you decide to piss a lot of people off, could you not do it to guys who have guns?"

About sixty-five of our own employees quit right away in protest, and more followed in later weeks, people up and down the organization. We have a cross-section of the country working with us, so it didn't surprise me that some were upset with us. I felt how emotionally charged this issue is even more personally. A great friend of mine—a friend of twenty-five years, a guy I'd gone on vacation and had Thanksgiving dinner with—sent me some text messages about how upset he was. Then he sent me a video of some guy in North Carolina talking nonsense—*you take my guns away, there's gonna be hell to pay*, etc. My friend wrote: "This is exactly how I feel." I was in no mood for it. We didn't communicate for months after that.

But the negative backlash, hot as it was, was overwhelmed by the positive response to our decision. People came into our stores with donuts, pizzas, and flowers for the staff. We got thousands of emails and letters. The manager of our store closest to Parkland emailed us the day after my TV appearances. "Before yesterday, my community continued to struggle with healing," he wrote. "That began to change at 7:15 AM yesterday. Thus far I have received 42 phone calls of support, and 17 walk ins that wanted to speak directly with the store manager."

People who needed nothing from us organized "buycotts" to give us business; one Los Angeles restaurant even offered a

10 percent discount to anyone with a Dick's receipt. Even Jim Cramer, the financial guy on TV, said, "I applaud anyone with a conscience." He doubled down on that later, saying that "if you're hunting with an AR-15, you're hunting humans."

And there was this: Walmart came out with its own announcement that they wouldn't sell guns or ammunition to anyone under twenty-one, either. Kroger announced that its Fred Meyer stores, forty-three of which sold guns, would bump up the minimum age, too—and Fred Meyer would stop selling assault-style rifles at its stores in Alaska, the only place it made them available. REI, the Seattle-based outfitters, stopped taking orders from Vista Outdoor, which owned such respected outdoor brands as CamelBak, Bell, Camp Chef, and Bollé, but earned most of its money making and selling firearms and aligned itself closely with the NRA.

We seemed to have started a shift. And momentum seemed to be building to something good.

# CHAPTER 20

# "BE BRAVE ENOUGH
# TO DO YOUR JOBS"

What did we hope would happen in the weeks after our February 28 announcement? Well, for starters, we hoped that the groundswell against assault-style rifles would build. That Congress would start debating in some meaningful way about them, and ultimately reinstitute the ban that kept them off the market for ten years. We hoped that while they were at it, they'd take a hard look at the inconsistencies of gun laws in general.

Consider that you have to be twenty-one to buy a handgun from a federally licensed firearms dealer, but you can lawfully buy a rifle—even an assault-style rifle—at eighteen. If you're buying from an *unlicensed* seller, federal law says you only have to be eighteen to buy a handgun, and there's no age restriction at all on shotguns and rifles.

Here's an inconsistency that makes even less sense: if I buy a rifle from a private seller on the Internet, I don't have to undergo a background check unless the seller lives in another state. The loophole at gun shows is well documented. A gun show can take place across the street from Dick's, and the rules for the sellers there will vary, depending on who they are. We and any other federally licensed dealers have to follow the same laws we'd follow in the store. But an unlicensed seller can show up with guns and sell them without background checks. Finally, there's this outrage: If you're on the no-fly list, you've been deemed too dangerous to sit on an airplane. But it won't stop you from buying a gun.

Where is the common sense here? It was this kind of inconsistency that convinced us we should put some muscle behind our talk about gun reform, so in March we made several trips to DC to speak with members of the House and Senate. A lot of the people we met had no grasp on the current laws, which was an unpleasant surprise. We met others who understood the laws but had no intention of changing them. A few others wanted such overreaching change that they had no hope of getting a dialogue going.

In general, the Democrats were sympathetic but told us they were blocked from action by the Republican majority in both houses of Congress. The Republicans said they didn't think there was need for reform. One of my conversations was with Senator Pat Toomey, a Pennsylvania Republican, our own man in Washington. It got pretty spirited. He told me he thought that if a gun is broadly distributed, it ought to remain on the market. That didn't make sense to me.

"Would you support a ban on assault-style rifles?" I asked him.

"No," he said.

"Would you support a ban on high-capacity magazines?"

"No," he said.

"Would you support a requirement that everyone has to be twenty-one to buy a gun?"

"No," he said.

I stood and thanked him for his time.

That was by no means the only meeting I had that left me frustrated. I sat down with one Democratic congressman from a California district that had just seen its own mass shooting. "You know what I think we ought to do?" he asked me. "We ought to get some guys from the Golden State Warriors to come shop in your store for basketball shoes, and we'll use that to build awareness of gun violence." I was puzzled by the suggestion. "That doesn't do much for me," I said.

"Well, another thing we're thinking about is organizing a bike ride around building awareness of gun violence," he said. "You could sponsor it. Or, if you wanted to, maybe you could come out and ride in it."

"Congressman, I have no interest in sponsoring a bike ride," I told him. "I have no interest in coming out and riding in it, either. What I'd like is for you and your colleagues to find a solution to this problem—to come together with intent to fix it." A couple minutes later his assistant came in and announced he was needed on the House floor for a vote, and the congressman left.

A common thread running through several of these conversations was that it would be unfair to require all gun purchasers to be twenty-one when men and women can serve in the military at eighteen. Believe me, I'm tremendously grateful for those young people who choose to put on a uniform; I salute their bravery and patriotism. But we're talking apples and oranges, because there's a meaningful difference between a young marine or army private who's been properly trained in the use of his or her rifle and an eighteen-year-old civilian with a bug up his ass and $200 in his pocket. Besides, it's not as if eighteen-year-olds in the military walk around with guns in their hands 24/7. On base, the guns are locked up. When you get down to it, the whole military argument against age restrictions holds no water.

But that didn't keep people from making it. In the end, we didn't get much traction in our trips to Washington. No one in Congress really wants to do anything about this issue, and we realized that our presence wasn't bringing the change we sought. We aren't finished: we promised to keep the conversation going when we met with the families of slain students and survivors in Parkland—a visit made at their invitation, and during which I saw firsthand that they were every bit as courageous and committed as they'd seemed on TV. They were inspirations. We will keep pushing for reasonable gun reform, no matter how long it takes.

Congress actually took one tiny step in the right direction. In an omnibus budget bill they adopted in March, the brave souls on the Hill authorized the Centers for Disease Control and Prevention to conduct research on gun violence. They didn't fund it, but they allowed it, which they hadn't done in years. The National Rifle Association wasn't pleased.

Still, we weren't where we wanted to be in keeping the issue in Washington's face, so in April we hired a DC lobbying firm to help guide us. And let me tell you: if we were toxic before, now we were doubly so. Our lobbying prompted Springfield Armory to sever ties with Dick's—to announce, in other words, that it would no longer supply guns for us to sell, because of all the disagreeable things we'd done. The company especially disliked our new age requirement, which it felt violated "a sacred right," according to Springfield, "fought for and secured by American patriots and our founding forefathers."

Point of information: it's Founding *Fathers*.

A few days later, MKS Supply, makers of the Hi-Point and Inland Manufacturing brands of firearms, announced it wouldn't do business with us, either, because we were compromising America's "God-given freedoms."

"In recent months, Dick's Sporting Goods and its subsidiary, Field & Stream, have shown themselves, in our opinion, to be no friend of Americans' Second Amendment," the company's president, Charles Brown, wrote in a press release. He was wrong about that: we believe strongly in the Second Amendment; we just believe, as Justice Anton Scalia once said, that the second, like all amendments, is not without limitations. "Dick's Sporting Goods and Field & Stream, in purportedly doing all of these things, have demonstrated that they do not share our values." That part he got right. We don't share their values.

A day later, O. F. Mossberg & Sons, makers of shotguns, announced they would not supply us, either. "Make no mistake, Mossberg is a staunch supporter of the U.S. Constitution and our Second Amendment rights," Iver Mossberg, the company's CEO, said in a statement, "and we fully disagree with Dick's Sporting Goods' recent anti–Second Amendment actions."

I did not take any of this personally. If we got our way on assault-style rifles, these companies would lose an important stream of revenue. Then again, they gave up another significant revenue stream by cutting us off, because we'd been one of the top three or four firearms retailers in the country for years; they sold a lot of guns through Dick's. But it was their call to make. We never asked them to change their minds.

But we did invite them to Pittsburgh, along with other gun manufacturers, to talk about our position. Some declined to even speak with me. Others talked with me on the phone but made it clear that they wouldn't meet in person. The CEOs at Mossberg and Sturm, Ruger sent me emails indicating that we had nothing to discuss. But some made the trip—I won't name names—and we met in a conference room at the Store Support Center to hash things out.

They shared their point of view, sometimes forcefully, but they were absolute gentlemen. They agreed that the country has a gun problem and that it needs a solution. My sense was that none knew what that might be, but whatever it was, it had to come in baby steps, and they felt we'd tried to do too much, too quickly. Bottom line, they said we should return assault-style rifles to the shelves and that we owed gun makers an apology. We weren't about to do any of that, so at meeting's end we agreed to disagree. I give the guys who came a lot of credit. It was gutsy.

We made another decision that enraged many in the gun rights fraternity. It struck us as hypocritical to return all the MSRs we had in stock to the manufacturers, because that would simply put them back on the market to sell through different hands. We believed these rifles should be off the street. So after brief debate, we decided that the only way to make sure the rifles were gone for good was to destroy them and eat the cost. Which would be substantial: we had roughly $5 million worth of inventory.

That's what we did. We sawed $5 million worth of rifles into pieces, then turned the scrap over to a metal recycler. The National Shooting Sports Foundation, the trade organization that came up with the "modern sporting rifle" moniker, expelled us from membership. The response from other gun people was surreal. Some acted as if we'd killed their best friends. Seriously: I got notes from people that read as if the rifles were people. "What a waste," the NRA lamented, "and what a strange business model."

All of this was prelude. We knew we'd take a financial hit, and a big one; experience told us as much. And indeed, in the first quarter of 2018, our comp sales were down about 2.5 percent from the same period a year before. Our second-quarter comp sales fell dramatically, by 4 percent, and third-quarter by 3.9 percent. Although this was significant, it was pretty much what we'd expected.

But as I wrote in an opinion piece in the *Washington Post*, there were principles at stake. "This issue transcends our company's bottom line," the column read. "We suspected that speaking out would have a negative impact on our business. But this was about our values and standing up for what we think is right.

"A group of us in corporate America have taken a stand, made hard choices and enacted reforms on our own because we firmly believe it's the right thing to do for our kids and for our country. The kids in Florida and across the nation have taken a stand and been brave enough to make their voices heard. The majority of Americans are demanding that members of Congress take a stand and be brave enough to do their jobs."

We'd been mulling how we should position our hunting category in a post-Parkland landscape and whether it might be time to reduce its importance. About 30 percent of the chain—and by early 2018, we had 732 Dick's stores, with another eight about to open—did very well in firearms; it's a regional business. It might make sense, we thought, to concentrate our firearms sales in those markets and look at reducing or phasing out the category elsewhere.

So eight months after Parkland, in October 2018, we launched an experiment. We removed guns from ten Dick's stores in markets where hunting didn't move the needle. We replaced them with a range and depth of other merchandise that we judged to be particularly suited to each place. In Boston, for instance, we doubled down on outerwear, licensed merchandise, and baseball gear. In a couple of Florida stores we enlarged baseball, saltwater fishing tackle, and athletic apparel.

We'd always customized our selection by region, but here we were sharpening our focus to an almost bespoke selection by individual store. The results were a pleasant surprise. Those ten stores did extremely well, significantly outpacing the other stores in their regions. So, encouraged, we planned to reallocate the gun space in another 125 stores in 2019, and to likewise localize the assortment in each. Our fallout with the gun industry might turn out to be a blessing.

Our long history of supplying hunters is something we're proud of at Dick's, and I don't think we'd ever want to stop it altogether. But I can see the day coming when we sell guns in only a fraction of our locations. And it's a safe bet that we will trade exclusively in those weapons designed for real sport. As for Field & Stream, we're studying ways we might tweak the formula to better serve outdoors enthusiasts who don't hunt.

I thought about my dad a lot while we struggled over the MSR issue. I wondered what Dick Stack would have made of the controversy. On the one hand, I imagine he'd have been panicked that we took such a public stand; after all, he wasn't much of a risk-taker after Hillcrest, and I think he would have freaked out that we'd alienated customers and vendors, let alone lost some revenue.

But I think he'd also be proud. He set our corporate example of marrying what we do to the communities we serve—it all started with his leading the drive to improve Little League in Binghamton. Plus, he was a principled guy who would approve of our trying to save lives, and while we have no way of measuring such a thing, we believe that our policy on raising the age for all gun purchases has done that. And though he was the con-summate salesman, and able to win over virtually anyone who walked through the door, I think he would have agreed that you can't please everyone—and that we can't let the potential loss of some disgruntled customers rewrite the philosophy that guides us.

And really, that's what this entire experience comes down to. These were *our* decisions, about how to run *our* business, based on *our* company's conscience. I'm confident that in his two-fisted, suffer-no-malarkey style, my dad would have done the same thing, and that neither market forces, nor threats, nor ugly e-mails, nor boycotts would have dislodged him from the course he judged to be right.

I don't think he would have needed a guarantee of success to proceed, either. We certainly didn't know whether we'd get Congress to act when we took up the MSR issue, and to date, it hasn't happened in any satisfying way. But you know what? Gun sales were down nationally in 2018. On Black Friday that year, traditionally a huge day for gun purchases, the FBI's NICS back-ground check program received 182,093 queries. That was down from 203,086 a year before, and down from the two previous years, too.


This is a fascinating time to be in retail. With Amazon and many brands going direct-to-consumer via the Internet, the industry is in a state of serious upheaval. Everybody now walks around with a store in his or her pocket—a whole range of competing stores, actually—and as we all sell similar products, our chal-lenge at Dick's is to work out the logistics of making our selection easy to access, purchases a snap to make, and delivery fast and cheap—all while, at the same time, differentiating ourselves from the other guys.

Our brands are key to that differentiation. We carry a larger selection of top-quality brands than anyone. We carry a greater selection within those brands, too. As we saw retail going through consolidation, we realized we had to preserve that—and that our survival depended in part on making ourselves as important to our vendors and brands as they were, and are, to us. We had to be more important to Nike, Callaway, and Under Armour than department stores and smaller bricks-and-mortar retailers were, and ultimately, than Amazon was. If a customer asked Callaway where she should buy her clubs, we wanted them to answer, "Dick's." And in return, we'd hold them up to our customers as something really special.

We've always cultivated win-win relationships with our brands. When Kevin Plank was just getting Under Armour started, I remember walking through one of our stores with him, talking about how we could help each other grow. We continued the conversation in his office in Baltimore, and the agreement that emerged from those talks was that we'd always treat each other *unfairly*. This guided our relationship for better than a decade. We provided Under Armour with key space in our stores, included them in a lot of our marketing, and helped them test new products they wanted to bring to market. They invested in fixtures and marketing for us, created exclusive products for us, and put their own employees on-site to ensure that the presentation of their product was perfect.

We've since formalized these sorts of relationships. A few years ago, we realized we needed to reduce the number of brands we carried—we had too many brands offering similar merchandise. So we established a new set of terms and conditions under which we would do business with them. We created strategic partnerships with brands such as Nike and Callaway. We'd overtly move market share to them—we'd put their product on the endcaps and in our power aisles, where they'd be impossible to miss by anyone walking into our stores. We'd market their product and, in many cases, put a team together to focus exclusively on their business. In return, they'd provide us with certain advantages— such as offering exclusive products or shoe color combinations sold nowhere else, and co-investing in marketing campaigns.

They often supply fixtures that create an in-store environment for their products.

These strategic partnerships are important to us. We're truly in this together. To drive that home, and preserve the special character of these pairings, we have no more than two in each category. In footwear and apparel, it's Nike. We have strategic partnerships with the North Face, and with Yeti, and with others, too.

Callaway is a great example. Within four months of becoming our strategic partner, Callaway was our number-one golf ball brand. They introduced their Chrome Soft, "the ball that changed the ball," through Dick's. They debuted their Tru-VisTruvis ball, which is painted like a soccer ball, in our golf departments, and we were aggressive about marketing and merchandising it.

Bruce Parker would probably keel over if he saw how well we work together. Callaway even came to us and said they wanted to get involved in our Sports Matter initiative. They created a green-and-white Sports Matter Truvis ball. Two dollars from the sale of each dozen go to the Dick's Sporting Goods Foundation. Last year, we sold more than two hundred thousand dozens of those balls. That's a real partnership.

For every brand that we form such a bond with, there are many that we don't. The majority of our suppliers have a more standard transactional relationship with us, and there's certainly nothing wrong with that. We get along well and work together, but we don't see their success as foundational to ours, and they don't consider our health as necessary to their own. Both sides have less invested in the partnership.

Still, all of our brands are important to us, and that won't change. Beyond that, I can't predict what the future holds. You'll hear some retailers lament that things aren't as they were five or ten years ago. I don't bother. Those days are gone. The sooner you grasp that, I figure, the sooner you can get to adapting.

We're up for it. We'll adapt as we need to. In the meantime, we'll strive to set ourselves apart by doing what we've always prided ourselves on: whether virtually or in person, we'll offer great customer service and top-quality gear, and we'll do it at a good price. My dad might feel lost in the uncertain and fast-changing retail environment of today, but he'd get that part.

So here we are, a really large company. As I write this, Dick's is closing in on 750 stores in 47 states. Plus, we run 94 Golf Galaxy stores and 35 Field & Stream stores. Our sales are approaching $9 billion per year. We've reached the point where only three brands we do business with are bigger than we are—Nike, Adidas, and VF Corporation, which makes Vans, Smartwool, the North Face, JanSport, and a lot of other outdoors brands. I never imagined such a day when I was arguing with my dad over getting popular sneakers in the Court Street store.

But then, that might be the least of the surprises since then. Last year I marked the fiftieth anniversary of my first day's work at Dick's as a thirteen-year-old, a kid who most desperately wanted to be anywhere but there, in the store my dad had started twenty years before. In a few months I'll reach a milestone in my long career at Dick's: the point at which I'll have run the business for as long as my dad did. Thirty-six years.

I did not foresee, in 1984, that we'd become national advocates for youth sports and team play, or involve ourselves in helping underfunded athletic programs, or get into the movie business. I certainly didn't expect that we'd become a flashpoint in the national debate about gun safety. There's so much I didn't imagine, couldn't imagine, that has come to pass.

In most respects, Dick's bears little resemblance to our humble operation in Binghamton and Vestal. When I took over the company, our floor space totaled twenty-one thousand square feet, and that was after we moved into the old Acme building. That's less than half of the retail area in any one of our Dick's or Field & Stream locations today, and smaller than many of our Golf Galaxy stores. Just in terms of physical footprint, we're two thousand times bigger.

Overseeing all that space has required our ranks to grow from twenty people to a workforce of more than forty thousand, with expertise not only in the products we sell but in complex logistics, social media marketing, nutrition, government affairs. Keeping all those stores filled with merchandise has required us to expand our warehouse from the tiny prefab shed out back of Court Street to a chain of immense distribution centers stretching across the country.

One thing that's remained the same: I still get out to visit our stores as often as I can. I learn something important on every trip. And a few familiar faces remain at the company. Larry Schorr is still a key player, as he has been since we bought the company from my dad. He's been instrumental in guiding us through many tough decisions and a confidant of mine through good times and bad. Today, he's the lead director on our board—the only remaining director, besides me, from the informal group I assembled in 1984.

Bill Colombo remains on the board, as well. Of all the gifts that my college education gave me, his friendship has turned out to be the best and most important. Dick's would not be the company it is today without Bill's wonderful smarts and skills.

Tim Myers has held a dozen different jobs at Dick's over the years. Today, he's the company's liaison for the Dick's Open: he travels the country talking to golf pros, convincing them to play at the annual tournament in Binghamton, which is still held at the golf course I often played with Gramp. He and my sister Kim still live in the Triple Cities, a few minutes' drive from Court Street. Kim ran for Congress in 2016 in New York's Twenty-Second District, and lost what turned out to be a hotly contested three-way race. Her politics and mine don't have a tremendous area of overlap, but I thought she'd have been a first-class member of the House and a great voice for the people of the Southern Tier.

Her campaign literature included a short biography. "I grew up working with my dad and my siblings in my family's business, Dick's Clothing and Sporting Goods," it read, "running the cash register, filing gun records and stocking shelves. That is where I learned the values of hard work, integrity, determination and giving back to my community." Amen to that.

A piece of the company's heart remains in Binghamton, and I imagine it always will. Store Number 1, in the old Acme, is by far the smallest Dick's in the chain, but it does very well, considering. Across the parking lot stands 345 Court Street, which is hallowed ground within Dick's. It's empty at the moment, but we have plans for the place. We're going to do something interesting there to commemorate the company's story.

We've tried to share our success with our hometown. A few years ago we realized that we needed another distribution center, the biggest of the bunch, to better service the Northeast and our growing e-commerce traffic. Our logistics group considered a number of attractive locations, but I wanted to build it in Binghamton. It opened last year in Conklin, just southeast of town and less than a mile from the first distribution center we built back in 1990, with a first-phase footprint of 650,000 square feet, employing more than two hundred people. We're in the process of expanding it to just shy of a million square feet, at which point nearly five hundred people will work there. It thrilled me to be there on opening day.

We transplanted a little of Binghamton when we built our new headquarters in Pittsburgh, too. We built the road into the property, and the city told us we could give it any name, and the building any address, that we wanted. That was easy. The Store Support Center is located at 345 Court Street. And if you visit the food court inside, you'll find the individual stations bear familiar names—Annie's Pizza Kitchen, named for my mom's mom; the Oakridge Grill, named for the street where my dad built his house; and Dutch's Deli, named for Gramp. The sit-down restaurant is called the McNamara Grill, after the South Side Binghamton street on which both of my parents grew up.

And there's a little reminder of home in our nearly eight hundred stores. Walk into any Dick's, and you'll find a big print on the wall, that picture of my dad and my uncle Ed standing in the original Dick's Bait and Tackle. My dad barely out of his teens. The inventory sparse. The store almost unimaginably snug around them.

Dad looks happy in the picture.

Proud that he's there.

And full of hope that he might make that little shop work.

# ACKNOWLEDGMENTS

Writing this story has taken me back through more than seventy years of history at Dick's, and reacquainted me with so many people who have contributed to the company since its earliest days as a tiny, seat-of-the-pants operation on the east side of Binghamton. The first and foremost contributor, obviously, was my father, to whom this book is dedicated. He started Dick's, and when it failed, started it again—then did me the favor of ruining my teenage summers while teaching me the business that's been central to my life. He lived the American dream, and he bequeathed it to me.

There was also my grandmother, who gave my dad $300 out of a cookie jar to start the company. Without her love and confidence in him, there'd be no story to tell. Dad's success would have been unlikely, too, without Bob Aiken and the core staff of guys who worked at Court Street for twenty years or more. And Dad wouldn't have been nearly so successful in life without his Donna.

The team that built Dick's into the largest sporting goods retailer in the country includes some of my best friends—Mike Hines, Joe Schmidt, and Bill Colombo. Larry Schorr has been a key player in every twist and turn we've taken since Dad sold the company. Tim Myers has been a strong and steady presence since we were both in high school. Many vendors whom we've partnered with have helped us grow, too—Elliott Hill and Ed

# ACKNOWLEDGMENTS

Haberle of Nike; Kevin Plank at Under Armour; Mark King at Adidas North America and Herbert Hainer at Adidas-Group; Chip Brewer (and yes, in his own way, Bruce Parker) at Callaway; and many, many others. I thank them all.

In telling this story, I relied on help from gentlemen who know the craft of storytelling far better than I do. First, Jerry Tarde helped me meet the right people to make this book a reality. My writer friend Earl Swift helped me transform a pile of disjointed memories into a logical narrative, a sometimes painful but ultimately rewarding process. He was patient, kind, and relentlessly good-humored throughout. Putting a book together is hard work, but we had quite a few laughs along the way.

My agent, David Granger, has looked out for me with care, ferocity, and a sharp, quick mind that never fails to impress. He has my everlasting thanks for treating me with such TLC.

And Rick Horgan, my editor at Scribner, has been enthusiastic about this story from the start, has been a hands-on and always helpful participant in its assembly, and a great collaborator with whom to work. Thank you, Rick.

These guys would agree, I'm sure, that two other people were essential to this book's completion. My executive assistant, Vanessa Ellis, was the glue that held the effort together. She was as important to the completed manuscript as she is to the everyday operation at Dick's—which is to say, irreplaceable. And my sister Kim helped chase down facts, dates, and names lost to memory, and offered helpful comments on the early drafts.

My greatest thanks go to my family, to whom I owe and dedicate my life. To Denise, the mother of my children, thank you for partnering with me to raise five wonderful human beings. To Michael, Brian, Katie, Maggie, and Mary, you've kept me going during innumerable difficult and trying times. You are the joys of my life.

To Donna and Ryan, thank you for another chance at love. I'm thrilled to be experiencing this adventure with you.

## ACKNOWLEDGMENTS

Thanks again to all. This has been a wonderful journey. I have so enjoyed the ride. And when I look into the future I feel optimistic about Dick's Sporting Goods, the United States, and our world. Our best days are ahead of us.

I believe that.